Passages in Modern Sculpture

Rosalind E Krauss

THAMES AND HUDSON

In memory of my father, Matthew Epstein

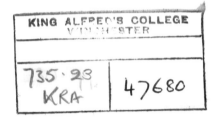
First published in Great Britain in 1977 by
Thames and Hudson Ltd, London

Printed and bound in the U.S.A.

acknowledgments

The process of acknowledging the intellectual debts a
writer incurs in the making of a book is often identical
with the explanation of how a given project was arrived
at and why it took its particular form. In the case of this
work, two groups of individuals helped to shape my sense
of the need and purpose for a critical history of modern
sculpture. First of all, there were my students—at M.I.T.,
Princeton University, and Hunter College—to whom my
efforts at clarifying certain issues and developing a language of description were initially addressed. For their
patience and endurance I am obviously grateful. But more
than that, it was their probing questions and their un-
willingness to accept partial explanations that led me to
reconsider the adequacy of what might be called the

canonical view of twentieth-century sculpture's development. In response to their need for clarity, and mine, I was motivated to write this book.

In attempting to achieve that clarity, I had recourse to several sources of powerful intellectual aid from colleagues and friends among critics, scholars, and sculptors. Leo Steinberg, whose essay on Rodin (now collected in *Other Criteria*) I had read in the early 1960s, first demonstrated to me the impossibility of a view by which modern sculpture was seen as being antithetical to Rodin's work. My treatment of Rodin in these pages owes a tremendous debt to that essay, and while specific passages by Professor Steinberg are cited within the text, I wish to acknowledge here the more general dependence I have had on his conception of Rodin's relation to modernism.

To Annette Michelson I am indebted not only for the cumulative effect of the critical essays she has been publishing on sculpture and film over the last ten years but for the many conversations during which she has frankly and generously criticized my own work. The effect of her thinking has had a great deal to do with the importance which issues of temporality assume in the discussion that follows.

More generally, the community of exchange with fellow critics, made possible by my associate editorship of *Artforum* from 1971 to 1975, was incalculably valuable. In addition to my connection with Annette Michelson and Jeremy Gilbert-Rolfe, I wish to acknowledge the importance of my association there with John Coplans and Robert Pincus-Witten. The criticism of the latter, written and oral, continually called to my attention aspects of contemporary sculptural production which I had tended to overlook.

The task of assessing the sculpture of the past decade has meant evaluating my own sense of the import of that work in the light of conversations with several of the sculptors who made it, particularly Richard Serra, Robert Smithson, Mel Bochner, and Robert Morris. For their friendship and generosity, both past and present, I am extremely grateful.

At different stages of its development, parts of this text were read by, and discussed with, some of my friends in the art-historical community, particularly Nan Piene, whose work on kineticism I have found consistently illuminating, and Andrée Hayum. For their suggestions and those made by Karen Kennerly and the painter Susan Crile, I am deeply indebted. My editor at Viking, Barbara Burn, provided the help and encouragement necessary to a project of this kind. I am grateful for her tact and expertise.

Since this book is, in large part, addressed to students, it is my hope that it reflects a sense of those questions and demands raised by the initial encounter with aesthetic objects. To my own parents, Matthew and Bertha Epstein, who first sharpened my own sense of this experience, both as a problematic and a pleasurable one, I offer my deepest thanks.

Dimensions indicate height if there is only one figure, height preceding width if there are two, and height, width, and depth if there are three.

contents

introduction 1

1 Narrative Time: **the question of the *Gates of Hell* 7**

2 Analytic Space: **futurism and constructivism 39**

3 Forms of Readymade: **Duchamp and Brancusi 69**

4 A Game Plan: **the terms of surrealism 105**

5 *Tanktotem*: **welded images 147**

6 Mechanical Ballets: **light, motion, theater 201**

7 The *Double Negative*: **a new syntax for sculpture 243**

notes 289

bibliography 299

index 303

Passages in
Modern
Sculpture

introduction

Although it was written in the eighteenth century, Gotthold Lessing's aesthetic treatise *Laocoön*[1]* applies directly to the discussion of sculpture in our time. For in the course of his argument, Lessing feels it is necessary to ask about the very nature of sculpture and to wonder how we can define the unique experience of that art. If these same questions have become even more necessary to ask, that is because twentieth-century sculpture has repeatedly taken forms that have been difficult for its contemporary viewers to assimilate into their received ideas about the proper task of the plastic arts. This was as true of the objects Brancusi, Duchamp, or Gabo made in the 1920s

---

* Superscript numbers refer to the notes beginning on page 289.

as it is of the work of many sculptors of the past few years. The issue of what might properly be considered a work of sculpture has become increasingly problematic. Therefore, in approaching a study of sculpture in this century, it is helpful to examine, as Lessing did two hundred years ago, the general category of experience that sculpture occupies.

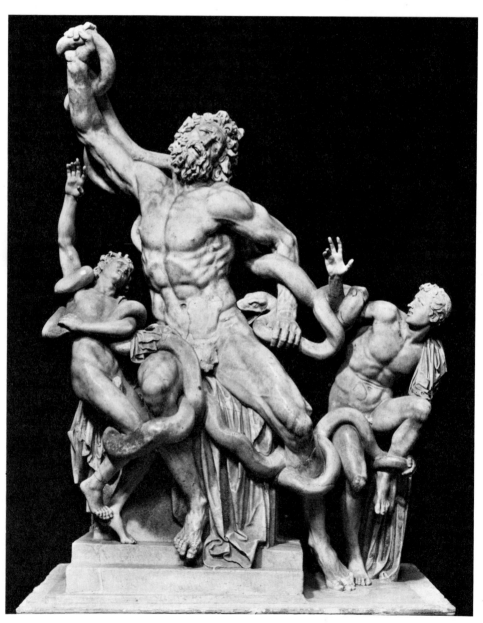

In trying to discover this in the *Laocoön*, Lessing begins by defining the limiting conditions of the separate arts. He asks himself if there is an inherent difference between a temporal event and a static object and, if so, what this difference means for the art forms that concern themselves with the one or the other type of construction. By posing this question, Lessing engages in what is called normative criticism. He is trying to define norms, or objective criteria, by which to define what is natural to a given artistic enterprise, and by which to understand what are its special powers to create meaning. Therefore, in answer to the question "what is sculpture," Lessing asserts that sculpture is an art concerned with the deployment of bodies in space. And, he continues, this defining spatial character must be separated off from the essence of those art forms, like poetry, whose medium is time. If the depiction of actions in time is natural to poetry, Lessing argues, it is not natural to sculpture or painting, for the character of the visual arts is that they are static. Because of this condition, the relationships formed between the separate parts of a visual object are *simultaneously* given to its viewer; they are there to be perceived and taken in all at once.

By the 1930s this sense of a natural opposition between an art of time and an art of space had become a basic starting point from which to assess the unique accomplishments of sculpture. In *Modern Plastic Art*,[2] the first book to deal seriously with twentieth-century sculpture, its author, Carola Giedion-Welcker, is entirely concerned with the spatial character of the sculptural task. Her enthusiasm for the modern achievements of that art arises from her sense of the increasing purity with which sculpture was concentrated on the spatiality of the medium —to the exclusion of any other concerns. In her eyes, sculpture's special resources for meaning issued naturally from the fact that it was made from inert matter, so that its very basis concerned an extension through space rather than time. What she observed happening throughout modern sculpture was the conspicuous forging of a relationship between this inert material and a system of patterning imposed upon it. So that in the static, simultaneous space of the sculptural body there was set up a comparison between two forms of stillness: the dense,

1. *Anonymous:* Laocoön and His Sons, *First century B.C. Marble 84". Museo Vaticano, Rome. (Photo, Alinari)*

3

immobile substance of the object and a lucid, analytic system that had apparently shaped it. She saw two major ways through which this crystallization of matter had been carried out by the end of the 1930s. Sculptors had analyzed static material "either by means of a deliberate simplification of volumes or in terms of the disintegration of mass through light."[3] Brancusi's work was her example of the capacity of the carver to reduce material toward volumetric simplicity, while Naum Gabo's served as the clearest exponent of the constructor's use of light to open matter up to an analysis of its structure.

But if we are interested in examining the differences between Brancusi and Gabo, it is not enough to speak simply of the opposing systems they used for deploying matter through the abstract, simultaneous space that we suppose is the one sculpture naturally inhabits. We are forced increasingly to speak of time. Brancusi's arrangement of form implies a different temporal condition from that of Gabo: its meaning arises from an entirely different set of appeals to the viewer's consciousness of his own time as he experiences the work. In the *Laocoön* Lessing had, of course, understood this. To his famous distinction between the temporal and spatial arts, he had added an important caveat: "All bodies, however, exist not only in space," he had cautioned, "but also in time. They continue, and at any moment of their continuance, may assume a different appearance and stand in different relations. Every one of these momentary appearances and groupings was the result of a preceding, may become the cause of a following, and is therefore the center of a present action."[4]

The underlying premise of the following study of modern sculpture is that, even in a spatial art, space and time cannot be separated for purposes of analysis. Into any spatial organization there will be folded an implicit statement about the nature of temporal experience. The history of modern sculpture is incomplete without discussion of the temporal consequences of a particular arrangement of form. Indeed, the history of modern sculpture coincides with the development of two bodies of thought, phenomenology and structural linguistics, in which meaning is understood to depend on the way that any form of being

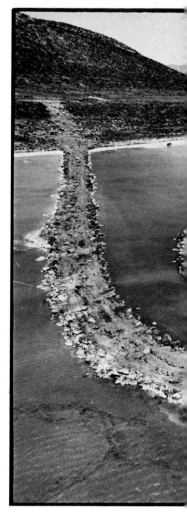

2. *Robert Smithson (1938–73):* Spiral Jetty, *1969–70. Black rock, salt crystal, earth. Rozelle Point, Great Salt Lake, Utah. (Photo, Gianfranco Gorgoni)*

4

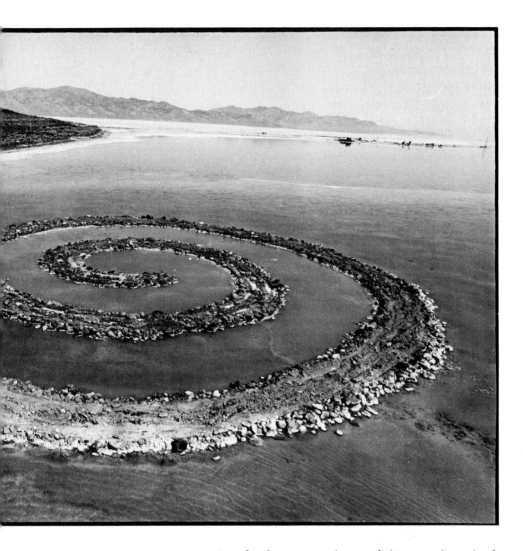

contains the latent experience of its opposite: simultaneity always containing an implicit experience of sequence. One of the striking aspects of modern sculpture is the way in which it manifests its makers' growing awareness that sculpture is a medium peculiarly located at the juncture between stillness and motion, time arrested and time passing. From this tension, which defines the very condition of sculpture, comes its enormous expressive power.

The aim of the following study is critical and theoretical, as well as historical. My intention is to investigate the formal organization and expressive concerns of a limited but representative number of works from within the development of modern sculpture. Therefore, the method used has more to do with the process of the case-study than with the procedures of a historical survey. These case-studies are intended to develop a group of concepts that is not only revealing of the sculptural issues involved in the particular works in question but can also be generalized to apply to the wider body of objects that form the history of sculpture in the past century.

It is my hope that the gains to be derived from a detailed examination of a single work, or group of related sculptures, will off-set the losses this has meant for a wholly inclusive historical survey. There are many sculptors, some of whom have produced work of high quality, who have been left out of this text, while others, some of lesser merit, have been included. Guiding these choices was a decision to address the primary issues that distinguish modern sculpture from the work that comes before it. So, for example, the continuation into the twentieth century of a traditional treatment of the human figure is not given a place in these pages alongside the other movements that are discussed. But it is my contention that the questions that bear on a decision to depict the human form, whether by means of a primitivist, gothic, or archaic vocabulary, are not central to the subject of this book. There will be readers who will see this as too narrow a conception of modern sculpture. However, the complex manifestations of a modern sensibility are what I have undertaken to explore. And it is my hope that the issues set forth in the following text will act as a set of meaningful probes into the large mass of sculptural production through which this sensibility has been given form.

Narrative Time: 1
the question of the
Gates of Hell

October, Eisenstein's epic film of the Soviet Revolution, opens with a shot of a statue, harshly lit against a dark sky. It is a statue of Nicholas II, the Czar of Russia (fig. 3), which the film-maker explores detail by detail, building it into an image of imperial power. In the scene that follows this beginning, a crowd rushes into the square which the monument occupies. Tying ropes around it, the insurgents topple the statue from its mount, performing an act by which Eisenstein symbolizes the destruction of the Romanov Dynasty.

In that first scene Eisenstein sets up the two poles of his film: the two opposing metaphors that establish both his analysis of history and the space in which it occurs. The crowd and the real space through which it moves are asked to represent the hero of the Revolution; while

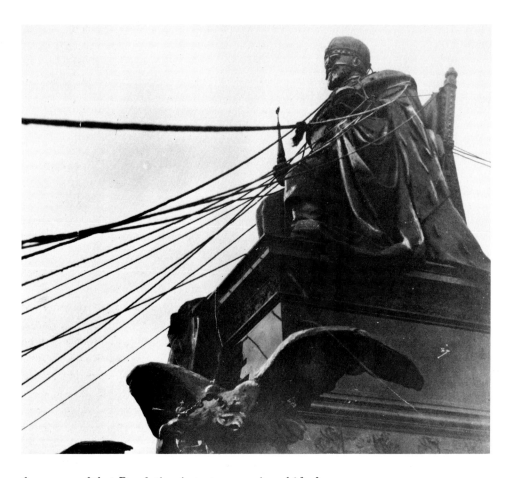

the enemy of that Revolution is cast as a series of ideologies and formal spaces, each one symbolized by means of statuary. In the film's re-creation of the struggle to retain imperial power in Russia, sculptures are made into surrogate actors; and there is consistent identification of particular icons with particular political views.

A compelling instance of this identification occurs when Eisenstein introduces the figure of Kerensky, the elected President of the Provisional Government who has assumed dictatorial powers. As Kerensky stands at the doorway to the throne room of the Winter Palace, Eisenstein cuts back and forth between shots of him and shots of a peacock. Significantly, the object to which Kerensky is compared is not a live animal, nor is it a static representation made of china, say, or tapestry. The peacock Eisenstein shows, in a whir of glittering, metallic plumage, is an automaton—an intricately constructed mechanical bird. And what Eisenstein wants the viewer to see, in the space of that flash of the bird's precisionist movement, is not an image of personal vanity but the symbol of an impoverished, outmoded rationalism. As an automaton, the bird represents the rationalist argument about the Great Chain of Being, where God as the First Cause of the universe was likened to the supreme clockmaker. In this analogy the very existence of the clockwork (symbolizing the artfulness of human contrivance) was used as proof of the logic and "Good Design" of an inherently just world.[1] For Eisenstein, this argument was identified with a political philosophy opposed to change and intent on using "things as they are" to legitimize oppression. When Kerensky enters the throne room, he does so to restore capital punishment to the laws of Russia.

In other sections of the film Eisenstein exploits other kinds of sculpture: images of Napoleon, figures of Christ, and primitive idols.[2] At one point he shows female soldiers, who are defending the Winter Palace against the coming Bolshevik attack, eying two works by Rodin: *The Kiss* and *The Eternal Idol.* Using these sculptures in their marble versions, Eisenstein photographs them to look like soft mounds of flesh, which the women observe with a rapt, ecstatic fascination. Through this device Eisenstein films a sentiment he obviously abhors: a cloying nostalgia for past fantasies of love.

The point of these sculptures—and of all sculpture—for Eisenstein is not its mimetic quality, not its capacity to imitate the look of living flesh, but its power to embody ideas and attitudes. It is Eisenstein's most basic assumption that sculpture, all art, is fundamentally ideological.

One of the ironies about the virtual museum of sculptural representations employed in *October* is the inclusion of Rodin. For his career, which ended in 1917, on the very eve of the Revolution Eisenstein's film celebrates, produced an art intensely hostile to rationalism. As a whole, Rodin's sculpture was the first extreme attack on the kind of thinking represented by the mechanical bird, an ideology that was deeply implanted in neoclassical sculpture, and persisted in almost all nineteenth-century sculpture up to the work of Rodin. The rationalist model,

3. *Sergei Eisenstein (1898–1948):* October *(still), 1927–28. (Photo, Courtesy Film Stills Archive, The Museum of Modern Art, New York)*

on which neoclassism depends, holds within it two basic suppositions: the context through which understanding unfolds is time; and, for sculpture, the natural context of rationality is the medium of relief.

Logical arguments—procedures such as "if X, then Y" —follow a temporal development. At the heart of such reasoning is the notion of causality, of the connection between effects and their causes which depend for their very relatedness upon the passage of time. In the eighteenth and nineteenth centuries ambitious painters and sculptors accepted without dispute the notion that time was the medium through which the logic of social and moral institutions revealed itself—hence the exalted position they gave to history painting as a genre and to historical monuments. History was understood to be a kind of narrative, involving the progression of a set of significances that mutually reinforce and explicate each other, and that seem driven as if by a divine mechanism toward a conclusion, toward the meaning of an event.

Therefore, when François Rude undertook a sculptural commission for the Arch of Triumph, he understood his task as transcending the simple representation of a moment from the French Revolution. The aspirations behind *La Marseillaise*, also known as *Departing Volunteers* (fig. 4) of 1833–36, were to fashion the composition into a kind of temporal cut that would knife through the disarray of historical incident and uncover its meaning. This aspiration, which Rude shared with his contemporaries, had been articulated at the end of the eighteenth century by Gotthold Lessing. The work of visual art, "in its coexistent compositions," Lessing argued, "can use but a single moment of action, and must therefore choose the most pregnant one, the one most suggestive of what has gone before and what is to follow."[3] In *La Marseillaise* Rude does capture that moment of absolute pregnancy, of forms focused to a point of utter sharpness from which meaning will then be seen to spread outward, connecting this particular composition to the events that form its past and its future.

In order to achieve this focus, Rude organizes the composition along two axes: a horizontal axis that divides the frieze of soldiers in the lower half of the work from

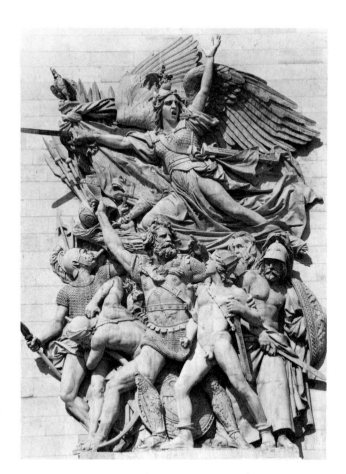

4. *François Rude (1784–1855):*
La Marseillaise, 1833–36. Stone,
ca. 504″ x 312″. Arch of
Triumph, Paris (Photo,
Giraudon)

the splayed form of the winged victory that fills the upper
register; and a vertical axis that plumbs the space from
the head of the victory down the center of her body
through the vertical juncture between the two central
soldiers. The meaning of the composition—and consequently of the moment it depicts—revolves around the
point where these two axes join. Rude produces the feeling of movement rotating around the vertical axis by overlapping the bodies in the lower register to form a semi-
circle. The line of soldiers seems to be issuing from the
far right, out of the very ground of the arch, and to be
moving forward as it proceeds to the left. The point at
which that wave of bodies crests is the point of contact
with the vertical axis, as the two central figures recognize
the symbol of victory. At that juncture, as they mirror
the image suspended above them, the soldiers seem to

11

arrest the horizontal flow of movement through space and time. By exploiting the formal device of symmetry, Rude creates an icon that will stand for a particular moment: the dawning of consciousness about the meaning of liberty. And then, leftward along the horizontal frieze, the figures seem to continue their movement, this time into the future.

The organization of *La Marseillaise* is essentially narrative. The varying degrees of relief, the isolation of the limbs of the figures by means of drapery in order to intensify the rhythmical effect of the paired gestures, the tension between the lateral movement implied by the lower register and the iconlike rigidity of the upper figure—all are ways in which Rude structures the narrative for the viewer. And what is crucial for a reading of this narrative is that the work is in relief. For, by its very nature, the medium of relief makes the reading of the narrative possible.

The frontality of the relief forces the viewer to place himself directly before the work in order to see it, and thus guarantees that the effect of the composition will in no way be diluted. Further, the medium of relief depends upon a relationship between the sculpted figures and their ground. Since this ground behaves like the illusionistic background of a painting, it opens up a virtual space through which the figures can appear to move. Into this movement—this apparent emergence from background to foreground—the sculptor can project the temporal values of the narrative. Most important, the medium of relief links together the visibility of the sculpture with the comprehension of its meaning; because from the single viewing point, in front of the work, all the implications of gesture, all the significance of form, must naturally devolve.

Relief thus makes it possible for the viewer to understand two reciprocal qualities simultaneously: the form as it evolves within the space of the relief ground and the meaning of the depicted moment in its historical context. Even though the viewer does not actually move around the sculpture, he is given the illusion of having as much information as he would if he could circumnavigate the forms—perhaps even *more*, since within a single percep-

5. *Auguste Rodin (1840–1917):* Gates of Hell, *1880–1917. Bronze, 216″ x 144″ x 33″. Philadelphia Museum of Art. (Photo, A. J. Wyatt, staff photographer)*

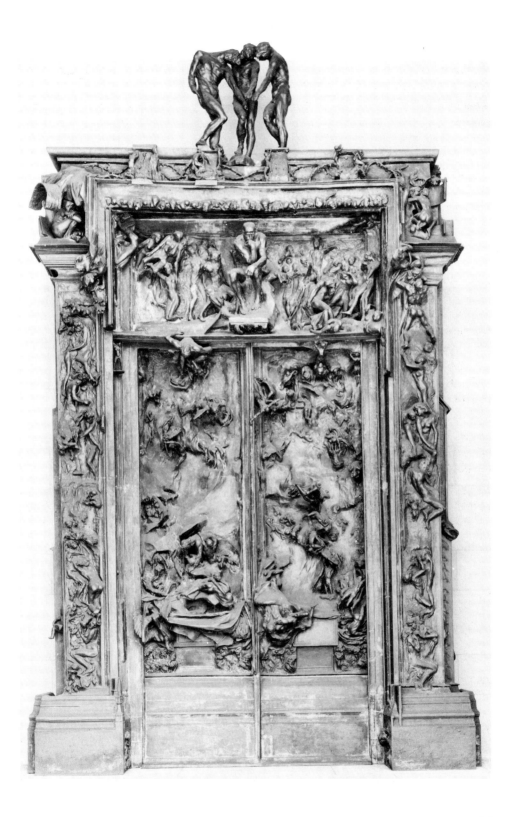

13

tion he sees both the development of the masses and their capacity to signify. If the sculptor's attitude to the relief is that of an omniscient narrator commenting upon the cause-and-effect relationship of forms in both historical and plastic space, the viewer's corresponding attitude is spelled out by the nature of the relief itself: he assumes a parallel omniscience in his reading of the work in all its lucidity.

Indeed, the nineteenth-century theorists who wrote about sculpture demanded that all form, whether free-standing in space or not, must achieve the clarity that seems to be the very essence of relief. "All details of form must unite in a more comprehensive form," Adolf von Hildebrand writes. "All separate judgments of depth must enter into a unitary, all-inclusive judgment of depth. So that ultimately the entire richness of a figure's form stands before us as a backward continuation of one simple plane." And he adds, "Whenever this is not the case, the unitary pictorial effect of the figure is lost. A tendency is then felt to clarify what we cannot perceive from our present point of view, by a change of position. Thus we are driven all around the figure without ever being able to grasp it once in its entirety."[4]

This, then, is the sense in which the mechanical bird, *October*'s golden automaton, is tied to Rude's sculpture of *La Marseillaise*. The automaton is part of a proof about the order of the world. Man's capacity to create the bird is taken to herald his capacity to understand, by analogy, the endeavors of the world's Creator. His own art of contrivance is seen as giving him a conceptual foothold on the logic of a universal design. Just as the clockwork bird carries with it the aspiration to understand, by imitation, the inner workings of nature, Rude's relief aspires to comprehend and project the movement of historical time and man's place within it. The narrative art of relief is Rude's medium, which makes this work paradigmatic for all of nineteenth-century sculpture . . . except for Rodin.

Yet, one might ask, why not for Rodin as well? In a sense Rodin's career is entirely defined by his efforts on a single project, the *Gates of Hell*, which he began in 1880 and worked on until the time of his death—a project for which almost all of his sculpture was orig-

6. *Rodin:* Gates of Hell *(architectural model), ca. 1880. Terra cotta, 39½" x 25". Musée Rodin, Paris. (Photo, Geoffrey Clements)*

inally fashioned. Like *La Marseillaise*, the *Gates of Hell* (fig. 5) is a relief, the sculptural decoration for a monumental set of doors that were to serve as the entrance for a projected museum.[5] And, again like *La Marseillaise*, the work is tied to a narrative scheme, having been commissioned as a cycle of illustrations of Dante's *Divine Comedy*.

In the beginning Rodin pursued a conception of the *Gates* that accorded with the conventions of narrative relief. His early architectural sketches for the project divide the face of the doors into eight separate panels, each of which would carry narrative reliefs arranged sequentially. The obvious models for this format were the great Renaissance doorways, particularly Ghiberti's *Gates of Paradise*, the portal for the Baptistry of the Cathedral of Florence. But by the time Rodin had finished the third architectural model in terra cotta (fig. 6), it was clear that his impluse was to dam up the flow of sequential time. In that model the divisions between the separate panels are nearly all erased, while at the same time a large, static icon has been implanted in the midst of the dramatic space. Composed of a horizontal bar and a vertical stem, topped by the looming vertical mass of *The Thinker*, this cruciform image has the effect of centralizing and flattening the space of the doors, subjecting all of the figures to its abstract presence.

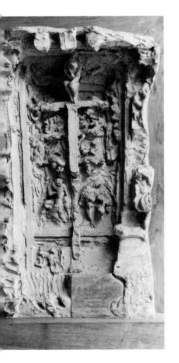

In its final version the *Gates of Hell* resists all attempts to be read as a coherent narrative. Of the myriad sets of figures, only two relate directly to the parent story of *The Divine Comedy*. They are the groupings of *Ugolino and His Sons* and *Paolo and Francesca* (fig. 7), both of which struggle for space on the lower half of the left door. And even the separateness and legibility of these two "scenes" are jeopardized by the fact that the figure of the dying son of Ugolino is a twin of the figure of Paolo.[6] This act of repetition occurs on the other door, where at the lower right edge and halfway up the side, one sees the same male body (fig. 8), in extreme distention, reaching upward. In one of his appearances, the actor supports an outstretched female figure. His back is arched with the effort of his gesture, and the strain across the surface of his torso is completed in the backward thrust of his head and neck. This figure, when cast and

15

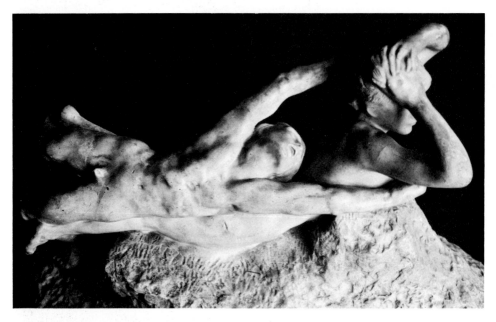

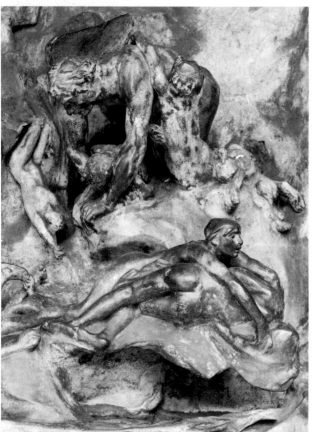

7. LEFT *Rodin:* Gates of Hell *(detail of lower left panel).* Philadelphia Museum of Art. *(Photo, A. J. Wyatt, staff photographer)*

8. FAR RIGHT *Rodin:* Gates of Hell *(detail of right panel).* *(Photo: Farrell Grehan)*

9. NEAR RIGHT *Rodin:* The Prodigal Son, *before 1889. Bronze, 55⅛" x 41¾" x 27⅝".* Musée Rodin, Paris. *(Photo, Bruno Jarret)*

10. ABOVE LEFT *Rodin:* Fugit Amor, *before 1887. Marble, 17¾" x 15" x 6¾".* Musée Rodin, Paris. *(Photo, Adelys)*

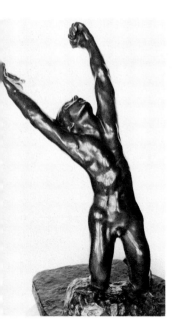

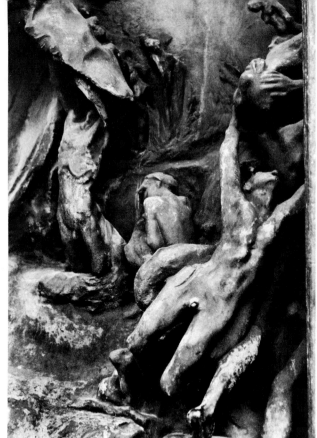

exhibited singly away from the doors, is called *The Prodigal Son* (fig. 9). When coupled with the female and reoriented in space in relation to her body, the male figure becomes part of a group called *Fugit Amor* (fig. 10). On the surface of the right door, the *Fugit Amor* couple appears twice, unchanged except for the angle at which it relates to the ground plane of the work. The double appearance is extremely conspicuous, and the very persistence of that doubling cannot be read as accidental. Rather, it seems to spell the breakdown of the principle of spatio-temporal uniqueness that is a prerequisite of logical narration, for doubling tends to destroy the very possibility of a logical narrative sequence.

At the top of the *Gates* Rodin again has recourse to this strategy of repetition. There, *The Three Shades* (fig. 11) are a threefold representation of the same body—three identical casts radiating away from the point at which their extended left arms converge. In this way *The Three Shades* act to parody the tradition of grouping triple figures that was central to neoclassical sculpture.

17

Wanting to transcend the partial information that any single aspect of a figure can convey, the neoclassical sculptor devises strategies to present the human body through multiple views. His interest in multiple vantage points comes from a conviction that he must find an ideal viewpoint, one that will contain the totality of information necessary for a conceptual grasp of the object. To say, for example, that one "knows" what a cube is, cannot simply mean that one has seen such an object, since any single view of a cube is necessarily partial and incomplete. The absolute parallelism of the six sides and twelve edges that is essential to the meaning of the cube's geometry can never be revealed by a single look. One's knowledge of the cube must be knowledge of an object that transcends the particularities of a single perspective in which only three sides, at most, can be seen. It must be a knowledge that, in some sense, enables one to see the object from everywhere at once, to *understand* the object even while "seeing" it.

In classicism the transcendence of the single point of view was often explicitly dealt with by using figures in pairs and in threes, so that the front view of one figure

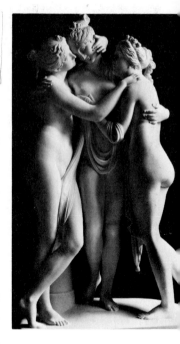

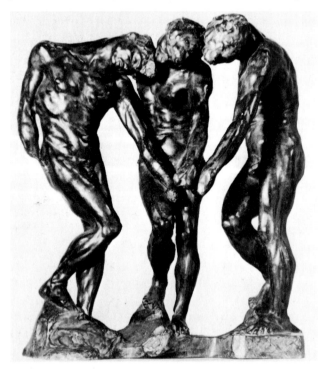

11. LEFT *Rodin:* The Three Shades, *1880. Bronze, 74¼" x 71" x 30". Musée Rodin, Paris.*
12. ABOVE *Antonio Canova (1757–1882):* The Three Graces, *1813. Marble. Hermitage, Leningrad. (Photo, Alinari)*

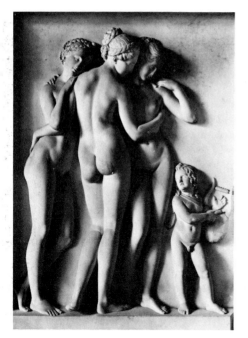
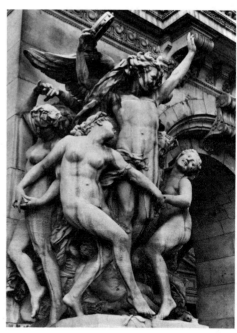

13. LEFT *Bertel Thorwaldsen
(1768–1844)*: The Three Graces,
1821. Marble. Palazzo Brera,
Milan. (Photo, Broggi)
14. RIGHT *Jean-Baptiste
Carpeaux (1827–75)*: The
Dance, 1873. Terra cotta, 90″ x
56″. Opera, Paris. (Photo,
Arch. Phot. Paris)

would be available simultaneously with the back view of
its mate. Without destroying the uniqueness of the individual form, there arises, then, a perception of a generic
ideal or type in which each separate figure is seen to
participate; and from this—displayed in sequence, in a
series of rotations—the *meaning* of the lone body is
established. During the early nineteenth-century, in both
Canova's and Thorwaldsen's neoclassical sculptures of
The Three Graces (figs. 12 and 13), one finds the main-
tenance of this tradition along with the meaning that
underlies it. The viewer sees not a single figure in rotation but, rather, three female nudes who present the body
in three different angles. As in relief, this presentation
arranges the bodies along a single, frontal plane, so that
it is legible at a glance.

The persistence of this strategy as a desideratum for
sculpture occurs decades later in Carpeaux's ensemble
for the façade of the Paris Opera. There, in *The Dance*
(fig. 14) of 1868–69, the two nymphs that flank the
central male figure perform for the viewer in much the
same way as Canova's *Graces* had done. Mirroring each
other's posture, the two figures rotate in counterpoint,
simultaneously exposing the front and back of the body
to view. With the symmetry of their movement comes a

19

satisfaction about the wholeness of one's perception of the form, and about the way it fuses with the notion of balance that suffuses the entire composition. Even though *The Dance* breaks with the surface qualities of neoclassical style, it carries on the underlying premises, and satisfies in every way Hildebrand's dictum about the need for all sculpture to conform to the principles of relief.

It is Rodin's lack of conformation to these principles that makes *The Three Shades* disturbing. By simply repeating the *same* figure three times, Rodin strips away from the group the idea of composition—the idea of rhythmic arrangement of forms, the poise and counterpoise of which are intended to reveal the latent meaning of the body. The act of simply lining up identical markers of the human form, one after the other, carries with it none of the traditional meaning of composition. In place of the intended angle/reverse-angle of Canova or Carpeaux, Rodin imposes an unyielding, mute, bluntness on his *Shades*. This he does in the artless, almost primitive, placement of the three heads at the same level, or in the strange repetition of the identical but separate pedestals on which each member of the group stands. The artful arrangements of Canova and Carpeaux had made the external views of their figures seem transparent to a sense of internal meaning. But Rodin's apparent artlessness endows his figures with a sense of opacity. The *Shades* do not form with each other a relationship that seems capable of signification, of creating a sign that is transparent to its meaning. Instead, the repetition of the *Shades* works to create a sign that is totally self-referential.

In seeming to refer the viewer to nothing more than his own triple production of the same object, Rodin replaces the narrative ensemble with one that tells of nothing but the repetitive process of its own creation. The *Shades*, which stand as both an introduction and a climax to the space of the doors, are as hostile to a narrative impulse as the "scenes" that occur on the face of the doors themselves.

The corollary to Rodin's purposeful confusion of narrative is his handling of the actual ground of the relief. For the ground plane of the *Gates* is simply not conceived of as the illusionistic matrix out of which the figures emerge. Relief, as we have seen, suspends the full volume

15. NEAR RIGHT *Thomas Eakins (1844–1916):* Spinning, *ca. 1882–83. Bronze, 19″ x 15″. Philadelphia Museum of Art. (Photo, A. J. Wyatt, staff photographer)*
16. FAR RIGHT *Adolf von Hildebrand (1847–1921):* Archery Lesson, *1888. Stone, 50″ x 44″ Wallraf-Richartz Museum, Cologne.*

of a figure halfway between its *literal* projection above the ground and its *virtual* existence within the "space" of the ground. The convention of relief requires that one not take literally the fact that a figure is only partially released from its solid surrounds. Rather, the ground of relief operates like a picture plane, and is interpreted as an open space in which the backward extension of a face or a body occurs.

Throughout the nineteenth century, sculptors continually tried to provide the viewer with information about those unseen (and of course unseeable) sides of whole objects imbedded within the relief ground. Given the unassailable frontality of relief, information about the concealed side of the figure had to come simultaneously with the viewer's perception of its front. One strategy for doing this we have already seen: the acting-out of the body's rotation through several figures, as in Canova's *Three Graces*. This information was also supplied, and increasingly so throughout the nineteenth century, by the intentional use of actual shadows cast onto the relief ground by the raised figurative elements. In

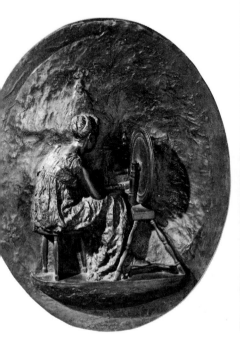

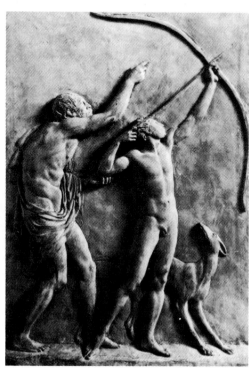

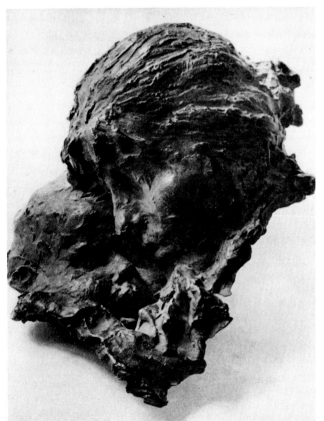
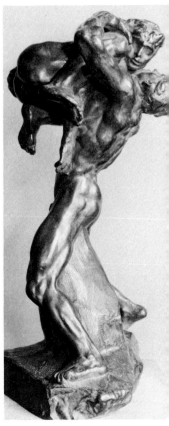

Thomas Eakins' bronzes of contemporary genre scenes
(fig. 15) or Hildebrand's antiquarian plaques (fig. 16),
there is a unifying formal impulse. Whether one looks
at the work of an ardent realist or of a determined
classicist, one sees that forms are marshaled so that the
shadows they cast will direct the viewer's attention to the
buried and unseen sides of the figures.

In a sculpture by Medardo Rosso, which is contemporary with Rodin's early work on the *Gates*, the use of
cast shadow operates as it does in Rude or Eakins or
Hildebrand. For Rosso's *Mother and Child Sleeping*
(fig. 17) contains not two but three figurative elements.
The first is the gently swollen circle of the infant's head.
The second is the voluptuous fabric of the side of the
female face in which the concave and convex forms of
forehead, cheek, and mouth are gathered into the simple
contour of the profile. The third, which lies between
them, is the field of shadow cast by the mother onto the

face of the child. What is striking about this shadow is that it does not function, as one would expect, by injecting a quantity of open space into the clenched forms of the sculpture, nor by serving as a fulcrum of darkness on which two light-drenched volumes are balanced. Instead, the shadow produces visual testimony about the other side of the woman's head.

The exposed surfaces of the faces, which carry the continual reminder of the sculptor's touch as he modeled them, become, because of the shadow, the most intense and poignant area of touch: the contact between the hidden cheek of the mother and the buried forehead of the child. It is as though Rosso felt it was not enough simply to excavate figures from the ground of the relief; he also supplies data about the realms of interaction so immersed within the material of the sculpture that neither the probe of his fingers nor our gaze could reach them. It is surely part of Rosso's meaning that beyond the brilliance of his modeling, which permits light to open and penetrate his surfaces, lies an unseeable area of the form about which he is compelled to report.[7]

In Rodin's *Gates*, on the other hand, cast shadow seems to emphasize the isolation and detachment of full-round figures from the relief ground and to enforce one's sense of the ground as a solid object in its own right, a kind of object that will not permit the illusion that one sees through it to a space beyond.

In addition, the shadow underlines the sense that the figures are intentionally fragmented and necessarily incomplete, rather than only perceptually incomplete, as in Rosso. For the first time, in the *Gates*, a relief ground acts to segment the figures it carries, to present them as literally truncated, to disallow them the fiction of a virtual space in which they can appear to expand. The *Gates* are, then, simultaneously purged of both the space and time that would support the unfolding of narrative. Space in the work is congealed and arrested; temporal relationships are driven toward a dense unclarity.

There is still another level on which Rodin worked this almost perverse vein of opacity: this is the way he related, or *failed* to relate, the outward appearance of the body to its inner structure. The outward gestures made by Rodin's figures do not seem to arise from what one

17. LEFT *Medardo Rosso (1858–1928):* Mother and Child Sleeping, *1883. Bronze, 13⅞".* Private collection.
18. RIGHT *Rodin:* "Je suis belle," *1882. Bronze, 29½" x 15¾" x 11¾". Musée Rodin, Paris. (Photo, Adelys)*

23

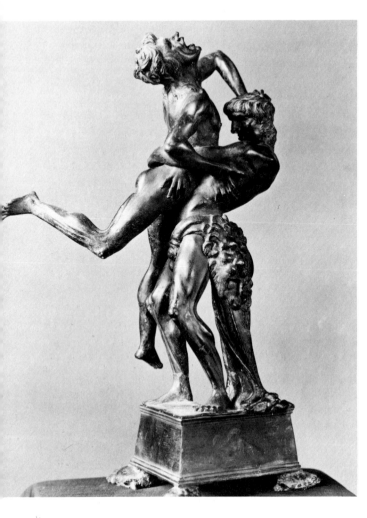

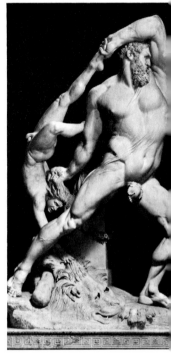

knows of the skeletal substructure that should support
the body's movement. One has only to compare, for
example, Rodin's group called "*Je suis belle*" (fig. 18)[8]
with a more classicizing work, Pollaiuolo's *Hercules and
Antaeus* (fig. 19), to see how this occurs. In both, a
standing male nude supports a second, airborne figure.
The moment of struggle that Pollaiuolo shows is fully
explained in terms of the body's system of internal support. The pressure of Hercules' arms encircling and
crushing Antaeus at a point on his spine causes a reaction
in which Antaeus is arched and splayed; while Antaeus,
pushing down on Hercules' shoulders, forces the doubling
backward of the lower form. Every action of the two
figures involves a thrust and counterthrust that reveal the

response of the skeletal system to external pressure. Clearly, in this work, gesture is both a result of that inner system and a revelation of it.

The clarity of contour that one finds in the Renaissance bronze is heightened and exaggerated when one turns to a neoclassical work that exploits the same gestural system of weight and support. Canova's *Hercules and Lichas* (fig. 20) explores the relationship between two struggling bodies within an even more radically defined single contour, and from an even more explicit frontality. The satisfaction one has in considering Canova's work is the satisfaction that comes from a sense of resolution—a sense that one's own particular vantage on the work, looking at its front, allows one to know with absolute certainty the mechanics of stress that consume the two bodies and invest the sculpture with meaning. The contour that unifies the figures resolves itself into a single wedgelike shape—its leading edge thrusting forward against the backward drag of the force resisting it.

This clarity of contour is the first thing one misses in *"Je suis belle,"* for Rodin has obscured it by seaming together the chest of the male and the torso of the female he supports. The bodies are therefore fused into a single contour that makes the reciprocity of their gesture highly ambiguous. The arched back and spread feet of the male figure indicate that it is both falling under the weight of the load it bears and rising to grasp or catch the other figure. Reading simultaneously as collapse and expansion, the gesture contains an ambivalence that one's knowledge of the body's structure cannot grasp rationally. Similarly, the female figure, doubled over into a ball of flesh, projects the feeling of both weight and buoyancy. One cannot penetrate to the skeletal core of the body to discover the meaning of these gestures.

It is not simply that one is looking at the group from an incorrect angle but that, unlike the Canova or the Pollaiuolo, Rodin's work has no angle of view that would be "correct"—no vantage point that would give coherence to the figures. The opacity that Rodin imposes on the relief ground of the *Gates*, and on the unfolding of narrative relationships upon it, is the same opacity that he here builds into the bodies of his figures: an opacity between the gestures through which they surface into the

19. TOP *Antonio Pollaiuolo (1429?–98):* Hercules and Antaeus, *ca. 1475. Bronze, 18".* Museo Nazionale, Florence. (Photo, Alinari)

20. BOTTOM *Canova:* Hercules and Lichas, *1812–15 (original 1796). Marble, 138".* Gallery of Modern Art, Rome. (Photo, Anderson)

world and the internal anatomical system by which those gestures would be "explained."

This opacity of gesture in *"Je suis belle"* is even more apparent in the single figure of *Adam* (fig. 21) and in its threefold appearance as the *Shades* surmounting *The Gates of Hell.* In *Adam* one notices the extreme elongation of the figure's neck and the massive swelling of its shoulder. One sees the way in which these two parts of the body are worked into an almost level plane, as though an enormous weight has pulled the figure's head around and out of joint so that the shoulder strains backward to aid in its support. And the relationship of the legs—one stiffened, the other flexed—does not give the relaxed effect of contraposto, in which the weight taken up by one leg releases the other into an easy curve. Instead, the bent leg of the *Adam* is racked and pulled, its thigh drawn out to nearly twice the length of the other.

What outward cause produces this torment of bearing in the *Adam?* What internal armature can one imagine, as one looks on from the outside, to explain the possibilities of their distention? Again one feels backed against a wall of unintelligibility. For it is not as though there is a *different* viewpoint one could seek from which to find those answers. Except one; and that is not exactly a *place* from which to look at the work—any of Rodin's work—but, rather, a condition. This condition might be called a belief in the manifest intelligibility of *surfaces,* and that entails relinquishing certain notions of cause as it relates to meaning, or accepting the possibility of meaning without the proof or verification of cause. It would mean accepting effects themselves as self-explanatory —as significant even in the absence of what one might think of as the logical background from which they emerge.

21. Rodin: Adam, *1880. Bronze, 75½" x 29½" x 29½". Philadelphia Museum of Art.*

The significance of what I have called this "condition" can be gauged by the force of its challenge to the normal picture one has of the self and the way that self relates to other selves. For we normally think of the self as a subjectivity with special access to its own conscious states, an access simply denied to others outside it. Because each individual registers sensory impressions upon his or her own mechanisms of touch or sight, what I see or hear or feel is available to me with a special kind of immediacy

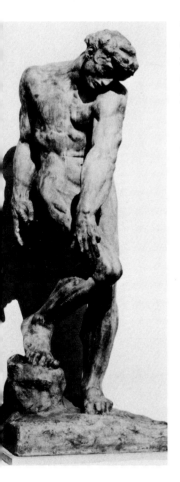

that is unavailable to anyone else. Similarly, my thoughts seem to be transparent to my mind or my consciousness in a way that is direct and present only to me. It would seem that what I think can be merely inferred by another person, can only reach him indirectly if I choose to report on my thoughts.

This picture of the self as enjoying a privileged and direct relationship to the contents of its own consciousness is a picture of the self as basically private and discrete. It is a picture which conjures up a whole set of *meanings* derived from a range of private experiences to which each of us has subjective access, meanings that exist prior to our communication with each other in the present. They are, one might say, the very foundation on which such communication must be built, the background from which it must arise. It is only because I have this experience prior to my contact with another person that I can know what he means in his various acts, his various gestures, his various reports.

If this observation is transferred to the realm of sculpture, it would seem that a sculptural language can only become coherent and intelligible if it addresses itself to these same underlying conditions of experience. I know that certain contractions of muscles in my face occur when I experience pain and therefore became an expression of pain, a representation of it, so to speak. I know that certain configurations of the anatomy correspond to certain acts I perform, such as walking, lifting, turning, pulling. Thus it would seem that the recognition of those configurations in the sculptural object is necessary for the meaning of that object to be legible; that I must be able to read back from the surface configuration to the anatomical ground of a gesture's possibility in order to perceive the significance of that gesture. It is this communication between the surface and the anatomical depths that Rodin aborts. We are left with gestures that are unsupported by appeals to their own anatomical backgrounds, that cannot address themselves logically to a recognizable, prior experience within ourselves.

But what if meaning does not depend on this kind of prior experience? What if meaning, instead of preceding experience, occurs *within* experience; what if my knowledge of a feeling, pain for example, does not depend on a set of sensory memories but is invented freshly and uniquely each time it occurs for me? Further, what if, in order to experience it, I must feel my body's very registration of it in relation to the way another person watches me and reacts to my gestures of pain? And, with regard to someone else's sensations, we might ask whether there is not a certain sufficiency in the expression of them that he makes, one that does not require our consultation of our own private lexicon of meanings in order to complete them, to comprehend them—whether, in fact, his expression does not enlarge our own lexicon, adding to it a new term, teaching us something new in the very originality of its occurrence.

This picture of meaning being synchronous with experience, rather than necessarily prior to it, is one that was developed by Edmund Husserl (1859–1938), a philosopher working at the time of Rodin's mature career.[9] Addressing himself to what has been called "the paradox of the alter ego," Husserl questioned the notion of a self that is essentially private and inaccessible (except indirectly) to others. If one were to believe in this notion of the private self, he argued, each of us would be one person to ourselves and someone else for another. In order for the "I" to be the same entity both for myself and for the person to whom I am speaking, I must become myself as I manifest myself to others; my self must be formed at the juncture between that self of which I am conscious and that external object which surfaces in all the acts, gestures, and movements of my body.

Although Rodin had no contact with Husserl's philosophy, so far as we know, his sculptures manifest a notion of the self which that philosophy had begun to explore. They are about a lack of premeditation, a lack of foreknowledge, that leaves one intellectually and emotionally dependent on the gestures and movements of figures as they externalize themselves. Narratively, in relation to the doors, one is immersed in a sense of an event as it coalesces, without the distance from that event that a history of its causes would bestow. With the *Gates* as a whole, as with each individual figure, one is stopped at the surface.

The surface of the body, that boundary between what we think of as internal and private, and what we acknowl-

22. NEAR RIGHT *Rodin:* Man's Torso, *1877. Bronze, 20⅞" x 11" x 7⅛". Musée du Petit Palais, Paris. (Photo, Bulloz)*

23. FAR RIGHT *Rodin:* The Walking Man *(backview detail), 1877. Bronze, 33⅛". National Gallery, Washington, D.C. (Photo, Henry Moore)*

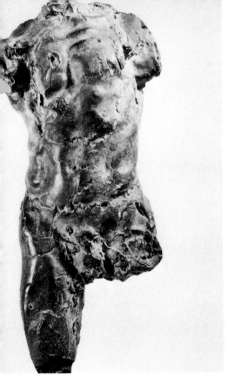
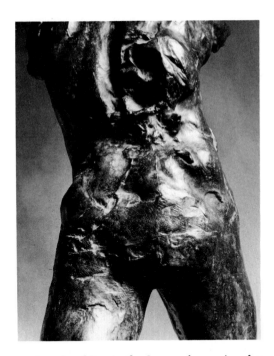

edge as external and public, is the locus of meaning for Rodin's sculpture. And it is a surface that expresses equally the results of internal and external forces. The internal forces that condition the surface of the figure are, of course, anatomical, muscular. The forces that shape the figure from outside itself come from the artist: the act of manipulation, artifice, his process of making.

Certain sculptures by Rodin could almost serve as illustrations for a manual on bronze-casting, so clearly do they document the procedures of formation. Sculptures such the *Torso* of 1877 (fig. 22) are riddled with the accidents of the foundry: air-pocket holes which have not been plugged; ridges and bubbles produced in the casting stage which have not been filed away—a surface marbeled with the marks of process that Rodin has not smoothed out but left, so that they are the visual evidence of the passage of the medium itself from one state to another.

This documentation of making is not limited to the accidents of molten bronze during casting. Rodin's figures are also branded with marks that tell of their rites of passage during the modeling stage: the lower back of *The Walking Man* (fig. 23) was deeply gouged in its malleable clay form and the indentation was never filled

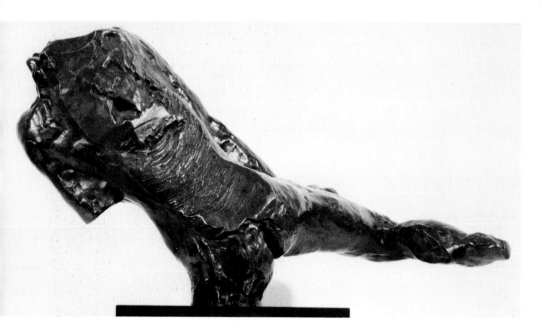

in; the *Flying Figure* (fig. 24) shows a knife cut that has
sliced part of the calf muscle on the extended leg—but
no additional clay has replaced this loss; and the lower
back and upper buttocks of the same figure bear the
mark of some heavy object that has brushed the clay
when wet, flattening and erasing the anatomical development, making the surface testify only to the fact that
something has dragged its way over it.[10]

Again and again Rodin forces the viewer to acknowledge the work as a result of a process, an act that has
shaped the figure over time. And this acknowledgment
becomes another factor in forcing on the viewer that
condition of which I have spoken: meaning does not
precede experience but occurs in the process of experience itself. It is on the surface of the work that two
senses of process coincide—there the externalization of
gesture meets with the imprint of the artist's act as he
shapes the work.

Nowhere in Rodin's oeuvre is this lodging of meaning
in the surface as eloquently and directly effected as in the
Balzac monument (fig. 25), which Rodin produced on
commission in 1897. Although Rodin's preliminary studies
for the work are of a nude figure, the final version completely swathes the body of the writer in his dressing
gown. The arms and hands can barely be detected under-

24. ABOVE *Rodin:* Flying
Figure, *1890–91. Bronze,*
20¼" x 30" x 11¾". Musée
Rodin, Paris. (Photo, Eric
Pollitzer)

25. NEAR RIGHT *Rodin:* Balzac,
1897. Bronze, 117" x 47¼" x
47¼". Collection, The Museum
of Modern Art, New York.
(Photo, Rosalind E. Krauss)

26. ABOVE RIGHT *Rosso:* The
Golden Age, *1886. Wax over*
plaster, 17⅝". Galleria d'Arte,
Rome.

30

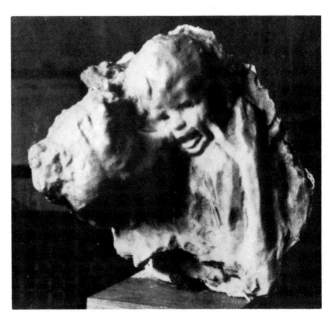

neath the robe as they reach from inside to hold it fast; and so little does the gown display of the body, as the fabric plunges from shoulders to toes with the empty arms of the garment reinforcing the verticality of its fall, that Rilke was moved to describe the head of the *Balzac* as something entirely apart from the body. The head seemed to be "living at the summit of the figure," Rilke wrote, "like those balls that dance on jets of water."[11]

Rilke's metaphor, in its stunning accuracy, points to the way in which Rodin engulfs the *Balzac* body within a single gesture which becomes a representation of the subject's will. Wrapping his gown around him, the figure *makes* his writer's body through that momentary, ephemeral arrangement of surface; he molds his own flesh into a columnar support as though his genius, concentrated into the contracted features of his face, were being held aloft by a single act of determination.

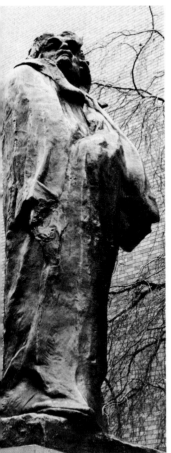

It is the intervention of a piece of cloth between viewer and sculptural figure which, like the *Balzac*, characterizes the work by Medardo Rosso that is closest in spirit to Rodin's own. An Italian contemporary of Rodin, Rosso spent the last twenty years of his career in France, where he was intensely envious of Rodin's growing reputation. Feeling that much of what was "original" in Rodin's art was shared and even anticipated in his own, Rosso

31

pointed to his own elevation of the *bozzetto*, or rough sketch, into the stature of "finished" work. He saw his own roughened surfaces, eloquent with the imprint of his fingers as he worked them and his own presentation of gesture through fragmentation of the body, as furthering that claim.

Yet, as we saw in the 1883 *Mother and Child Sleeping*, Rosso's work from the early part of his career remains within the traditional vein of sculptural relief. No matter how ruffled and bruised the skin of *The Golden Age*, 1886 (fig. 26), or *Veiled Woman*, 1893, these surfaces do not achieve the kind of self-sufficiency and opacity that Rodin's do.[12] They continue to refer beyond themselves to an unseen side, to a previous moment in the narrative chain, to project inward toward an internal emotional condition. Only in much later work—in the 1906–07 *Ecce Puer!* (fig. 27)—does Rosso draw close to the deepest resources of Rodin's art.

The story surrounding this late work places its origins in a visit Rosso paid to some friends in Paris. There he caught a glimpse of the young son of the family half hidden behind the curtained entry to the living room, shyly listening to the adults talking within. Surprised by Rosso's glance, the boy started back, and Rosso discovered

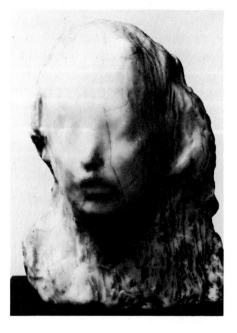
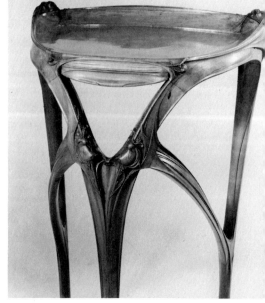

in that visual melee of drapery, shadow, and expression a momentary fusion of timidity and curiosity. In that fleeting moment Rosso learned what the ambivalent set of feelings looked like. With *Ecce Puer!* Rosso expresses both that knowledge and the act of its coalescing. The child's features are veined by the folds of curtain which groove the wax surface of the sculpture, so that the solidity of the flesh is irretrievably softened by a depiction of the speed with which the apparition formed and disappeared before the artist's eyes. Thus, the surface that obscures and shrouds the image of the child simultaneously carries the meaning of the boy's expression. *Ecce Puer!* begins and ends in this surface; nothing is implied beyond it.

This emphasis on surface and the way meaning is lodged within it by factors that are partly external— whether the accidental pattern of light or the casual impress of the artist's thumb—were not restricted to the two great sculptural personalities of the last decade of the nineteenth century and the first decade of the twentieth. Although Rodin and Rosso brought this to its fullest pitch of meaning, one finds evidence of a corresponding sensibility within the decorative arts of the time, particularly within the style called *art nouveau*. Whether we are talking about the metal inkwells and candlesticks of Victor Horta or Henry Van de Velde, or the carved furniture of Hector Guimard (fig. 28), the decorated vases of Louis Tiffany and Emile Gallée, or the architectural façades of Antonio Gaudí, we find a design style that does not concern itself with the internal structure of an object. Generally speaking, *art nouveau* presents volume with an undifferentiated sense of the interior, concentrating instead on its surface. As in the sculpture of Rodin and Rosso, the surfaces of these objects bear evidence of an external process of formation. They are executed in such a way that we feel we are looking at something that was shaped by the erosion of water over rock, or by the tracks of waves on sand, or by the ravages of wind; in short, by what we think of as the passage of natural forces over the surface of matter. Shaping those substances from the outside, these forces act with no regard to the intrinsic structure of the material on which they work. In the furniture of the French and Belgian *art-nouveau* designers, one never finds a clearly stated distinction between vertical, load-bearing members and horizontal surfaces. The juncture between table top and table leg flows into a single curve that is expressive only of the application of some kind of external pressure—like wind bending reeds, or the tides shaping the stems of water plants.

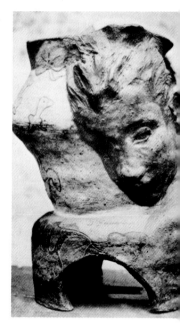

The designs with which Tiffany veins the surfaces of his glass objects likewise obscure functional or structural divisions, such as the separation between foot, body, neck and lip of a vase. Instead, one finds patterns derived from other natural, membranous tissue—feathers, flower petals, cobwebs, leaves—grafted onto the swollen exterior of the glass, expressing an even pull of tension over the surface.

In the three-dimensional work of another late-nineteenth-century artist there is a corresponding vision of sculptural expression as the surface decoration of hollow vessels. Most of Paul Gauguin's sculpture, whether carved or modeled, occurs as the application of anatomical fragment to the surface of hollow shapes. Consistent with the impulses of *art nouveau* in general, the external articulation of these vessels—as in the pot here (fig. 29) or *The Afternoon of a Faun*—indicates nothing of the internal structure of the object, so that the arrangement of one part of the face of the object in relation to another has no feeling of being rationally or structurally compelled. The bulges and swells of these surfaces speak not so much of a composition that could logically be known beforehand as they do of magical or primitive forces which the artist has discovered in the act of creating the particular constellation of images within any given object. Gauguin's sculpture makes reference to narrative only to generate a sense of irrationality, or mystery. Gauguin presents the pieces of a story but without a sequence that would give the viewer a sense of accurate or verifiable access to the meaning of the event to which the artist alludes.

The procedures that Gauguin uses to deny the viewer access to the narrative meaning of his sculpture are close to Rodin's procedures on the *Gates of Hell*. Violently fragmenting the various protagonists within the narrative ensemble, enforcing the discontinuity and disruption with which they move across the surface, a relief such as *Be in Love, You Will Be Happy* (fig. 30) subverts the traditional logical function of that mode of sculpture.[13]

As we have seen, Rodin used yet another strategy in the *Gates* (fig. 5) to defeat the conventional meaning of narrative, and that was to repeat figures, as he had done with the *Shades* (fig. 11), and to present these identical units, one next to the other. This kind of repetition forces a self-conscious account of process to usurp attention from the object's role in the overall narration. It was this kind of reference to the process of creation that informed the sculpture of Rodin's most progressive follower—Henri Matisse.

Working for the most part with small-scale bronze figures, Matisse explored much of the territory Rodin had already covered. The surfaces of his figures follow the older artist's example in the testimony they bear to the procedures of modeling: the gouging and pinching, the minor additions and subtractions of material, the traces of thumb and hand as they worked the clay. Matisse's inclination to express the human form through anatomical

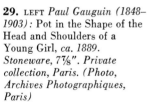

29. LEFT *Paul Gauguin (1848–1903)*: Pot in the Shape of the Head and Shoulders of a Young Girl, *ca. 1889. Stoneware, 7⅞". Private collection, Paris. (Photo, Archives Photographiques, Paris)*

30. RIGHT *Gauguin:* Be in Love, You Will Be Happy, *1901. Painted wood relief, 28⅛" x 28¾". Courtesy Museum of Fine Arts, Boston. Arthur Tracy Cabot Fund.*

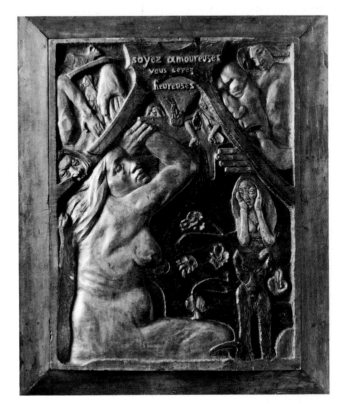

fragments derives from Rodin, as do certain actual poses taken from Rodin's work, such as the way Matisse's *Serf* repeats the stance of Rodin's *Walking Man*. In addition, one finds sculptures by Matisse—such as *Standing Nude with Arms Raised* (1906) and *The Serpentine* (fig. 31) (1909)—that express the arms and legs of the figures as undifferentiated rolls of clay—echoing Rodin's figurines of dancers in which representation of the body is arrested at the first stage of a sketch done in clay coils (fig. 32). Indeed, it was out of this fascination with process that Matisse's most original and radical formulation of the possibilities of sculpture came.

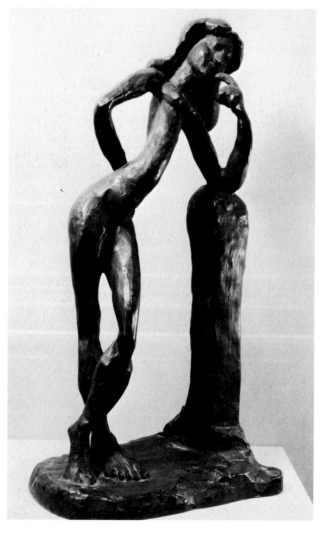

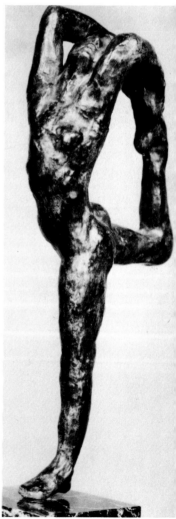

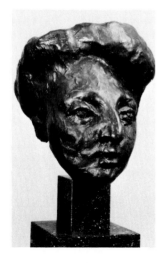

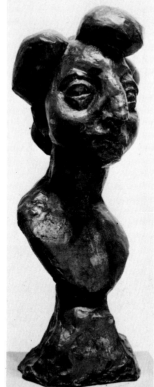

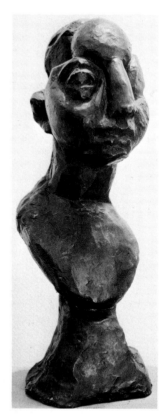

31. FAR LEFT *Henri Matisse (1869–1954):* The Serpentine, *1909. Bronze, 22¼". Collection, The Museum of Modern Art, New York. Gift of Abby Aldrich Rockefeller.*

32. NEAR LEFT *Rodin:* Dance Movement A, *ca. 1910–1911. Bronze, 28" x 8¾" x 13⅛". Musée Rodin, Paris.*

33. ABOVE LEFT *Matisse:* Jeannette, II, *1910–13. Bronze, 10⅜". Collection, The Museum of Modern Art, New York. Gift of Sidney Janis.*

34. ABOVE CENTER *Matisse:* Jeannette, III, *1910–13. Bronze, 23¾". Collection, The Musuem of Modern Art, New York. Acquired through the Lillie P. Bliss Bequest.*

35. ABOVE RIGHT *Matisse:* Jeannette, V, *1910–13. Bronze, 22⅞". Collection, The Museum of Modern Art, New York. Acquired through the Lillie P. Bliss Bequest.*

In 1910–13 Matisse modeled five versions of a female head, producing the series of *Jeannette I–V* (figs. 33, 34, and 35), which arranges in linear progression the artist's analysis of physiognomic form. In this series, Matisse takes the notion of a linear string of events—that conception which we have been calling narrative—and reorients it to become a kind of analytic ledger on which is written the account of formal conception and change.

With the serialization of the head of *Jeannette*, one finds oneself very far from the kind of concentration of many historical moments into a single "pregnant" image that was found in Rude's *La Marseillaise* (fig. 4). Instead, one is confronted with a single perception prolonged over the various moments of its development—each one projected as a separate image. *Jeannette I–V* is the logical completion of what the *Shades* had begun; the ambition to interpret and condense the meaning of history has contracted to a presentation of steps in an object's formation.

Analytic Space: 2
futurism
and
constructivism

This is a story told by the poet Filippo Marinetti, who shaped it into a narrative circle, to hold, like a ring, the stony-hard facets of the first *Futurist Manifesto*. It was winter, 1909. Marinetti and some friends were together late one night. The setting was Marinetti's house in Milan, with its lush interior of Persian carpets and filigreed lamps. To all of them, the ambience seemed at cross-purposes with the direction of their lives, and they resented its silence, its capacity to encompass and reflect the immense starlit sky, the muffled watery echoes of the canals, the ominous stillness of stone palaces. They resented the harmony it created with an Italy replete with memories of antiquity, an Italy oblivious to the gathering forces of industrialism.

Their conversation began to reflect this resentment;

they spoke of the fact that beyond the slumbering quiet there were men who were even then at work, and they conjured images of violent labor: ". . . stokers feeding the hellish fires of great ships," or men fueling the power of locomotives roaring through the night. This longing for noise and speed to shatter the still silence in which they felt smothered was answered by the sudden sound of trolley cars beneath their window. Galvanized, Marinetti shouted to his companions to follow him—to drive out into the dawn light. "There's nothing," he cried, 'to match the splendor of the sun's red sword, slashing for the first time through our millennial gloom!"[1]

They crowded into automobiles and began a breakneck drive through the streets of the city. Incited by speed, Marinetti began to long for an end to "domesticated wisdom," to what had already been thought, to what was already known. As if in reply, his race with experience ended in upheaval, as his car, swerving to avoid a collision, overturned in a ditch.

For Marinetti, this clash with danger was the necessary conclusion to his experience: "O! Maternal ditch," he exclaimed, "almost full of muddy water! Fair factory drain! I gulped down your nourishing sludge; and I remembered the blessed black breast of my Sudanese nurse. . . . When I came up—torn, filthy, and stinking— from under the capsized car, I felt the white-hot iron of joy deliciously pass through my heart!"

That story—of exasperation with the values of an honored past, and of a forward, almost desperate rush toward a radical baptism in the waters of industrial waste—is the prose setting for the declarative points of the *Futurist Manifesto*. The *Manifesto* itself proclaims a love of speed and danger. It states a new cult of beauty in which "a racing car . . . is more beautiful than the *Victory of Samothrace*." It advocates the values of aggression and destruction, calling for the dismantling of museums, libraries, academies—of all those institutions dedicated to the preservation and prolongation of the past. Written in 1909, the *Manifesto* was the first of a long series of proclamations by which the Italian futurists attempted to affect the course of European art.

Aside from the specifics of its actual content, the extraordinary aspect of that *Manifesto* arises from the strategy of its presentation. For, unlike other aesthetic tracts— one might think of Hildebrand's *The Problem of Form* or Worringer's *Abstraction and Empathy*—this text breaks through the decorum of objective argument to locate the reader within the temporal unfolding of narrative. Its medium is the story, and it is through the straightforward rush of events in time that the author wished to create its impact. The manifesto proper arises at a specific juncture within the story, becoming the objective result, a revelatory experience. As such, it attempts to project the shape of a future set of events or values. In that sense, one could compare the *Manifesto*, even though it is a verbal structure, to the Rude relief of *La Marseillaise* (fig. 4). One could, that is, see it as related to that same condition of powerfully distilled narrative. Except that, in place of a sequence that leads to and climaxes in political revolution, Marinetti substitutes the forward march of industrialism. His story is about the trajectory of his own consciousness converging with the path of technological development. Their point of intersection is made physically explicit in the image of his immersion in the ditch of factory sludge—his body literally embraced by the by-products of industrial progress. The *Manifesto*, placed at the story's center, results in a call for the notion of speed as a plastic value—speed has become a metaphor for temporal progression made explicit and visible. The moving object becomes the vehicle of perceived time, and time becomes a visible dimension of space once the temporal takes the form of mechanical motion.

Given the static nature of the sculptural object, it might seem that sculpture is the least likely medium to use to represent time unfolding through motion. Yet Umberto Boccioni, the futurist artist most dedicated to the reformulation of sculptural style, did not think so. For him, the problem became one of fusing two separate modes of being, in which the object would participate. The first of these modes involved the structural and material essence of the object—what one might call its inherent characteristics. This aspect Boccioni referred to as "absolute motion." The second mode he called the object's "relative motion." By this he meant the contingent existence of the object in real space, as a viewer changed positions relative to the object and saw new groupings form between it and neighboring objects (fig. 37). "Relative motion" also refers to the distentions and changes in shape that would occur once a figure at rest was precipitated into movement. In order to represent the synthesis between absolute and relative modes of being, Boccioni spoke of the necessity of creating "a sign or, better, a unique form that would replace the old concept of division with a new concept of continuity."[2]

The first sculpture to work out this synthesis was made by Boccioni in 1912. Called *Development of a Bottle in Space* (fig. 36), it is a still-life arrangement of a table, bottle, dish, and glass.

Extraordinarily enough for a work about the submersion of objects within the flow of space and time, *Development of a Bottle*—like Rude's *La Marseillaise*—is structured to be seen frontally, like a relief, and it is dominated by a revelatory, iconic shape, or, in Boccioni's own terms, "a sign." For the *Bottle*, as Boccioni conceives it, is made up of a series of bottle-shaped profiles or shells which have been fitted inside each other like Chinese boxes. However, unlike the Chinese boxes, the front face of this sum of nested bottles has been cut away. Therefore, in order to perceive the relationship between the forward edges of these half-cylinders, the viewer is immobilized at a single vantage point, since it is only from the front that the series of exfoliations—and their meaning—can be seen.

Facing the front plane of the sculpture, then, the viewer is made aware of a particular opposition embodied or represented by the work—an opposition between a static, hollow center and the depiction of a moving or shifting exterior. For Boccioni has modeled the nested, cutaway shells of the bottles so that they seem to have been rotated slightly in relation to one another. The rotation tightens and becomes more extreme toward the top of the form, where the shells revolve, at different speeds, around the shaft of the bottle's neck. At times one can imagine that the shells would completely obscure the hollow center of the object, and at other moments, like the one caught and held by this particular configuration, the shells leave the

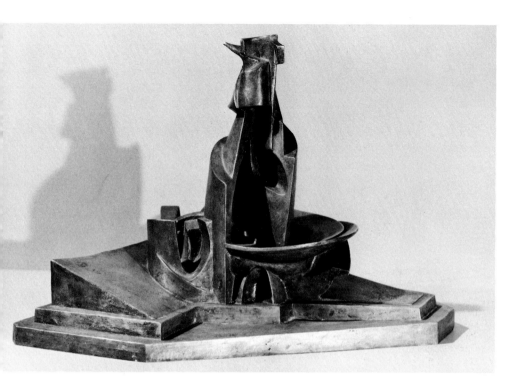

center available to sight. And while the external sheaths of the object are thus arranged in an illusion of continual motion, the innermost center around which they turn is understood to be completely at rest.

This center, unlike the jagged and incomplete shells of the bottle's exterior, is a concavity edged by a simple, unbroken profile, and functions as an ideal shape that seems to guarantee the object's integrity—a kind of radiance or emanation from within. If we return to Boccioni's categories of relative and absolute motion, we realize that this image of stillness, running like a ridgepole through the interior of the work, reads as a symbol of invariance. That is, the central profile characterizes the structural essence of the object—in terms of a shape of irreducible simplicity—which endures beyond the surface changes of "relative motion": the contingencies of light, placement, or the happenstance of the observer's point of view.

Development of a Bottle in Space is thus a work that equates the concerns of sculpture with concerns about how things are known. It attempts to outrun the partial information that any single view would allow a perceiver

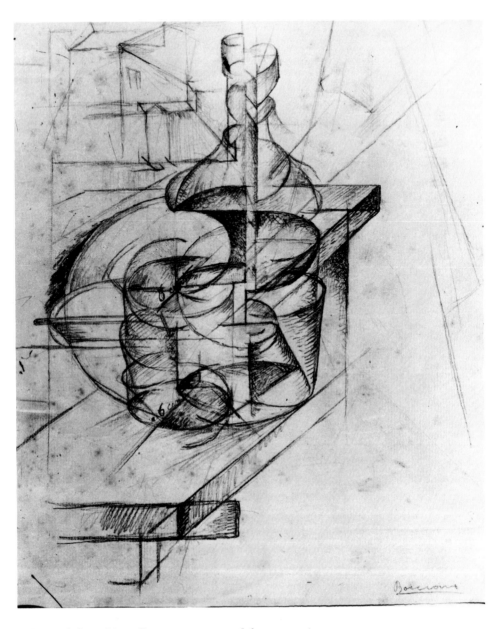

to have of that object. It seems to proceed from a notion
of the poverty of brute perception since, in any one
moment of seeing, much of the actual surface of the
bottle will be obscured from view. By overcoming that
poverty, the bottle can be known in terms of a full conceptual grasp of the thing, a grasp which supersedes the
incompleteness of any single, isolated perception. "Knowing" the bottle must be—in the terms of the idealist view

that the sculpture embodies—a function of a kind of synthetic vision that integrates all those partial and in themselves unintelligible angles of vision. The sculpture dramatizes a conflict between the poverty of information contained in the single view of the object and the totality of vision that is basic to any serious claim to "know" it. One resolution to that conflict would theoretically come if one redefined the viewer's "real" stance relative to the object: picturing his position in terms of an infinitely mobile intelligence, capable of enveloping all aspects of the bottle at once. That is the resolution proposed by Boccioni's work.

If the frontality of the relief-like presentation of *Development of a Bottle in Space* physically immobilizes its viewer, pinning his observation of it to a single facet, the representation of the spiraling shells conceptually frees him from this physically static position. It allows him to become a disembodied intelligence circulating through an ideal space to grasp the thing from all sides at once, and to collapse this conceptual circumnavigation into a single, infinitely rich and complete moment of intellection. The moment of contact with the sculpture is extended and thickened into an encounter that is pregnant with an accumulation of past and future relationships between viewer and object.

For the futurists, this intellectual domination of things is prescribed by their own point in history. As they wrote in 1910: "Who can still believe in the opacity of bodies, since our sharpened and multiplied sensitiveness has already penetrated the obscure manifestations of the medium? Why should we forget in our creations the doubled power of our sight, capable of giving results analogous to those of X-rays?"[3] *Development of a Bottle in Space* is an emblem of this "sharpened and multiplied sensitiveness." For it not only treats the viewer as a consciousness capable of encompassing the object's exterior in a single instant but it also guarantees the unity and clarity of this knowledge by giving him access to the object's very core. The simple, bottle-shaped contour that resides at the center of the work acts like a compressed, schematic "idea" of the structure of the bottle—an intellectual emblem of its essence. The futurists' demand for the immediacy of this knowledge is underlined by their

37. *Boccioni:* Table and Bottle and Block of Houses, *1912. Charcoal drawing, 13" x 9⅓". Castello Sforzesco, Milan. (Photo: Archivio Fotografico)*

written reference to X-ray vision, as they turn to science to peel away the mute surfaces of things that make them unintelligible. *Development of a Bottle* dispenses with the unintelligible, and becomes an argument on the side of a conquering intelligence.

Yet for all of futurism's claims to have turned away from the art of the past, Boccioni's ambition for sculpture is clearly not new. We have seen it operating in the neo-classic display of the figure in terms of the three simultaneously given views of its exterior; we have read of it in Hildebrand's treatise on sculptural form; we have encountered it in the shadowy testimony Rosso gives to the nether side of an object—knowledge of which is made to exist in an inextricable fusion with its front face.[4] What is new in futurism is that this idealism is married, early in the twentieth century, to the concept of technology. Their notion is that locked within the functioning of machines, embodied in the ratios between gears and levers, physicalized by mechanical motion, one will find a direct and rational model for the energy produced by the conquests of thought. Futurism transforms a classical meditation on beauty into a technologically informed vision of power.

Of course, in the light of the futurists' strident advocacy of the beauty of machines, and their professed distaste for that inventory of subject matter into which traditional art had poured its own sets of standards and values, Boccioni's use of conventional still life as the basis for his sculpture may seem incongruous. (As incongruous as the fact that Boccioni wrought his first, fully realized work in bronze in spite of the *Manifesto*'s specifying the priorities for sculpture as being, among others, the use of antitraditional materials such as glass, sheet metal, wire, or electric lights.)[5] However, the choice of subject is undoubtedly an index of Boccioni's growing knowledge of and respect for cubism, and his sense that the success of the cubist painters stemmed from the attitude with which they carried forward their work as a form of research. From early 1911, with the very first report on cubism to appear in Italy, the futurists had been impressed to learn that this research was conducted with the common studio paraphernalia of still-life objects. The

Italian critic Soffici had written of Picasso that he "goes around the objects themselves, considers them poetically from all angles, submits to and renders his successive impressions; in sum, shows them in their totality and emotional permanence with the same freedom with which impressionism rendered only one side and one moment."[6]

In the fall of that year the futurists had gone briefly to Paris to see the new French art for themselves, an acquaintance that was strengthened by longer contact the following year. So, in some sense Boccioni's *Bottle* is predicated both on his native convictions and on his subsequent assessment of Picasso's enterprise. The *Bottle* is a partial attempt to detach a cubist-based object from its illusionistically bound pictorial situation and immerse it in the life of the three dimensions of real space.

Boccioni's endeavors, which took place in the winter of 1912–13, were contemporaneous with Picasso's own experiments with liberating the still-life components of his paintings from the confines of absolute two-dimensionality. Comparing Picasso's reliefs to Boccioni's *Bottle* becomes an interesting exercise in the divergence of aesthetic premises. For no two sets of objects could be, in actual intent and in formal result, less similar. Boccioni was bent on giving the stationary viewer a kind of conceptual leverage over his fixed point of view by structuring into the sculpture an illusion of spiral motion, but Picasso's relief-objects are left as static and immobile as the wall surface against which they are seen. If Boccioni had carved the center of the bottle into a discrete shape that would confer an essential unity onto the object, Picasso's constructions (figs. 38–40) fail to deliver that "sign" of unity through which the essence of the object can be grasped. So the stationary viewer of the Picasso relief is not released from the object's front and propelled around its sides. He is left with the reality of his placement and the resulting lack of the futurist form of knowledge. There is no singular shape lying at the core of these constructions which the viewer can read as the generative idea that operates beyond the disarray of their assembled, perceptual facts.

Instead, Picasso constructs his reliefs from two types of perceptual fact which interlock across the surface of the work. The first of these is a combination of planes and shadow-filled gaps between planes. Through this treatment, which occurs in the 1914 *Violin* (fig. 38), for example, the shape of the object—its contour or profile— is utterly dispersed. And what we encounter instead is something like a corrugated plane—a surface that has become dense with the cues of tactile experience: shadow and texture. Interwoven through this array of tactile cues is a second visual element, which one might characterize as decorative pieces drawn from a language of description. For the musical instruments and still-life objects from which Picasso's reliefs are built carry on their surface the fragments of a pictorial language.

In the case of *Violin*, Picasso decorates some of its planes with a mesh of line that refers to the function of crosshatching in drawings or paintings. In two-dimensional representations, crosshatching is used to shade or model surfaces, giving to them an illusion of volume. Because *Violin* is already three-dimensional, shading or hatching is of course superfluous to it. Realizing this functional redundancy, the viewer is aware of the crosshatching as an ossified element: a refugee from the descriptive language of another medium (painting or drawing) which seems to have no real function within a work of sculpture. Furthermore, Picasso places two shallow troughs on either side of the work's center, one smaller and lower than the other. Representing the sound holes of the real instrument, these rectangular pieces work also as elements from the language used in a picture to indicate depth. They are cues to the diminution in size and the oblique relationship of forms that occur in the "picturing" of objects separated from one another in space. Another instance of this can be seen in the construction, *Guitar* (fig. 39), where Picasso arranges the strings so that instead of extending parallel along its face the way they would in an ordinary instrument, they converge to a point. And this convergence reads unmistakably as a means of indicating perspective—that is, as a device to project the illusion of depth onto a flat surface. In all these cases the fragments of descriptive language fail to integrate the separate planes of the constructions into a single, coherent object. In their calculated failure to do so, they take on a kind of frozen existence much the way the words in

38. *Pablo Picasso (1881– 1974)*: Violin, *1914. Painted lead, 38" x 26¼". Estate of the artist.*

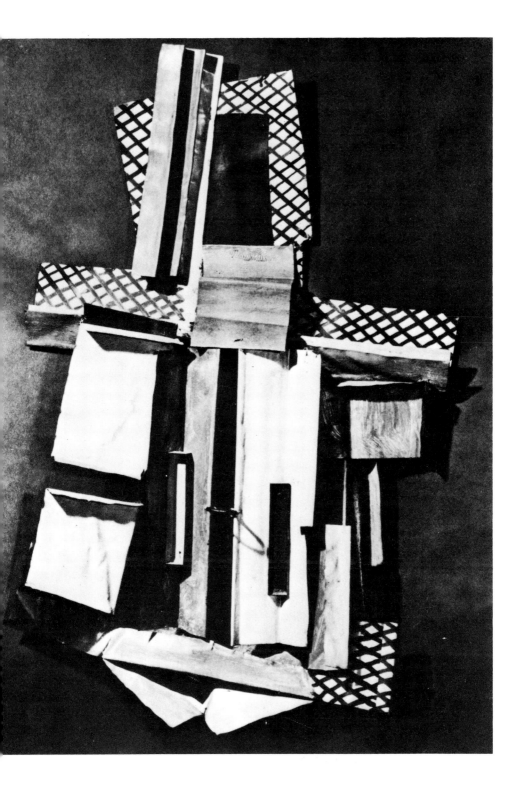

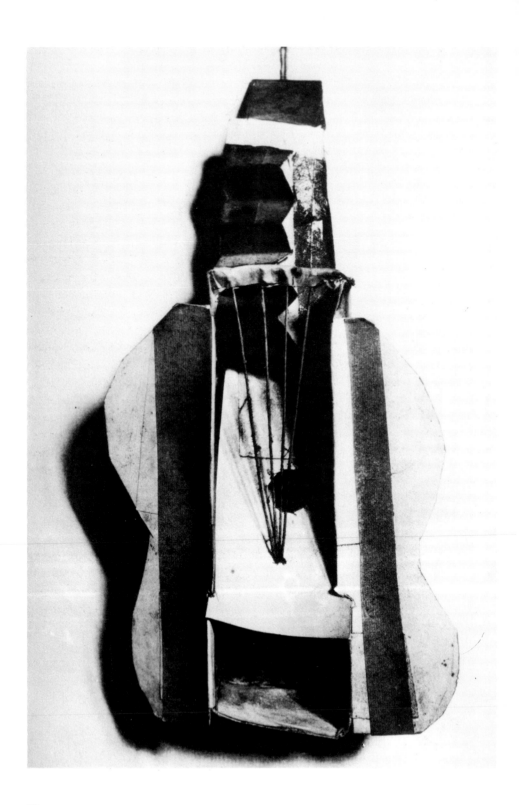

cubist collages, deprived of a linguistic context in which to perform, turn into inert objects.

Spread side by side in these reliefs, then, is an array of material and set of descriptive elements that have been forced to become merely decorative because they are deprived of their normal role within representation, namely, the means for structuring brute perception, for providing a grammar by which the viewer can order and make sense of the experience of his world. Insofar as Picasso presents us with two orders of experience, his reliefs are not unlike Boccioni's *Bottle*. The divergence—and it is a profound and absolute one—between Picasso's reliefs and futurist sculpture is in Picasso's conception of the relationship between the two orders. Boccioni had pictured the conceptual order as transcending the materials of experience—projected into the heart of those essentially inert materials by the formulating consciousness of the viewer. Picasso, on the other hand, weaves the two orders together, presenting them side by side, displaying them both as perceptual orders and as occupants of literal space. Picasso's reliefs do not present a moment of organization that lies *beyond* the surface of the object—an ideational center which we can intellectually occupy to give the object a significance that transcends our perception of it. He insists that there is a logic immanent *in* that surface and that conception arises with experience rather than prior to or apart from it.

The extraordinary lesson of the cubist reliefs of 1912–15, is similar, then, to the lesson of the *Gates of Hell*: that the partial experience of the external object is already fully cognitive, and that meaning itself surfaces into the world simultaneously with the object. In order to make this point, Picasso takes the language that had formerly been a part of the virtual space of illusionism—locked within the confines of pictorial space and thus separated from the real world—and makes that very language an aspect of literal space.

This was the sculptural statement that greeted the twenty-eight-year-old Russian artist Vladimir Tatlin, when he made his way late in 1913 through Europe to Paris to meet Picasso. The Russian avant-garde painters had by then become aware of both the futurist and cubist move-

39. *Picasso:* Guitar, *1914. Paper, 13¼" x 6½". Estate of the artist.*

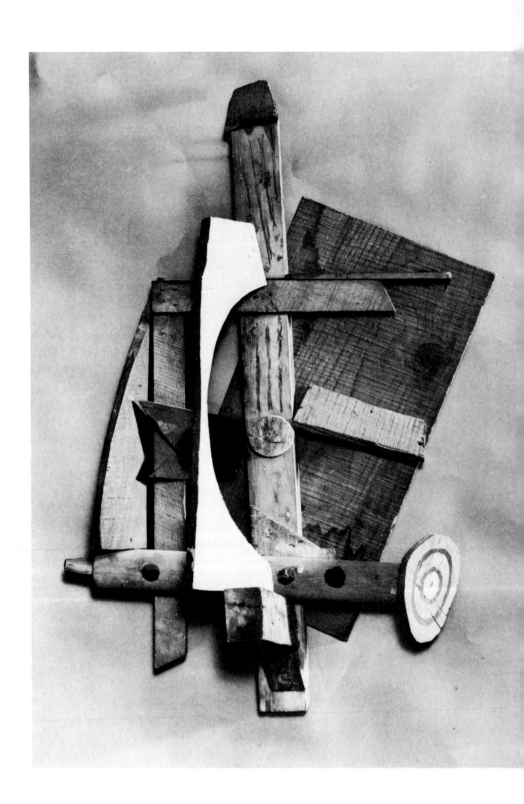

ments; in fact, the first *Futurist Manifesto* had been trans-lated into Russian and had begun to work its effects on Moscow artistic circles by 1910. Direct access to the art of Picasso and Braque had been made possible for Tatlin and Kasimir Malevich through the great contemporary collection of Sergei Shchukin, with the result that Tatlin had resolved to visit Paris, and, if possible, to apprentice himself to Picasso. It was a plan that Picasso himself would not accept, and Tatlin, too poor in 1913 to remain in Paris for more than a month, had to satisfy himself with frequent visits to the older man's studio. Back in Russia in 1914, Tatlin began work on a series of "counter-reliefs" made in imitation of Picasso's constructions out of sheet tin, cardboard, and wire. The exhibition of these reliefs in 1915 launched Tatlin on his career as Russia's most radical sculptor.

By now it is fairly obvious why the counter-reliefs caused such scandal, for they proceed in a direction diametrically opposed to the conclusions drawn by every other sculptor—including Boccioni—whom Picasso's cub-ism had influenced. Boccioni, as we have seen, took cubism's dismemberment and dispersal of the object and reconstructed out of it a model of ideal intelligibilty. In so doing, he had segregated his *Bottle* from real space—from the world in which we actually move—to install it firmly within something that can only be characterized as conceptual space. The realm that the *Bottle* inhabits transcends the poverty of partial vision. It is a realm through which many views are synthetically intercon-nected, and it is, in this sense, an operative model for the aspect of a viewer's experience that Boccioni assumes to be essential to any understanding of both space and the objects contained in it. Mirroring the mental space of the viewer's comprehension, the coherent space of the ana-lytically presented bottle is detached from the real space of the world. Both the mental space and the object which reflects its structure are understood to exist beyond the realm of inchoate matter that characterizes literal space. The illusionism which enshrouds Boccioni's *Bottle* is thus an illusion of motion which is in turn a model of conceptual integration. And for the illusion to operate, the bottle must be seen as transcending real space.

40. *Picasso:* Musical Instruments, *1914. Wood, 23¾" x 11⅛". Estate of the artist.*

41. *Vladimir Tatlin (1885–1953):* Corner Relief, *1915. Iron, aluminum, primer, 31" x 60" x 30" (destroyed; reconstruction made by Martyn Chalk, 1966–70, from photographs of the original). Fischer Fine Art Ltd, London. (Photo, Cuming Wright-Watson Associates Ltd.)*

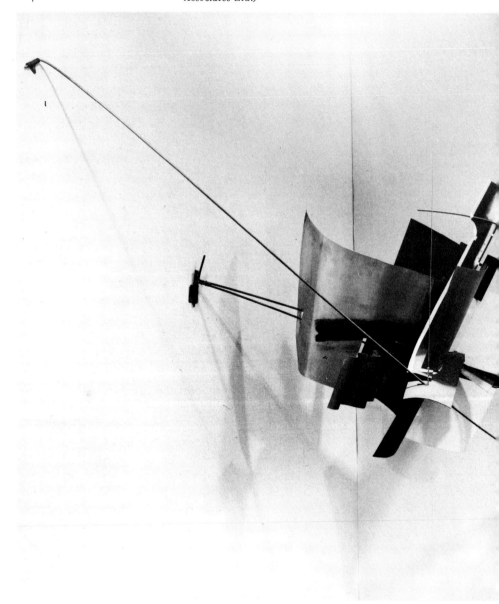

The radical quality of Tatlin's corner reliefs stems from their rejection of this transcendental space in two different ways, first in the anti-illusionism of their situation and second in the attitude they manifest toward the materials of which they are made. Each corner relief (fig. 41) is demonstrably organized in relation to the conjunction of two wall planes that Tatlin uses to support the work physically. This architectural integer—the corner —unlike the pedestal base of *Development of a Bottle*, is part of the real space of the room in which the counter-reliefs are to be seen. If the function of Boccioni's pedestal is to bracket the sculptural object from natural space, declaring that its true ambience is somehow different from the randomly organized world of tables, chairs, and windows, the function of Tatlin's corner is to insist that the relief it holds is continuous with the space of the world and dependent upon it for its meaning.

Thus, unlike the central spine of the *Bottle* which organizes the work around an imagined core, the central vertical element of the *Corner Relief* relates specifically to the vertical crease which marks the meeting of the two real walls. The *Relief* is read as a forward projection from that specific architectural element. The central vertical of the *Relief*, inclined toward the viewer and shaped like a blade, relates to a real ambience, much as the prow of a ship slicing through a body of water is understood in terms of its double relationship to the energized volume of which it is the leading edge, and the resistant medium of the ocean which yields to its purposive advance. The fact that the *Relief* itself is not symmetrical around its vertical core underscores this anti-idealist quality of the structure, declaring that the core is not the center of the work producing a series of emanations outward. Rather, it functions both to support the sculpture actually and to split the object visually into two independent halves. Because the configuration of one half cannot be inferred from the observable relationships in the other, one's experience of the Tatlin *Relief* is radically different from the experience of conceptual control that Boccioni's *Bottle* both promotes and allows. Tatlin has reversed his patterning and organizing of the visual data, so that one's experience of his reliefs is a heightened awareness of the specific situation they inhabit.

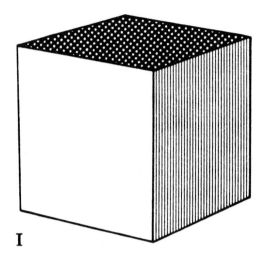

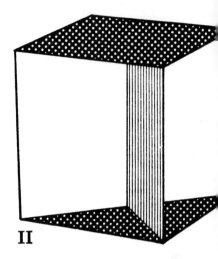

I   II

One symptom of this revised awareness of the inter-
dependence between the constructed object and the reality
of its situation appeared several months after the counter-
reliefs were first shown. At a Moscow exhibition called
"Year 1915," the painter Mikhail Larionov was installing
his own relief construction on a wall to which a motorized fan was already attached and his colleagues jokingly
asked if the fan were part of the work. Larionov followed
Tatlin's example in deciding that the logical answer must
be "yes" and reorganized his construction to incorporate
the mechanical object.

In addition to this externalization of the structural
logic of sculpture—a displacement of experientially available facts from the ideal and internal core to the visible
exterior—Tatlin's reliefs represent what he himself described as "a culture of materials,"[7] meaning that the
shaping of any section of the work would respond to the
real, structural requirements placed on that section. If
sheet metal gains greater compressive strength when it is
folded or rolled, then this fact accounts for curved elements within the work. Where great tensile strength is
needed in order to suspend the elements of the relief
freely in space, Tatlin employs wire. This attention to the
structural properties of materials is, of course, very far
removed from the kind of thinking that led Boccioni to

56

cast a meditation on the conceptual transparency of a bottle in solid bronze.

By 1920 the air in Moscow was rife with the crossfire of aesthetic ideologies. Naum Gabo, a Russian sculptor who was completely opposed to Tatlin's move "into real space and real materials," staged a campaign against productivism, as Tatlin's position was called, by printing five thousand copies of a manifesto stating his own convictions and posting it all over Moscow.[8] With the appearance of this document came a massive confusion of terms. For Gabo titled his statement *The Realistic Manifesto*, yet it is a tract that argued for the kind of sculptural idealism which we have seen operating in the work of Boccioni. Gabo's notion of "the real" was obviously directed toward the revelation of a transcendent reality rather than a manifestation of factual reality. To add to this lexical confusion, Gabo's analysis of matter entailed a construction of the object out of the intersection of simple flat planes. Because of the formal clarity with which Gabo revealed the work's structure, his objects, as well as his aesthetic theories, began to be designated as works of "constructivism," although the name constructivism was, by the early 1920s, the title Tatlin's colleagues and supporters used to describe their own program rather than Gabo's. (Throughout this text that practice, by now established for almost fifty years, will be continued. I will refer to the work of Gabo and Pevsner as constructivist, extending that term to include the Russian influence at the Bauhaus during the 1920s and early 1930s, specifically in the work of El Lissitzky and László Moholy-Nagy.) That the work of Gabo and his brother Antoine Pevsner should have garnered this title is due to the emigration of the two brothers from postrevolutionary Russia to Germany (Gabo) and France (Pevsner),[9] where their work came to seem logically connected to an aesthetic position in which the construction of the object would point toward an immediate, legible geometry.

The primary tool of this absolutism was the constructive principle that Gabo called "stereometry." Gabo presented this concept in its simplest form through a little diagram (fig. 42) that accompanied an article explaining

42. *Naum Gabo (1890–   ): Diagram showing volumetric (I) and stereometric (II) cubes. From* Circle *(London), 1937.*

the basis of the constructivist method. The diagram shows two images of a cube placed side by side. "Cube I" is an ordinary solid, which, like the objects we perceive in real space, presents us with a partial view of itself. Because it is closed, we see only three of its sides. "Cube II," however, is constructed differently. Its four side walls have been removed, and in their place, two diagonal planes knife through the interior of the form, intersecting at right angles at its very center. These two intersecting planes serve the purpose of simultaneously structuring a cubic volume—serving as an armature or support for the top and bottom plane of the figure—and permitting visual access to the interior of the form. What the second, opened cube revealed for Gabo was not merely the space ordinarily displaced by closed volumes but the core of the geometric object, laid as bare as the principle of intersection itself, making the figure comprehensible much the way a geometric theorem isolates and makes available essential propositions about solid objects.

Gabo had employed this stereometric device as early as 1915 when he began to fashion figurative sculpture from flat cardboard and plywood shapes. These profiles (figs. 43a and b) would always function to display the interlacing of shapes in three dimensions through the interior, or structural core, of the normally closed volume. The thrust of Gabo's work was thus toward the conceptual penetration of form—making it the structural counterpart of Boccioni's vision.

Like Boccioni's *Bottle*, Gabo's sculpture must be read as inhabiting a special, ideated space and it must appear to be conceptually transparent—presenting to the stationary viewer a summary of all the separate vantage points he would have were he to circumnavigate the exterior of the object. It is therefore not surprising to see the difference between a 1916–17 head by Gabo (fig. 44) and the corner constructions of Tatlin on which the head is based. Gabo retains the framed and specialized context of a relief ground out of which he projects the intersecting planes of the facial and cranial structure. The very point of Tatlin's use of the corner to submerge the sculptural elements in real space is revoked by Gabo, whose corner element has become an analytic stereometric space.

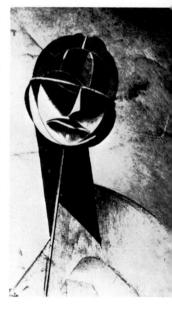

43a ABOVE and 43b ABOVE RIGHT *Gabo:* Constructed Head, *1915. Wood. (Original in U.S.S.R.; bronze version in collection of the artist.)*

44. BELOW RIGHT *Gabo:* Head of a Woman, *1916–17. Celluloid and metal, 24½" x 19½". Museum of Modern Art, New York.*

45. FAR RIGHT *Jacques Lipchitz (1891–1973):* Standing Personage, *1916. Bronze, 49¾". The Solomon R. Guggenheim Museum, New York.*

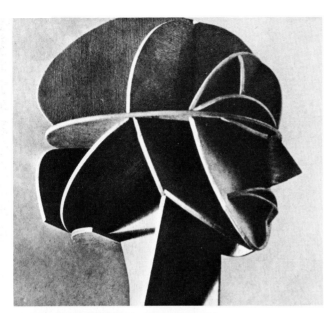

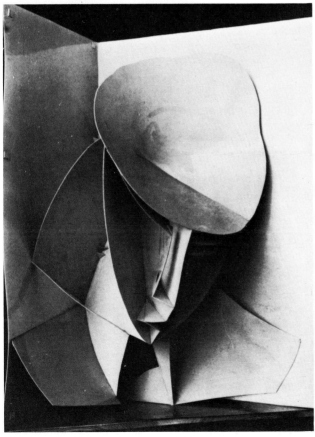

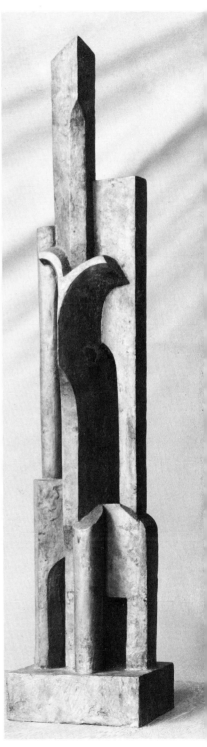

59

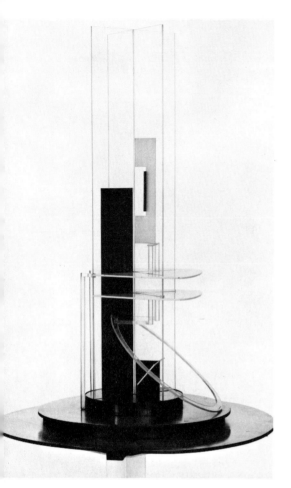

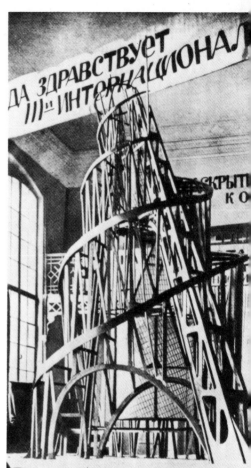

Tatlin's corner has been transformed into a theoretical
ninety-degree wedge cut from an ideal spheric volume—
one that would have to expand beyond the actual confines of the walls to contain the whole cranium of Gabo's
figure.

By the early 1920s, when Gabo began to use clear
plastics to fashion his work, this exploitation of transparent materials was obviously an extension of his intellectualist position. For the literal transparency of the
intersecting vertical planes of a work such as the 1923
Column (fig. 46) is merely the material analogue for the
underlying idea of the construction: namely, that one
must have access to the core of the object where the
principle of its structure—its rigidity and its coherence

as a volume—is lodged in the intersection maintained along its axial center.

Since Gabo thought of his *Column* as a miniature version of an object that could be re-created on an architectural scale, it is instructive to contrast it to Tatlin's projected architectural structure which was to serve as a *Monument to the Third International* (fig. 47), a model of which Tatlin built in 1919–20.[10] Tatlin conceived his tower, which was to be one-third again as high as the Eiffel Tower, as an external sheathing of steel girders to contain a vertical stacking of three great glass volumes which would function as assembly halls and offices. The exterior of the tower was cast in the form of two interlaced rising spirals, the visual appearance of which would correspond to and complement the revolving movement of the chambers they were intended to support. Tatlin planned that the lowest chamber, which was to be a huge glass drum, would slowly turn at the rate of one full revolution per year; the next highest, pyramidal chamber would make one complete turn in a month, and the topmost chamber—a cylindrical room—would make one revolution each day.

Tatlin's edict of "real space and real materials" results, then, in a work ideologically opposed to Gabo's model on the two points that we have been stressing. First, its structure has been displaced from the interior of the object to its exterior. It is obvious that there is no need to penetrate past the surface of the steel sheath to an internal place where a structural logic is secreted or hidden. Rather, the logic is carried by the surface, and the notion of a dualistic split between inside and outside is resolved through a visual unification of the meaning of the external structure and the experiential center of the work. Second, Tatlin's tower separates itself from Gabo's *Column* in promoting an entirely different attitude toward the notion of time. The transparency of Gabo's *Column*, like the split-open section of Boccioni's *Bottle*, presents the viewer with a perceptual synthesis in which past and future moments are collapsed. One view of the object is presented as the sum of all possible views, each one is understood to be a part of a continuous circumnavigation of the object spread out through space and time, but

46. FAR LEFT *Gabo:* Column, *1923. Plastic, wood, and metal, 41". The Solomon R. Guggenheim Museum, New York.*

47. NEAR LEFT *Tatlin:* Monument to the Third International, *model 1919–20 (now destroyed). (Photo, Nationalmuseum, Stockholm)*

unified and controlled by the special kind of information which the transparency of the object makes clear to the viewer. In this single view, the experience of time and space is both summarized and transcended. In contrast to this, Tatlin's tower is concerned with the experience of real time. Its inhabitants were to occupy chambers that would slowly turn in space. The chambers were to house legislative bodies and information centers—newspaper offices and radio and film studios—whose function would be to direct and record the development of a revolutionary political situation. The tower thus addresses itself to a temporal experience, the dimensions of which cannot be known beforehand. The tower is about the processes of a historical development rather than the transcendence of it. For Tatlin, technology is placed visibly at the service of a revolutionary ideology through which history might be shaped; for Gabo, it is a model of absolute knowledge through which the future is given rather than found.[11]

If we think back to the image that Eisenstein had used

48. *Gabo:* Translucent Variation of Spheric Theme, *1951 version of 1937 original. Plastic, 22⅜". The Solomon R. Guggenheim Museum, New York.*

49. ABOVE NEAR RIGHT *Antoine Pevsner (1886–1962):* Construction in an Egg, 1948. *Gilt bronze, 28" x 19¾" x 17¼". Albright-Knox Art Gallery, Buffalo, N.Y. Gift of The Seymour H. Knox Foundation, Inc. (Photo, Greenberg-May Prod. Inc.)*

50. ABOVE FAR RIGHT *El Lissitzky (1890–1941):* Proun-the-Town, 1921.

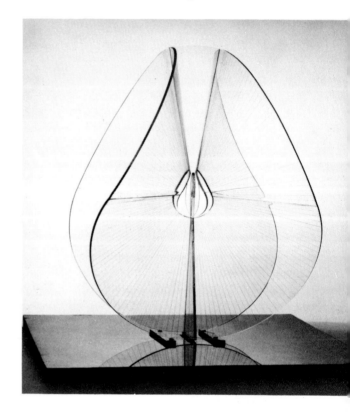

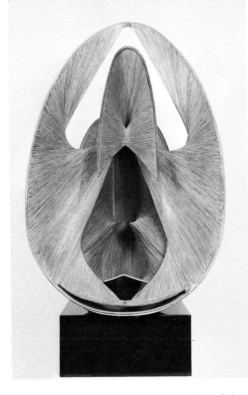
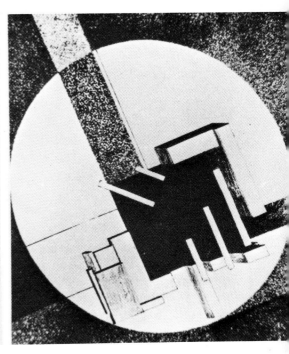

in *October*—the image of the clockwork bird—we realize
that the mechanical peacock takes on a particular meaning
and relevance in relation to the sculpture of Eisenstein's
contemporaries. In Gabo's aestheticizing of technology
there is a continuation of the attitudes embodied by the
automaton, while in Tatlin's manipulation of technology
there is an attempt to make it a part of dialectical process.

By the early 1920s that wing of Russian constructivism
we have been calling "idealist" or "intellectualist" had
begun to have repercussions in Western Europe. For one
thing, Gabo and Pevsner had left Russia for France and
Germany, where they continued to construct sculpture
which had the transparency and clarity of mathematical
models (figs. 48 and 49). For another, the idealist attitude
toward structure was carried westward into the Bauhaus
through the writings and paintings of El Lissitzky, whose
"elementarist" aesthetic was based, like Gabo's, on de-
materialized forms built up stereometrically through the
intersection of planes.

Lissitzky's impact (fig. 50) on the Bauhaus attitudes
toward form was effected indirectly through two men

whom he had met in Germany in 1921, and upon whom he had left a deep impression. One of these was the Hungarian artist László Moholy-Nagy, who went to the Bauhaus in 1923 to devise and teach the introductory course in materials and design. The other was the Dutchman Theo van Doesburg, a painter (fig. 51) whose attitudes toward three-dimensional form crystallized around Lissitzky's theories, and are reflected in a statement about structuré from 1924: "The new architecture is *anti-cubic*, that is to say it does not try to freeze the different functional space cells in one closed cube. Rather it throws the functional space cells . . . centrifugally from the core of the cube. And through this means, *height, width, depth and time* (i.e. an imaginary four-dimensional entity) approaches a totally new plastic expression in open spaces. In this way architecture acquires a more or less floating aspect that, so to speak, works against the gravitational forces of nature."[12] This statement reflects the constructivist determination that the object—whether it be architectural or sculptural—present itself more as a mental construct than a dense, material substance. The formal

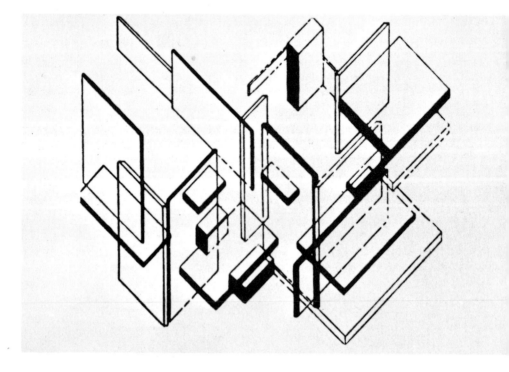

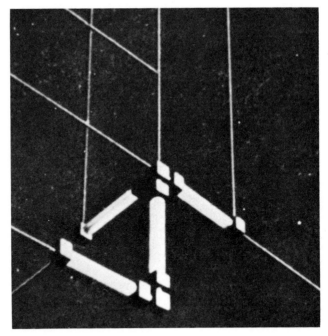

51. LEFT *Theo van Doesburg (1883–1931) and Cornelis van Eesteren (1897–   ): "The Relation of Horizontal and Vertical Planes," ca. 1920.*

52. RIGHT *Walter Gropius (1883–1969):* Hanging Lamp, late 1920s (now destroyed). Designed for Gropius office at the Bauhaus, Weimar.

values of apparent weightlessness and resistance to gravity signal van Doesburg's desire that the construction be assimilated into the ideational or conceptual terms of a mental space.

Van Doesburg's impact on the Bauhaus began after 1921, when he opened an atelier in Weimar adjacent to the Bauhaus studios. It was his presence during the years 1921–23 that made it imperative for Walter Gropius, the director of the Bauhaus, to call Moholy-Nagy onto his staff, a move that reoriented Bauhaus thinking in the direction of constructivism (figs. 52 and 53). The work of Max Bill, who was a Bauhaus student after the arrival of Moholy-Nagy, exemplifies the effect of this transplanted constructivism on sculptural practice (fig. 54). Bill's work, like that of Gabo and Pevsner, elaborates models for mathematical concepts into sculptural form. Bill's intention for these objects was that they express a "mathematical way of thinking" and that they impress the viewer as purely intellectual constructions. As one writer has expressed it, "Max Bill . . . attempts to overthrow the barriers between artistic intuition and scientific knowledge. He sees geometry, the mutual relations of surfaces and lines, as the primary foundation of all form. Herein

65

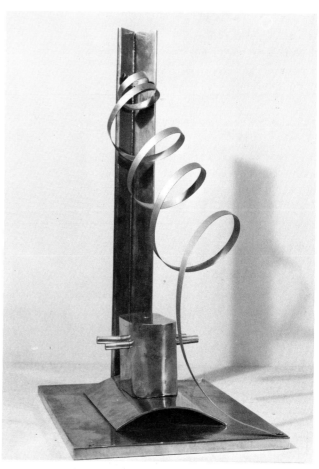

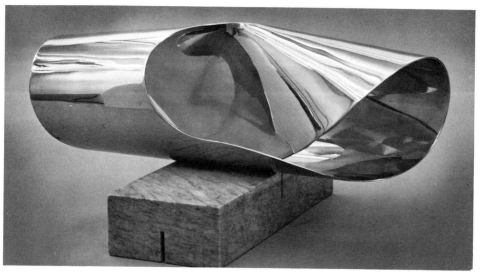

lies also the source of the aesthetic expression of mathematical figures. By giving concrete form to abstract thought—as in the mathematical models of space—he introduces an element of feeling into it."[13]

With this absolute dependence upon concepts drawn from science, the work of Bill and the other Bauhaus-related artists consolidates a particular position about the meaning of the sculptural enterprise. That position, as it has been emerging throughout this chapter, may be summarized as one that views sculpture as an investigatory tool in the service of knowledge. The ambition of men like Gabo, Lissitzky, Moholy-Nagy, or Bill is to dominate material by means of a projective, conceptual grasp of form. Their strategy is, time and again, to build the object out from what appears to be a generative core. Their insistence on symmetry, promoted by the use of this core, gives rise to the sensation that the entire work is available to the stationary viewer in a single, conceptually extended perception. Itself an analytic object, the sculpture is understood as modeling, by reflection, the analytic intelligence of both viewer and maker. And the production of the model is understood as being the proper goal of the making of sculpture.

There are alternatives to this conception of the sculptural enterprise, some of which are expressly critical of the assumptions embedded in it. Sculpture may, for instance, embody a much more speculative attitude about the relationship between art and "knowledge." During the teens, at the same time that the futurist and constructivist modes of sculpture were being developed and consolidated, the work of two other men were taking shape. These artists, Marcel Duchamp and Constantin Brancusi, present models of the meaning of sculpture that are explicitly antithetical to constructivism. Their work questions both the constructivist conception of what the sculptural object is and the validity of the whole notion of transparency. It is to those examples that one now must turn.

53. LEFT *László Moholy-Nagy (1895–1946)*: Nickel Construction, 1921. Nickel-plated iron, 14⅛" (including base). Collection, The Museum of Modern Art, New York. Gift of Mrs. Sibyl Moholy-Nagy. (Photo, Soichi Sunami for the Museum of Modern Art)

54. BELOW *Max Bill (1908–)*: Endless Loop I, 1947–49 (executed 1960). Gilded copper on crystalline base, 14¼" x 27" x 7½". Hirshhorn Museum and Sculpture Garden, Smithsonian Institution, Washington, D.C. (Photo, The Solomon R. Guggenheim Museum, New York)

Forms of Readymade: 3
Duchamp
and
Brancusi

One evening in 1911, four members of the Parisian avant-garde attended a bizarre theatrical presentation: Marcel Duchamp, Guillaume Apollinaire, Francis Picabia, and Gabrielle Buffet-Picabia went to see *Impressions of Africa*, a performance based on a novel by Raymond Roussel. "It was tremendous," Duchamp was later to say of that night. "On the stage there was a model and a snake that moved slightly—it was absolutely the madness of the unexpected. I don't remember much of the text. One didn't really listen."[1]

What Duchamp had seen was a staging of one of the curiosities of French literature. *Impressions of Africa* is the story of an elaborate gala to celebrate the investiture of an African king with the crown of a defeated, neighboring country. The festival, created by a group of shipwrecked Europeans who happen to be circus performers and scientists, is a series of spectacles, each one more fantastic than the next, and none having any narrative connection to the other. Yet the sense of discontinuity between these spectacles is dispelled once the viewer or reader grasps the theme underlying each of the festival's separate acts. Uniting them all is the image of a series of primitive machines geared toward a similar product: each one involves an intricate set of contrivances which end up making "art."

There is, for example, a painting machine: a photosensitive plate attached to a wheel mounted with many brushes. The landscape images that fall on the plate are registered and transmitted to the mechanism that drives the brushes, which, in turn, record the image in paint on canvas. And there is a music machine: a large worm (the "snake" of Duchamp's recollections) which releases drops of water from a trough by convulsions of its body. These drops fall onto the strings of a zither in exact patterns, producing musical compositions. Still another example is a tapestry machine: a paddle-driven loom suspended over a rushing stream moving like "some silent musical instrument, striking chords or playing arpeggios,"[2] and weaving a luminous, complex image of the flood scene from the Bible.

The literary space of *Impressions* is inhabited, then, by a group of people who have mechanized the routine of art-making. The biological and physical forces they harness become machines that create images—images that we recognize as the basis of the experience we identify as art. But by automating the production of art, the machines arrive at a result in which the structure of the image is absolutely disconnected from the psychological and emotional structure of the person who initiates the art, who sets the machine in motion. In that sense, Roussel seems to be generating an early version of that parody of art called "painting-by-numbers," a kind of coloring-book attitude toward the creation, or re-creation, of known masterpieces. If we feel that a kit containing an outline drawing of a work by Van Gogh, for instance, and tubes of paint with directions as to the placement of each color, is a parody of art, our reasons are very clear:

they come from our belief that everything about the original image is an expression of the inner feelings and thoughts of its maker. This includes the individual strokes of paint—their thickness and variation—as well as the peculiar physiognomy the artist gives to objects and the way he molds the space they occupy. The whole of the original painting carries, we feel, the autograph of its author; its importance to us is in the authenticity with which it bears the imprint of his very being. It is in that sense that we feel there to be a correspondence between the space of the image which we can see and the interior psychological and, therefore, invisible space of the author of the image. But, in fact, the whole of *Impressions*, like the kit, seems to be expressing a total disbelief in the notion that there must be an intimate, causal connection between an individual and what he makes, a thinker and his thoughts, or the content of a mind and the space it projects. The story is punctuated by images that ridicule a Western rationalism built on the necessity of logical connections. Set up in the center of the African village is a statue of Immanuel Kant portrayed as a kind of burlesque thinking machine: when a trained magpie perches on a lever next to the statue, intense lights inside the philosopher's skull are suddenly switched on in a parody of the blinding onset of reason.

Marcel Duchamp, one of those who saw this performance in 1911, was experiencing at this same time his own brand of restlessness and impatience with an art that celebrated rationalism. He had recently abandoned fauvism for cubism, but found himself equally alienated from his newly adopted style and from the men who practiced it and theorized about it. He tells of a meeting with Max Jacob and Apollinaire—two of the major spokesmen for cubism—and says, "It was unbelievable. One was torn between a sort of anguish and an insane laughter. Both of them were still living like writers of the Symbolist period, around 1880, that is."[3] For Duchamp, *Impressions* was something completely apart from Apollinaire's world. "It was no longer a question of symbolism," he said, "or even of Mallarmé—Roussel knew nothing of all that. And then this amazing person, living shut up in himself in his caravan, the curtains drawn."[4]

A year later Duchamp began to move away from cubism. At first this disaffection was expressed in heretical subject matter: Duchamp traded in the still-life artifacts and human subjects of orthodox cubism for a peculiarly mechanistic content. Instead of the bottles, newspapers, and nudes of Picasso, Braque, and Léger, his painting began to fill up with images of elaborate machinery to which he gave names such as *The Bride* and *The King and Queen Surrounded by Swift Nudes*. By 1913–14, Duchamp had become directly involved with industrial products themselves as he produced his first two "sculptures": a bicycle wheel which he mounted on a kitchen stool and a commercially produced rack for drying bottles which he merely signed (fig. 55). He had, in other words, entered into the mature phase of his career in which he was constantly obsessed with the question of what it is that "makes" a work of art.

The signed bottle rack, his first "readymade," was transferred from the realm of ordinary objects into the realm of art by the mere fact of its having been inscribed by the artist. In this case (as in the case of subsequent readymades, such as the snow shovel, called *In Advance of a Broken Arm* [fig. 56], of 1915, and the urinal, called *Fountain* [fig. 58], of 1917), the artist had clearly not fabricated or constructed the sculpture. He had, instead, selected an object from one of the almost infinite number of manufactured items that passively filled the space of his everyday experience. It was an object over the making of which he had had absolutely no control. Therefore, it could not be read as bearing the stamp of an act of creation, that is to say the object did not appear as something coming from the matrix of the sculptor's personally held ideas or emotions.

In that sense, Duchamp's "work" in putting such an object into the world of art was something like the actions of Roussel's machines in *Impressions of Africa*. For Duchamp's "work" was simply an act of selection. As such, Duchamp had made himself into a kind of switching mechanism to set in motion the impersonal process of generating a work of art—but one that obviously would not stand in a conventional relationship to him as its "author." The readymades became in that way part of

55. NEAR RIGHT *Marcel Duchamp (1887–1968)*: Bottle Rack *(readymade), 1914. Galvanized iron, 25½" (original lost). Galleria Schwarz, Milan.*

56. FAR RIGHT *Duchamp:* In Advance of a Broken Arm *(readymade), 1915. Metal and wood, 47¾" (original lost). Yale University Art Gallery, New Haven, Conn. Gift of Miss Katherine S. Dreier.*

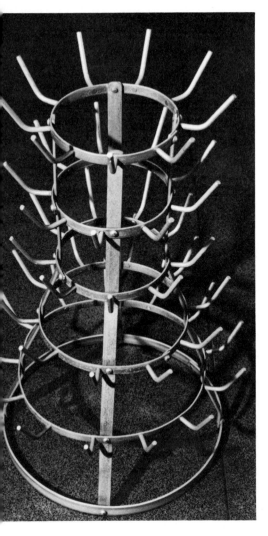 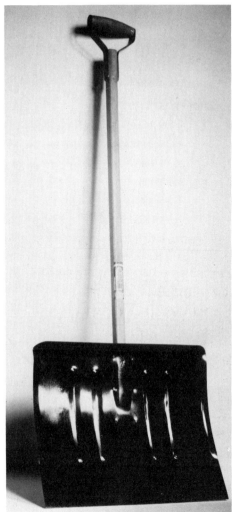

Duchamp's project to make certain kinds of strategic moves—moves that would raise questions about what exactly is the nature of the work in the term "work of art." Clearly, one answer suggested by the readymades is that a work might not be a physical object but rather a question, and that the making of art might, therefore, be reconsidered as taking a perfectly legitimate form in the speculative act of posing questions. In using the readymade to ask about the nature of art "work," Duchamp gravitated toward the Rousselian extreme expressed in *Impressions of Africa*.

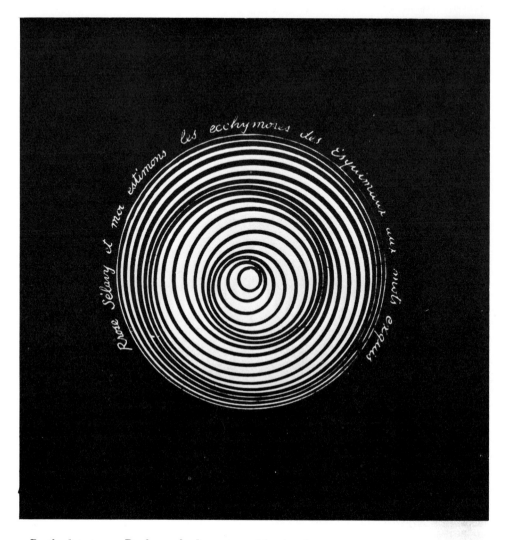
Rrose Sélavy et moi estimons les ecchymoses des Esquimaux aux mots exquis

By the late teens, Duchamp had penetrated further into what one might call Roussel's strategic thinking. For Duchamp had begun to produce as "works" elaborate word-plays in which sentences were constructed by the repetition and inversion of a small group of phonemes— making the homophonic phrases Duchamp called *Rrose Sélavy*. For example: *"Rrose Sélavy et moi estimons les ecchymoses des Esquimaux aux mots exquis"* (fig. 57). [Eros, that's life, and I esteem the bruises of the Eskimos who have exquisite words.]

The connection this bears to Roussel and *Impressions of Africa* is at a deeper level than the manifest content of the work Duchamp saw performed in 1911, although the explicit images of the art-machines stand as an example for the underlying productive strategy of the work. Each of the sections of *Impressions* was constructed from transformations of a text by means of puns or homophones. An example is a section derived from a poem by Victor Hugo, in *Les chants du crépuscule*, two lines of which read:

> Ô revers! ô leçon!—Quand l'enfant de cet homme
> Eut reçu pour hochet la couronne de Rome.
> [What an upset! What a lesson!—when the
>   son of this man
> Received as his rattle the crown of Rome.]

Roussel had taken these lines and changed them by phonetic regrouping. *"Eut reçu pour hochet la couronne de Rome,"* he transformed into "Ursule brochet lac Houronne drome." And the resultant words—"Ursula," "pike," lake," "Huron Indians" and "[hippo]drome"—became elements from which he constructed a story, or a part of a story around which a particular piece of the *Impressions* spectacle revolved.[5] Roussel thought of writing, then, as a kind of game for which he had devised an elaborate and binding set of rules. And this game, based on a ritualistic exercise of punning, became the obscure and hidden machine by which he constructed his work.

57. *Duchamp:* Optical Machine. *Plate from* 391, *No. 18, July 1924.*

An extreme example of this constructive technique had occurred in Roussel's short stories in which he set himself the task of beginning and ending the story with the same sentence, except for the transposition of two letters. In the changed context of the narrative, the second appearance of the nearly identical line would take on an entirely different meaning. One of these stories begins with the phrase "la peau verdâtre de la prune un peu mûre" [the greenish skin of the ripening plum] and ends with "la peau verdâtre de la brune un peu mûre" [the greenish skin of the aging brunette]. The tale Roussel fabricated to connect these two lines concerns an aging Spanish beauty's complexion which turned sickly as a result of poison taken through a piece of fruit.[6]

Only after Roussel had died did a text appear in which

the author released the code to this mechanistic construction. This book, *Comment j'ai écrit certains de mes livres* ["How I Wrote Some of My Books"], was published in 1935—long after Duchamp had begun to construct his own homophonic texts. But Duchamp had known—from reports about Roussel—the general direction of the author's technique, and through this information he was able to perceive something of the obsessiveness of Roussel's production. "What mattered," Duchamp said, "was an attitude, more than an influence, to know how he had done all that, and why. . . ."[7]

It seems to have been the very opacity of Roussel's work that fascinated Duchamp; for his books had been fashioned through an extreme automation of the artistic process—a mechanization that yielded two interrelated results. The first of these we have already indicated, namely, that the work is deprived of its conventional source of meaning. For the meaning of most art objects is lodged within a mesh of ideas and feelings held by the creator of the work, passed through the act of authorship into the work, and thereby transmitted to a viewer or reader of it. The traditional work is thus like a transparent pane—a window through which the psychological spaces of viewer and creator open onto each other. As we have seen, the mechanization of the art act becomes a barrier to this conventional right of access and, in being so, it promotes a second result. Having short-circuited the traditional functions of meaning, the work focuses all attention on the curiosity of its production. By "all attention," I mean here literally all—both the artist's and the viewer's; and by "curiosity of production," what is indicated is not a personal idiosyncrasy or quirk, but rather much more absolute aesthetic questions for which the work at hand becomes both the general statement and the specific example.

The 1917 *Fountain* (fig. 58) was a urinal that Duchamp had rotated ninety degrees so the side that would normally be connected to the wall is now the underside or base of the sculpture. In its new position, the work was then signed pseudonymously and dated: "R. Mutt/ 1917." Duchamp submitted the *Fountain* to the Independents show in New York, where it was, not surpris-

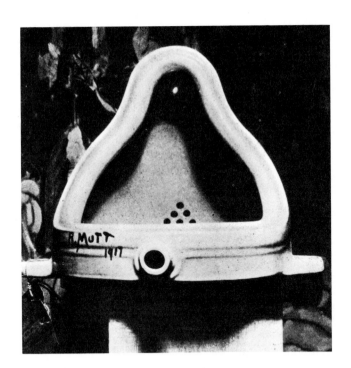

58. *Duchamp:* Fountain
(readymade), 1917. Porcelain,
24″ (original lost). Sidney
Janis Collection, New York.

ingly, suppressed (hidden from view by the organizers of the exhibition). The reasons for this were presumably twofold. The major one was probably that the sculpture was nothing but an ordinary object, and the less serious one was that, as a urinal, the object violated the bounds of good taste. But for Duchamp, the work was no longer a common object, because it had been transposed. It had been "flipped" or inverted to rest on a pedestal, which is to say that it had been repositioned, and this physical repositioning stood for a transformation that must then be read on a metaphysical level. Folded into that act of inversion is a moment in which the viewer has to realize that an act of transfer has occurred —an act in which the object has been transplanted from the ordinary world into the realm of art. This moment of realization is the moment in which the object becomes "transparent" to its meaning. And that meaning is simply the curiosity of production—the puzzle of why and how this should happen.

The nature of this recognition is unlike that of constructivist or cubist sculpture. It is not about deciphering the formal construction of the object, or about the way that parts can relate to one another in the nature of signs or integers of meaning. It is a recognition that is triggered by the object but is somehow not *about* the object. And, as a moment, it does not concern the time in which the object itself exists or in which the viewer experiences or understands it. That is, the moment does not resemble the linear passage of time from the seeing of the object to the cognition of its meaning. Instead of that kind of arc, the shape of this moment has much more the character of a circle—the cyclical form of a quandary.

Curiously, the shape that this moment takes (one of returning the viewer again and again to the beginning of the question of "why?") is related to the shape of the Rousselian "story" in which the last sentence is the "same" as the opening one. It is a shape that ironically undermines the "natural" course of a narrative which proceeds from beginning through middle to end. Turning back on itself, this inversion of narrative substitutes the strategy of a self-critical enterprise for the production of an outcome.

This circular shape to which Duchamp gave the experience of art takes its most literal form in the Rrose Sélavy productions which Duchamp actually mounted on revolving disks so that the homophonic phrases would seem not to reach closure.[8] (See for example fig. 57.) Instead, they could be read as an endlessly eliding transmutation of sound: "L'aspirant habite Javel et moi j'avais l'habite en spirale," in such a case. For *"en spirale"* reads as a transposition of the syllables of *"l'aspirant"* and thus promotes the sensation of the end of the sentence fusing or running into its beginning.[9] As with the sentences on all the other disks, the meaning of this one is elusive because of grammatical distortions and a strange use of verb and noun relationships. Because of this disruption in the straight grammatical surface of the sentence, the reader/hearer is encouraged to resort to the homophonic subtext, or puns, exuded by the sounds of the words as pronounced. And in the case of all the disks, this subtext is erotic in nature.[10] Thus, the disks carry out the injunction of the pseudonym which Duchamp used as the creator of the puns, all of which were signed by his self-appointed alter ego "Rrose Sélavy." This name, itself homophonically pronounced *"Éros, c'est la vie,"* translates into a statement about the sexual basis or erotic meaning of life. And it is this meaning that not only underlies the pronouncements of the disks but also seems to accompany the sculptural presence of many of the readymades.

Returning to the *Fountain* (fig. 58) one can see how an erotic subtext attaches itself to the object by way of the visual pun suggested by the shape of the object in its new orientation. For its position and isolation has the effect of anthropomorphizing the urinal, giving to the lax shape of its hollow interior the suggestion of a uterine form, and to its surface the implied curves of the female body.

It might be objected at this point that in suggesting this connection between the nude female torso and the shape of the inverted urinal, we are resolving the question Duchamp posed—namely, what "makes" the work of art—in favor of metaphor. That is, we are pointing to the artist's act of transformation, in this case from the industrial object into human image, as that which constitutes the work of creation. Yet in the case of the *Fountain*, the artist's creative act is so obviously minimal, the transformation itself so absolutely negligible (leaving the urinal exactly the same as all other examples of its kind), that instead of feeling that we have found an answer, we must confront a whole new set of aesthetic questions. The metaphor of the *Fountain* does not seem to have been wrought or fabricated by Duchamp but rather by the observer. So that the questions raised and set into relief are: what is the expectation of meaning which we carry to works of art? Why do we think of them as statements that must convey or embody a certain content? Further, if that content is generated by ourselves —by our own need to find a meaning—are we justified at all in believing that content to be causally connected to the producer of the object?

Thus, even when we have seen the metaphorical "statement" of the urinal, we are returned to the same perception of it that we had when we perceived it as "merely" a commercial object. We are returned, that is, to a perception of it as something disconnected from Duchamp personally, as something existing instead in the realm of impersonal questions posed. This tension between a psychically charged, erotic metaphor and a disembodied, conceptual question parallels another tension one feels when confronting the readymade. For the *Fountain*, with its shiny white porcelain curves and countercurves, has a sensuous presence that elicits one's normal visual response to works of art: a response that tends to promote an analytic examination. As we have seen with other sculpture, this analysis involves relating internal structure to surface, decoding the shapes made visible by edges and planes, or responding to the composition of mass and void. But the *Fountain* thwarts this analytic impulse. Faced with a readymade object, we can make no attempt at formal decoding. For, as we have been made to feel again and again, since it was not Duchamp who "intended" the formal relationships of the urinal, the work cannot be understood as having encoded the meanings carried by formal decisions. Duchamp's strategy has been to present a work which is irreducible under formal analysis, which is detached from his own personal feelings, and for which there is no resolution of one's efforts to decode or understand it. His work is not intended to hold the object up for examination, but to scrutinize the act of aesthetic transformation itself.

In the past fifteen years a series of monographic studies of Duchamp have appeared.[11] Among other things, they have generally seen their task as being a psychoanalytic unpacking of the imagery of his work. In doing so, they propose, with the author of *Psychopathology of Everyday Life*, that behavior that appears inadvertent and therefore meaningless is, on the contrary, an index of deeply held intentions on the part of the individual who displays it. Thus such phenomena as slips of the tongue, misplacing of objects, "mistaken" substitutions of words in personal correspondence all read as a veiled message in which desires or privately held feelings are encoded. Fueled by these Freudian insights, the Duchamp scholars have argued that no matter how seemingly disconnected the readymades are from the artist's aesthetic or formal intervention—and hence from the kind of stroke-by-stroke revelation of personality that one might feel tempted to see in the autographic character of, say, a painting by Van Gogh—Duchamp's choice of them reveals aspects of his personality as surely as would any other piece of apparently "meaningless" behavior.

Having pieced together Duchamp's persistent references to autoeroticism, his repeated use of the spiral as an emblem of turning back upon himself (in the *rotoreliefs* and the disks of *Anemic-Cinéma*, for example), or his fixation on androgyny in his appearances as Rrose Sélavy, the scholars have constructed a "history" of Duchamp by which they can project meaning on a work like *Fountain*. By means of this history, they are supplying the object with exactly the kind of narrative matrix that the work itself so skillfully and brilliantly destroys. For with *Fountain*, as with the other readymades, and everything else he made, Duchamp clearly intended to negate a traditional sense of narrative.

The operations of cause and effect or of a rational sequence of events, which we have seen as the touchstone of third-person narration, withers and dies as the viewer confronts the readymade, as he senses that it has dropped from nowhere into the stream of aesthetic time. And Duchamp celebrated this demise with what he called "the beauty of indifference," by which he expressed his determination to make art that was cut loose from personal affect. In performing radical surgery on the body of the narrative convention, Duchamp was clearly severing the object from that causal chain—whether historical or psychological—which we saw function in nineteenth-century sculpture. He was, further, making a situation that would be completely opaque and resistant to the classical assumption that objects are made to be naturally transparent to the operations of the intellect. He was undermining the medium of relief through which the ideological circumnavigation and containment of the object could be illusionistically promoted. In this sense Duchamp's paintings on glass become a brilliant *riposte* to the convention of the relief ground that we have already discussed. For, as we saw, the relief ground is not only a spatial context from which the sculptural object emerges; it is also a context of meanings, serving as a tissue of narrative relationships within which the object or objects are imbedded and can be understood.

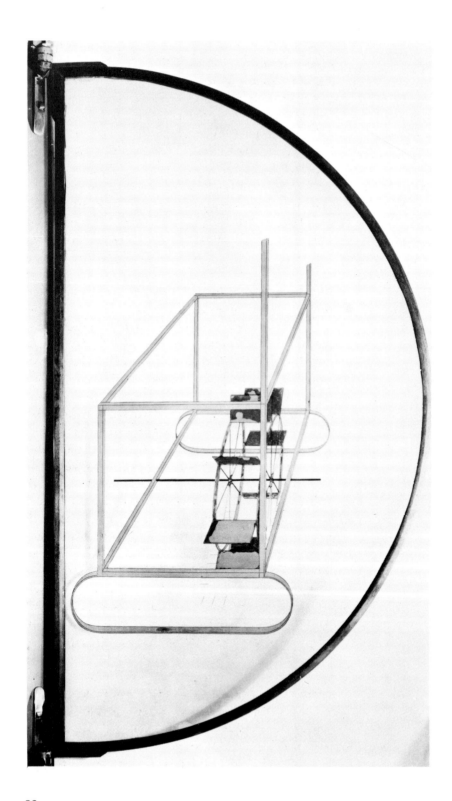

Contrary to this notion, a work such as the 1913–15 *Glider Containing a Water Mill in Neighboring Metals* (fig. 59) suspends an illusionistic object in a ground that is literally transparent. The glider and water mill of the title are painstakingly set forth in a perspective rendering applied to a pane of glass. This is mounted, with another pane laid over the image, in a semicircular metal frame hinge-mounted to the wall. The work is then swiveled so that it is perpendicular to this wall plane. Thus the image of the water mill appears to be an object free-standing in space, sandwiched between two pieces of glass like a butterfly or other biological specimen, presented as a bit of life which has been captured and congealed, suspended for the observer's scrutiny.

The glass "ground" of the *Glider* functions as the direct opposite of the conventional pictorial ground, which is conceptually transparent, allowing one to imagine the spatial development of the object it contains. Duchamp's ground is literally transparent, destroying the natural "suspension of disbelief," for one can in fact examine the object from all sides and see the sliver-thin flatness of the space it actually occupies. Furthermore, while the conventional ground provides a narrative matrix or context for the object distinct from the one in which the viewer himself stands, the transparent pane of the *Glider* breaks down this separation. Through the glass ground the viewer simply sees a continuation of his own space. And the effect of this is like the arbitrary placement of the readymade within the space of a gallery: it forces the viewer to focus on the strangeness of the aesthetic context *per se*. Like the specimen of the butterfly, the aesthetic act of bringing an object from a real context and placing it within a pictorial one is held up for scrutiny. In failing as an illusionistic matrix, the glass ground succeeds as a dialectical one, revealing the basis of a narrative tradition even while it rejects it.

As I have said, Duchamp scholars have struggled to replace some of the "ground" that the artist himself had cut away. They have tried to resupply the works with a background of psychological structure within which one can "read" these objects. To do this, of course, is to violate the strategic import of Duchamp's work; yet the tempta-

59. *Duchamp:* Glider Containing a Water Mill in Neighboring Metals, *1913–15. Oil and lead wire on glass mounted between two glass plates, 57⅞" x 31⅛". Louise and Walter Arensberg Collection, Philadelphia Museum of Art. (Photo, A. J. Wyatt, staff photographer)*

tion is irresistible, akin to reaching for a clue the artist himself has held out. For Duchamp said, "my work is breathing"—permitting scholars to see the details of his biography as pertinent to the meaning of his work. In 1923 Duchamp "stopped" being an artist and took up chess. Yet, all the while, he contributed to aesthetic discourse by holding up to the world the emblems of formal attack which were contained in the production of the readymades. He thus promoted a tension between the legendary quality of his own personality and life-style and the form of depersonalization which was the larger meaning of his art.

There is another artist whose career is exactly contemporaneous with Duchamp's, beginning late in the first decade of this century, climaxing in the early 1920s, and then continuing primarily to produce objects from already established images. Like Duchamp, this artist promoted a mythic persona behind which he moved and from which he issued aphoristic statements about his work. And there is also a startling detachment between this aura of personal myth and the depersonalized quality of the art. That man is Constantin Brancusi, of whom Sidney Geist has written, ". . . the work of Brancusi, early and late, is styleless. I have observed that the sculptures often need each other, but they do not need the sculptor or his personality. The effacement of self is known to art as the general sign of the classical artist; in Brancusi's case it is his signature. He often dwelt on the thought that 'There is a purpose in all things. To get to it one must go beyond oneself.' "[12]

It may seem that Duchamp's readymades are as far away as one can get from the sculptural achievements of Brancusi. The readymades are unworked and, for the most part, antirepresentational. They are common objects slipped into the stream of aesthetic discourse, as a series of questions to which there is no certain reply. Brancusi, on the other hand, maintained his art within the arena of representation; like many other sculptors he labored over the question of a work's resemblance to human or animal forms. Furthermore, almost half of his production involved the direct carving of stone or wood, making the task of transforming the raw material one of arduous and patient

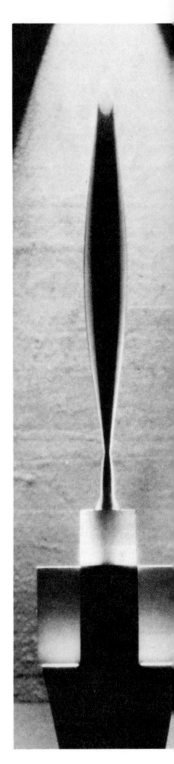

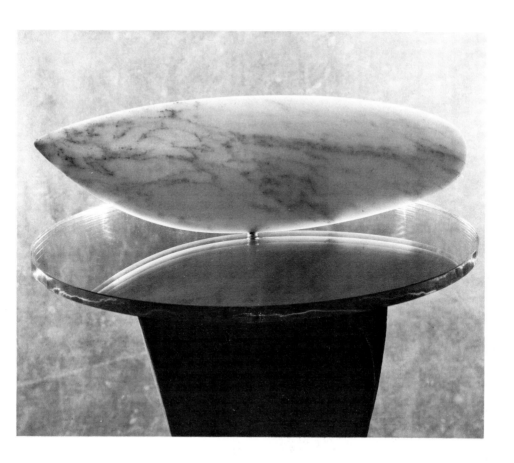

labor. Even when the objects were cast in bronze, they were painstakingly polished by Brancusi until their surfaces reached a shining finish of perfect reflectivity. We are tempted, then, to place these two figures, Brancusi and Duchamp, in mutual opposition—with Duchamp cast as the disturbing dialectician and Brancusi as the creator of objects that invite contemplation.

Yet, when we think about the objects Brancusi made— the nearly uninflected blade of *Bird in Space* (fig. 60), the smooth egg shape of *The Newborn,* the single fin of *The Fish* (fig. 61), the jutting cylinder of *Torso of a Young Man*—we realize that there is something peculiar about the nature of this contemplation to which the objects invite us. For it is a contemplation that is as unreceptive to analysis as the polished marble or bronze surfaces are to penetration. Given the unified quality of the single shapes, whether ovoid or finlike or voluted, there is no way to read them formally, no way to decode the set of their internal relationships, for to put it simply, no relationships exist.

In place of a part-by-part formal dynamic, there is in Brancusi's sculpture something one might call the deflection of an ideal geometry. That is, when confronting many of his works, one seems to be seeing simple spheres or cylinders or ellipsoids that have been deformed in some way. This deformation is slight enough so that it does not disturb the quality of the geometric volume as a whole—a unitary quality that is essentially unanalyzable (how does one formally analyze a circle, for example; how does one break it down into its constituent parts?). Yet the deformation is great enough to wrench the volume out of the absolute realm of pure geometry and install it within the variable and happenstance world of the contingent. Thus, instead of a pure ellipsoid, presented as an abstract object understood independently of the particularities of its placement or orientation (for it has no "top" or "bottom" surface), or of the material from which it is made, Brancusi gives the viewer *Beginning of the World* (1924). And, in that sculpture (fig. 62), placement is all.

62. *Brancusi:* The Beginning of the World, *1924(?). Polished bronze, 7½" x 10⅝" x 6⅝". Musée National d'Art Moderne, Paris. (Photo, Musées Nationaux)*

Polished to mirrorlike smoothness, the bronze "egg" is placed in the center of a circular metal disk. The effect of this conjunction of the object and the surface on which it rests is to insure a difference in kind between the reflections that will register on the lower portion of the form and those that will fall upon its upper half. Fraught with distorted patterns of light and dark reflected from the space of the room in which the object is seen, the smooth shape of the top half is contorted by myriad and changing visual incidents. The lower portion, on the other hand, simply reflects the underlying disk, and this reflection has the smooth, uninterrupted flow of a gradual extinction of light. Where the object touches base with the disk, the reflection it receives is the shadow of its own nether side cast back onto its surface, as if by capillary action. One therefore perceives the underside of *Beginning of the World*, outlined in velvety darkness, as a dis-

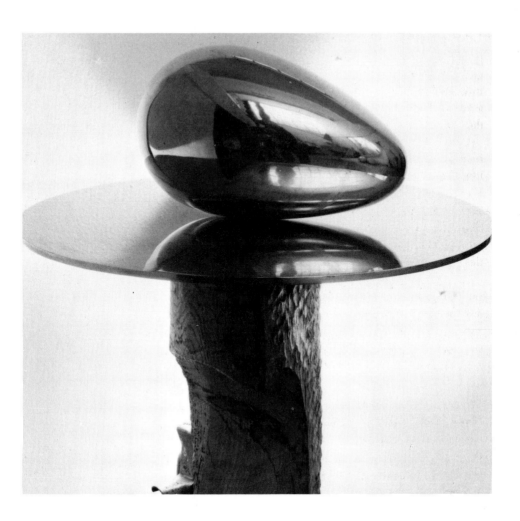

tinctly rounded curve in contrast to the upper surface of
the form, whose contour is flattened by the invasion of
light. It is this differential that gives to the geometry of
the form something of a kinesthetic quality that recalls
the feeling of the back of one's head, resting heavily on
a pillow, while the face floats, weightless and unencum-
bered, toward sleep (fig. 63).

The contemplation to which Brancusi's work invites us,
then, is far from the task of dismantling form to analyze
its internal relationships. Instead, it is a call for us to
acknowledge the specific way in which matter inserts
itself into the world—the way in which placement betrays
attitudes of being—so that a man sleeping appears both
to himself and to others as very different from when he

is, say, running, and these seem to be differences not merely of posture but differences in the essence of his form. Brancusi seems always to predicate the meaning of a sculpture on the particular situation which must modify the absolutes of its geometric form.

One finds oneself at this point in an area of almost insidious overlap between Brancusi and Duchamp. For like the readymade, the ovoid of *The Beginning of the World* (fig. 62) is a found object, a form that is in a real sense given to Brancusi rather than invented by him. Similarly the aesthetic act revolves around the placement of this discovered object which transposes it into a particular context from which it will "read" as art.

To review the long, slow development of Brancusi's career, toward the moment when he would conceive and accept *Beginning of the World* as a "work," is to see the series of decisions that the sculptor had to make as he traveled the path from a nineteenth-century conception of sculpture to the radical position of his own maturity. One might start in 1907, with a sculpture called *Torment* (fig. 64), the upper torso and head of a child, modeled in clay and cast in bronze.

Both in subject and in formal structure *Torment* reflects the influence of Medardo Rosso,[13] for this image of the child both physically fragmented and emotionally isolated within his own world of surprise or fear reminds one of the *Ecce Puer!* (fig. 27). Structurally *Torment* recalls as well Rosso's *Mother and Child Sleeping* (fig. 17) and particularly *The Flesh of Others* or *Sick Boy* (fig. 65), where the sculptural forms focus on a private inner reach explicitly buried beneath the surface of the body. *Torment* revolves around the structural contrast between exterior and interior, between what is open to inspection and can therefore be seen, and what is closed to examination and is consequently "visible" to the sculptural "subject" only. In Brancusi's work the child's head strains on its neck, backward and to one side, to meet its own contorted and raised right shoulder. Thus the left side of the child is one long, open, vertical axis —a languid contour in which skull, ear, neck and shoulder can all be seen distinctly. On the right side, these forms clench together into the nearly horizontal axis created

63. ABOVE *Brancusi:* Sleeping Muse, *1910. Gilded bronze, 6¼" x 11⅜" x 6¾". Musée National d'Art Moderne, Paris. (Photo, Musées Nationaux)*

64. FAR RIGHT *Brancusi:* Torment, *1907. Bronze, 14½". Private collection.*

65. NEAR RIGHT *Rosso:* Sick Boy, *1893. Wax over plaster, 11¼" x 10" x 7¼". Collection of Lydia K. and Harry L. Winston (Dr. and Mrs. Barnett Malbin, New York).*

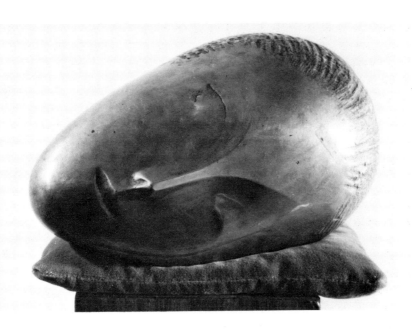

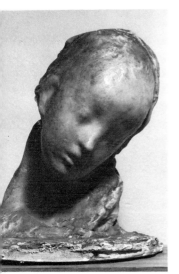

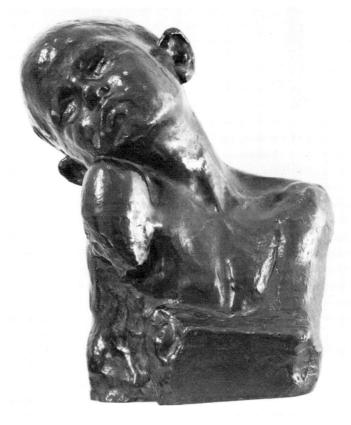

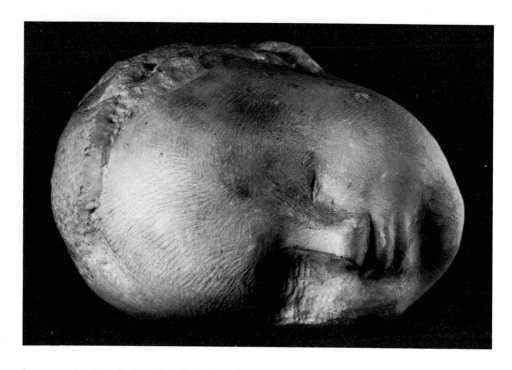

between cheek and shoulder. It is into that physical compression of form that the exterior surfaces of the right half of the body disappear, echoing the Rosso-like insistence on the essential privacy of the self.

There is as well an important comparison to make between this configuration and the treatment of the body one finds in works by Aristide Maillol, in whose studio Brancusi had begun his Paris career. In *The Study for "Thought"* of 1902 (fig. 66), for example, that same compression of the separate parts of the body occurs, as the head of the figure is forced into contact with the chest and thigh, resulting in an adjustment of the body toward a simplified, compact geometric volume. By creating a parallel between the disposition of parts of the figure and the cubic profile of the whole, Maillol concentrates our attention on a consonance between the internal structure of the body and its external form. As was true in neoclassical sculpture, this reciprocity betokens a belief that underneath the surfaces of objects lies the organizing premise from which they derive their meaning. As well, the adjustment of the volume toward geometric simples is an effort to locate this meaning in a world of ideal

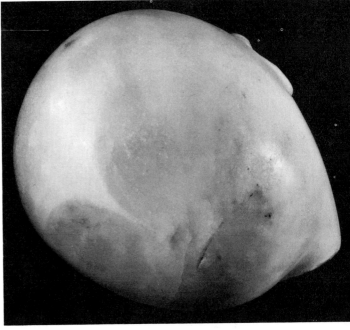

66. BELOW *Aristide Maillol (1861–1944)*: Study for "Thought," 1902. Bronze, 7" x 4½". Norton Simon Inc. Foundation. (Photo, Frank J. Thomas)

67. ABOVE LEFT *Brancusi*: Head of a Sleeping Child, 1908. White marble, 6½" long. Musée National d'Art Moderne, Paris. (Photo, Musées Nationaux)

68. ABOVE RIGHT *Brancusi*: Prometheus, 1911. Marble, 5" x 7". Philadelphia Museum of Art. (Photo, The Solomon R. Guggenheim Museum, New York)

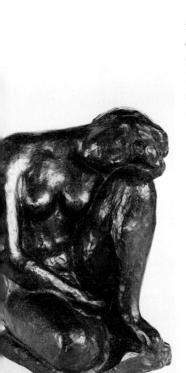

form. In *Torment*, Brancusi had shifted the terms of his employment of an internal structure from Maillol's idealist practice to the more psychological interests of Rosso. But *Torment* (which exists in two different versions) was only the first of a long series of meditations on the form of childhood (fig. 67).

By 1911 this image had undergone radical change. As *Prometheus* (fig. 68), the child's head has lost its shoulders and torso, retaining only a fragment of the bent neck attached, like the tail of a comma, to the spheric head. The separate planes of the face have been smoothed away to produce a marble surface of almost undisturbed convexity. The extremely shallow relief of the plane of nose and forehead against the eye socket and cheek has the quality of pattern registered impermanently on the surface, as though it were only a shadow cast into the smooth mass of the stone. In this sense, the sculptor explores a notion of sculptural detail as something imposed on the work from outside, which is like Rosso's late discovery of the importance of context in the *Ecce Puer!*

By the time Brancusi translated the marble *Prometheus*

into polished bronze (fig. 69), those faint changes in plane that produce a shadowlike sense of the facial features have become overwhelmed by a more absolute contextural "drawing": the effect of reflection which we saw in *The Beginning of the World.* In the polished version, the coloration of reflected lights and darks distinguishes the two hemispheres of the head in a way that is responsive to its placement and therefore to its meaning. Instead of expressing the composition of the face as the result of the real, internal structure of the skull, a structure that is bilaterally symmetrical, the composition of the reflections registers a startling asymmetry. The smooth, heavy, downside of the infant head resting prone on a horizontal surface appears different in kind from the upper side of the head which seems freed from the pull of gravity. What this opposition implies is an ephemeral line of division between two states of being—that of the dependent infant, too fragile even to support its own head, and that of a voluntary lifting of the body, in which the potential for self-supporting verticality can be read as a symbol for the ultimate independence of the will.

By 1911, therefore, Brancusi had simply changed the direction toward which *Torment* seemed to lead.

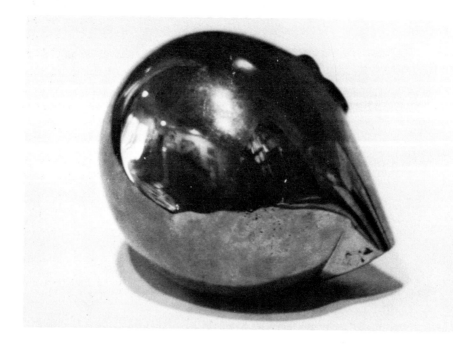

That is, he had foresworn the notion of an internal armature—echoing the body's own skeletal substructure—around which to organize the sculpted figure. He had, as well, rejected the meanings that such an internal organization tends to promote. Instead, he had turned to a sense of structure as something which the figure finds within a particular context, and what we have seen stemming from this decision is a kind of content consistent with this externalization of structure. The fact that one feels the *Prometheus* to be a complete object rather than a fragment of a body (like a severed head) attests to the self-sufficiency of the work, a self-sufficiency that is possible once the object is freed from all references to the internal anatomical armature on which *Torment* depends.

It is over the issue of what I have been calling "contextual drawing" that Brancusi's objects are most radically distinguished from that of other sculptors working at this time with the human body in highly simplified or fragmented forms. The drawing in works by Gaston Lachaise, for example, presupposes that anatomical subdivisions are manifestations of an internal structure which reaches outward at specific junctures to brake or tie back the voluminous bodies that seem in the process of ballooning toward a spheric simplicity (fig. 70). Or, in the sculpture of Amedeo Modigliani, where the extremely shallow incisions on limestone blocks etch the physiognomy of the head (in a manner from which Brancusi himself had learned), this drawing imprints the stone with a primitivizing language (fig. 71). As such, the drawing marks the work with a sign system that is anything but contextual.

By 1915, Brancusi fully consolidates the independence of the head as self-contained object with the work called *The Newborn* (fig. 72). In it, even the rudimentary neck of the *Prometheus* (fig. 68) has been shorn off to leave the contour of the sculpture a naked, uninterrupted ovoid. The only complications he allows to this smooth egg-shape are the lowering of one "cheek" to create a steplike ridge down the long axis of one side of the object, and the slicing away of an almost complete circular plane near one end of the ellipse. Suggesting an image of the newborn's face contorted by an open-

69. *Brancusi:* Prometheus, *ca. 1911. Bronze, 5½" x 6⅞" x 5½". Hirshhorn Museum and Sculpture Garden, Smithsonian Institution, Washington, D.C.*

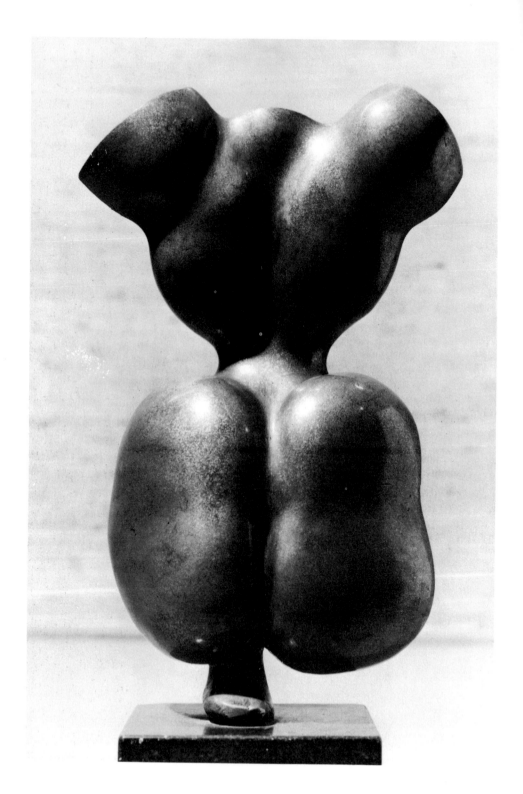

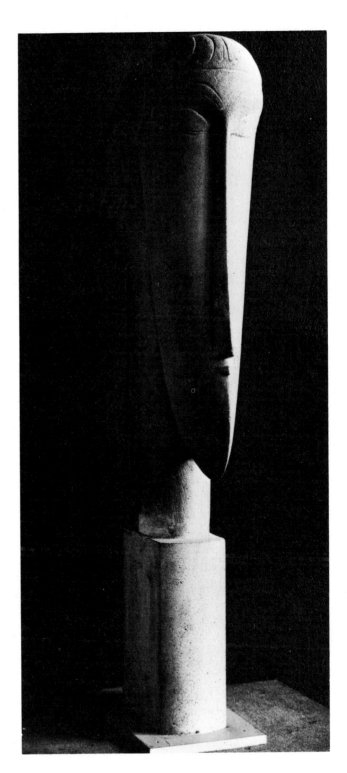

70. LEFT *Gaston Lachaise (1882–1935):* Torso, *1930. Bronze, 11½″ x 7″ x 2¼″. The Whitney Museum of American Art, New York. (Photo, Geoffrey Clements)*

71. RIGHT *Amedeo Modigliani (1884–1920):* Head, *ca. 1913. Stone, 24¾″ x 7″ x 14″. The Tate Gallery, London.*

mouthed cry,[14] these features also imply the much more primitive level at which life is born through the division of the single cell.[15]

Through the imagery of *The Newborn*, Brancusi radically declares the work to be a cell-like object which is detached, in terms of its content, from the structure of the complete body. In this isolation of body from figure, in this emphatic rejection of the internal armature and its classical meanings, one hears an echo of Rilke's description of Rodin's *Balzac* (fig. 25), when he spoke of the head as something that seemed to be "living at the summit of the figure like those balls that dance on jets of water." For Rilke was talking about a sculptural perception of the body which does not take for granted that the *meaning* of the body is the same as its anatomical structure. If the smooth tension of the skin of Brancusi's mature sculpture seems to repudiate the excesses of Rodin's elaborated and corrosive surfaces, if Brancusi's reductive shapes seem at variance to Rodin's complicated and twisted contours, this is only a superficial distinction of style. Brancusi himself said, "Without the discoveries of Rodin, my work would have been impossible."[16] And indeed the parallels are inescapable between that investment of meaning in a surface severed from the prior experience of a skeletal core which we have seen both in Rodin's art and in Brancusi's contextural notion of form.

The chain of development from *Torment* (fig. 64) to the *Prometheus* (fig. 68) and then *The Newborn* (fig. 72), a chain that ends in the final reductive statement of *The Beginning of the World* (fig. 62), consists of steps systematically taken over a period of eighteen years. The same patient labor, extended over a fifteen-year span, produced the series that begins with the first of Brancusi's single, standing birds, the *Pesarea Maiastra* (1910) and climaxes with the first bronze *Bird in Space* (1923). That development similarly proceeded from a work structured in terms of separate, articulated masses axially related to one another (fig. 73) to a final statement that is unitary —and thus hostile to part-by-part analysis—and does not permit itself to be read in terms of an internal armature (fig. 60).

The flamelike bronze shape of *Bird in Space* seems to

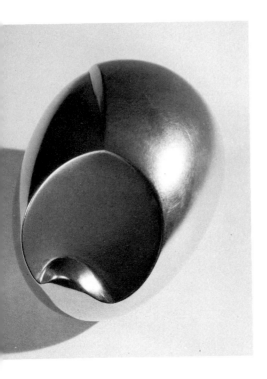

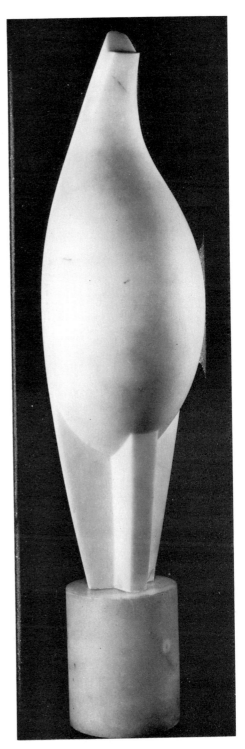

72. ABOVE *Brancusi:* The
Newborn *(Version I)*, 1915.
*Bronze, 5¾" x 8¼". Collection,
The Museum of Modern Art,
New York. Acquired through
the Lillie P. Bliss Bequest.*

73. RIGHT *Brancusi:* Bird,
1912(?). *White marble, 23¾",
marble base 6". Louise and
Walter Arensberg Collection,
Philadelphia Museum of Art.*

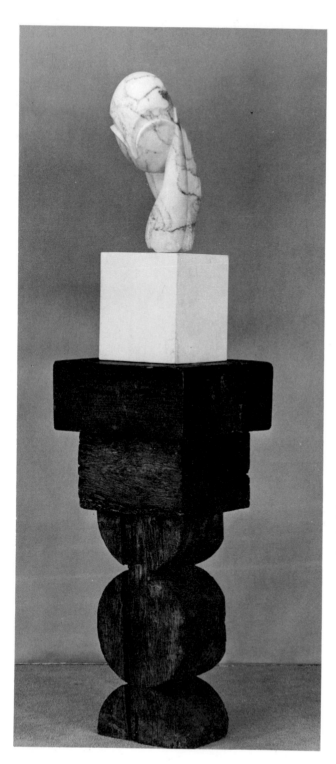

74. *Brancusi:* Mlle. Pogany
(Version II), 1919. Veined
marble, 17⅜″; base of
limestone and two oak sections,
48″. Collection of Mr. and
Mrs. Lee A. Ault, New York.
(Photo, The Solomon R.
Guggenheim Museum, New
York)

alter continually because of the way light falls on the elongated convexity of the sculpture's surface. As light strikes the tubular form, it tends to dissolve the vertical contours into an inexact, unstable gleam, fracturing one's sense of its absolute shape. Brancusi himself courted this dissipation of the edge of the work in the way he illuminated it for the photographs he took for its publication.[17] (See fig. 60.) Further, the convex surface focuses the shadows of the surrounding space into a dark stripe that runs vertically down the approximate center of the work. Because this vertical shadow is unstable with regard to the bronze mass, moving and shifting over its surface with the movements of the viewer, and because it is so obviously cast *onto* the work from outside rather than projected from within, it reads almost like a parody of the axial and internal armature of traditional, figurative sculpture. This is a parody which is continued in the bases that Brancusi provided for many of the birds—bases that consisted of forms piled or stacked one on top of the other. The separateness of these forms—faceted carved wood, cruciform stone, cylindrical marble—declares that even the grounds from which the sculptures rise are detachable, rearrangeable, contingent. There is, in other words, no given rationale for their configuration. To an extreme degree, *Bird in Space* joins hands with the late work of Rodin in expressing a sculptural consciousness of the body surfacing into gestures that in themselves express a moment in which the self is formed.

Regardless of aesthetic pedigree, however, the *Bird in Space* is a large, tubular metal object of startling simplicity. In 1926, it was one of twenty-six sculptures Brancusi shipped from France for exhibition at the Brummer Gallery in New York. The U. S. Customs officials, who examined the objects for duty-free entry as works of art, took one look at *Bird in Space* and saw the similarities it bore to a propeller blade or some other industrial object. They insisted on imposing a commercial import tax on the work, refusing to believe that it was sculpture.

All through his career, as Brancusi fanatically polished the surfaces of his bronzes to purge them of any sign of the hand-crafted studio object, he courted the finish of machine-made industrial products. And he obviously delighted in the beauty and severity of mechanically functional shapes. His insistence on translating every one of his marble sculptures into polished bronze dissipates the notion that the works were conceived as a celebration of the monolithic density of the natural stone, or rationalized in terms of the marble block. Brancusi's art was in no way guided by a "truth-to-materials" ethos in which, along with Henry Moore and Arp's sculpture, it was subsequently placed.[18] As a gifted technician, Brancusi exploited the natural properties of the materials in which he worked. So when he carved *Torso of a Young Man* (fig. 75), a cylindrical trunk mounted on two vestigial legs, he selected a piece of wood forked with the natural growth of its branches. Yet he would, just as often, act in violation of the apparent properties of his physical medium. Thus in the marble versions of *Bird in Space* he carved the juncture between base and shaft so slenderly that these works had to be fitted with an interior rod of metal before they could be submitted to the action of the chisel. And in the case of *Torso of a Young Man* (fig. 76), his translation of the wooden form into bronze dispenses with whatever formal meaning there might have been in exploiting the natural growth of the wood. The metallic version has none of the rationale of the carved one. The joints between stubby legs and torso have all the "naturalness" of pipe fittings, and the highly polished ensemble has the sleek streamlining of an industrial part.

Paired with the mechanical aura that surrounds this sculpture is the erotic quality of its design. In calling the work Brancusi's "first *torso as object*," Sidney Geist points to the fact that in this male torso there are no genitals, adding that "*Torso of a Young Man* is itself a phallus, geometrical, rationalized, sublimated."[19]

In this combination of the mechanical with the erotic, one finds yet another parallel between Brancusi and Duchamp. It is a parallel signaled by the customs case over *Bird in Space* and heightened by the fact that two years after Duchamp's *Fountain* was "censored" from exhibition in New York, one version of Brancusi's *Princess X* caused a scandal at the 1920 Salon des Indépendants in Paris and was removed from the galleries. Like *Torso*

75. BELOW *Brancusi:* Torso of a Young Man, *ca. 1916. Wood, 19". Louise and Walter Arensberg Collection, Philadelphia Museum of Art. (Photo, A. J. Wyatt, staff photographer)*

76. RIGHT *Brancusi:* Torso of a Young Man, *1925. Polished bronze, 18" x 40⅜" x 7". Hirshhorn Museum and Sculpture Garden, Smithsonian Institution, Washington, D.C.*

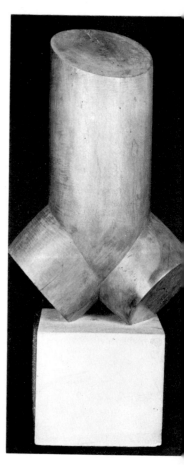

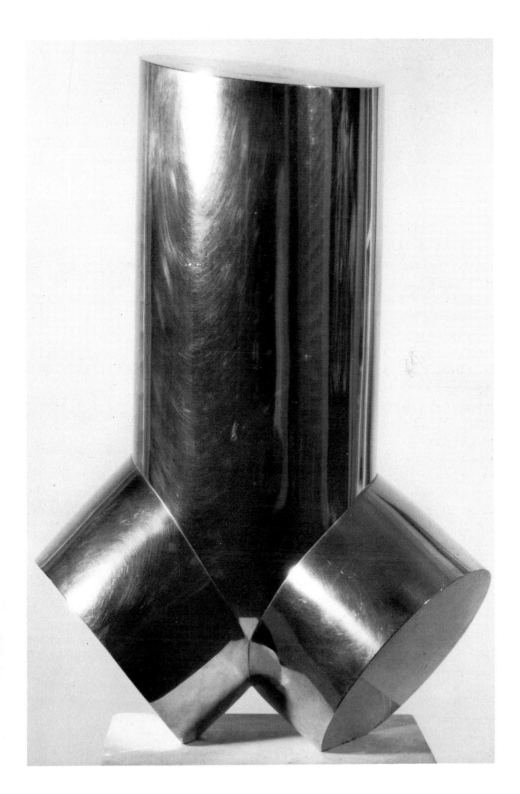

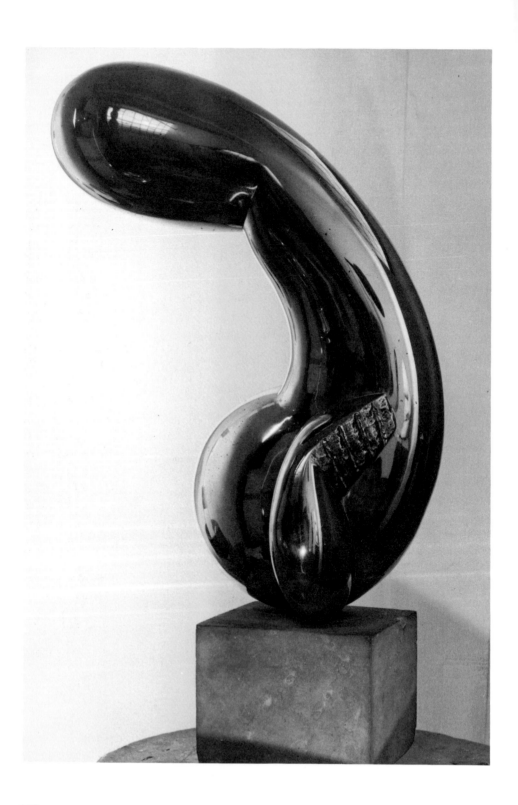

of a Young Man, Princess X (fig. 77) is a partial figure, the whole of which reads inescapably as a phallic object. The viewers of the exhibition protested its presence as obscene.

But the real sense in which the two men can be coupled in discussing the development of twentieth-century sculpture is that both of them took the same position on the question of sculptural narrative. Both of them rejected the technologically based role of analysis in sculpture, creating work that questioned the very role of narrative structure by gravitating toward that which is unitary and unanalyzable. The work of both men, therefore, stands aloof from the tendency we have traced from futurism and cubism into constructivist sculpture—a tendency to substitute for historical or psychological narrative the satisfactions of a quasi-"scientific" account of the structural organization of form.

No matter how different the level of realization of their work—Brancusi's so refined and elegantly crafted, Duchamp's so aggressive and formally offhand—both men stand apart from their contemporaries in ways that are similar to one another. Although surrealist sculpture, developing in the 1930s, exploited certain aspects of their work, the aims of surrealism were such that much of what was most radical in Duchamp's and Brancusi's conception of sculpture was either ignored or transformed. Indeed, it was not until the 1960s that Duchamp's concern with sculpture as a kind of aesthetic strategy and Brancusi's concern with form as a manifestation of surface assumed a central place in the thinking of a new generation of sculptors.

77. *Brancusi:* Princess X, *1916. Polished bronze, 23".* *Musée National d'Art Moderne, Paris. (Photo, Musées Nationaux)*

A Game Plan:
the terms
of surrealism

4

Take a newspaper.
Take some scissors.
Choose an article of the length
    you wish your poem to have.
Cut out the article.
Then cut out carefully each of the words in
    the article and put them in a bag.
Shake gently.
Then pull out each cutting one after the other.
Copy them down conscientiously
    in the order in which they left the bag.
The poem will resemble you.
And you will be a writer of infinite originality and of
charming sensitivity, although incomprehensible to the
masses.

—TRISTAN TZARA[1]

In 1920, when Tristan Tzara wrote down this recipe for composing poetry through the chance arrangement of sentence fragments pulled at random from a paper bag, the four-year-old dada movement, of which he was the impresario, had reached the height of its influence. In Paris, there were six periodicals through which dada writers and artists carried an unremitting attack on an aesthetic of rationality, or as Jean Arp put it, "Dada wished to destroy the hoaxes of reason and to discover an unreasoned order."[2]

If an ordered structure is the means of endowing a work of art with intelligibility, then a breakdown of structure is one way of alerting the viewer to the futility of analysis. It is a form of shattering the work as mirroring the rational powers of its viewer, a way to cloud up

105

the transparency between each surface of the object and its meaning, making it impossible for the viewer to reconstitute its every aspect through a single, concordant reading. Composition by means of chance disrupts the possibility of a work's having a coherent thread or core running through it to guarantee its intelligibility from the inside out. Dada's enemy was the a priori, the power of reason, and, most particularly, reason as a vehicle of power. For dada was a movement born out of horror at the destruction wreaked during World War I, which it viewed as the combined product of an overweaning technology and the lies of bourgeois rationalism. "The beginnings of dada," Tzara wrote, "were not the beginnings of art, but of disgust."[3]

Therefore, if in our schematic history of early twentieth-century sculpture we see a split developing between a sculpture of reason and a sculpture of situation, we can see how dada comes down on the side of the latter. Dada, which developed at the same time as the art of Duchamp and Brancusi, shared with the two men much of the same attitude toward the structural and temporal status of objects. For both Duchamp and Brancusi produced objects which are, in their striking wholeness and opacity, resistant to analysis. They are not conceived around a "core," to which their separate parts might be related— for they have no "core" of the kind we have seen in other work, whether it be that of neoclassicism or of Boccioni or Gabo; and the mute opacity of their surfaces tends to repel analytic penetration. Furthermore, Duchamp and Brancusi situated their sculptures within a temporal condition that had nothing to do with analytic narrative. The temporality of the readymade is that of the conundrum or the riddle; as such it is speculative time. And the temporality of Brancusi's sculpture is a product of the situation in which the work is placed—the reflections and counterreflections that tie the object to its place, making it the product of the real space in which the viewer encounters it. Unlike analytic time, in which the viewer grasps the a priori structure of the object, deciphering the relationship between its parts, and connecting everything to a structural logic or first cause, the alternative posited separately by Brancusi and Duchamp is that of

78. Duchamp: 3 Standard Stoppages, 1913–14. Threads glued to painted canvas strips, mounted on glass panels with wood, 50⅞" x 11⅛" x 9" (overall dimensions of wooden box). Collection, The Museum of Modern Art, New York. Katherine S. Dreier Bequest.

106

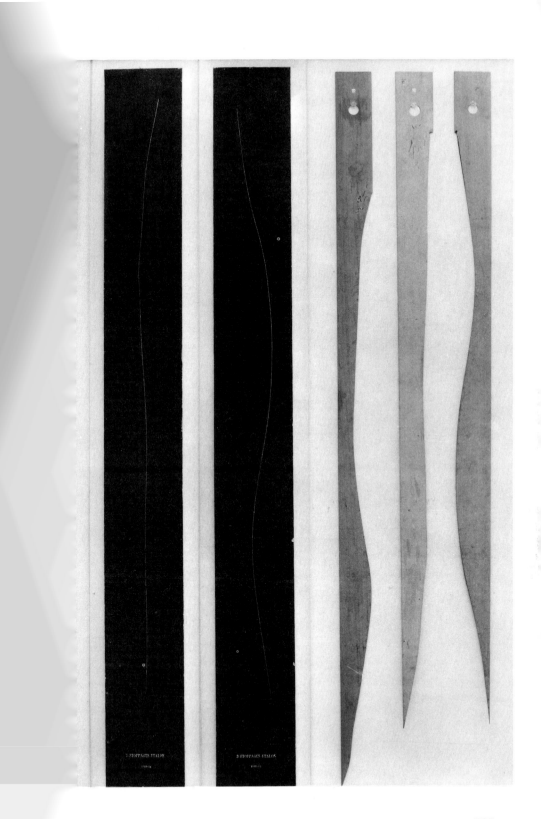

real time, or experienced time. It is the lived time through which one encounters the riddle, experiencing its twists and deviations, its resistance to the very idea of "solution." Or it is the experience of form as it is shown to be open to change through time and place—the contingency of shape as a function of experience.

If we return to Tzara's directions for composing poetry —his recipe in which the major ingredient is chance— we realize that his operation of pulling lines out "one after the other" is a radical strategy for forcing the writer to embrace experienced time. Given Duchamp's prior interest in composing by means of the "laws" of chance,[4] Tzara's gravitation toward this method is not surprising. But, in relation to the Duchamp precedent (fig. 78), the third to last line of Tzara's recommendation *is* surprising. For Tzara concludes that the poem which is created by the routine he describes "will resemble you," its author. This simple assumption on Tzara's part that the work of art will thereby reflect its maker contradicts the Duchampian position that the connection between object and author be wholly arbitrary. Duchamp welcomes this arbitrariness as a way of voiding the possible resemblance between the made object and its maker. So "the poem will resemble you" is a wrench that Tzara throws into Duchamp's argument from the "laws of chance," making it cease to function as a machine to depersonalize the work of art.

But 1920—when Tzara issued that directive about making a poem—was the year he transferred the base of his operations from Zurich to Paris. It was the point at which he consolidated his connection with the young Parisian poets who were editors and writers for the magazine *Littérature*: Louis Aragon, André Breton, and Philippe Soupault. It was also when Breton first fastened on the word "*surréaliste*," which had been coined by Apollinaire in the play *Les Mamelles de Tirésias*. Over the course of the next three years Breton was to grow increasingly involved with the provocative meaning he read into that term, sensing in it the basis for the new aesthetic position he would outline in the 1924 *Manifesto of Surrealism*. So 1920, the year of Tzara's affiliation with Breton and the others, was the beginning of an association with elements that were inherently different from the Zurich-based beginnings of dada. And his recipe for making a poem shows, in that phrase "the poem will resemble you," the infiltration of a somewhat alien line of thought.

To grasp the direction of that line of thought, one must remember that Breton's wartime experience was very different from Tzara's isolation in neutral Switzerland. Breton had served as a medical orderly in a hospital in Nantes for shell-shock victims. There, with some knowledge of Freud's *Interpretation of Dreams* behind him, Breton had spent long hours talking to soldiers who were severely disturbed, creating a situation in which their unconscious projections were more available than they otherwise would have been. Emerging from this with a firm conviction that the unconscious operates with a totally different kind of energy from that of the conscious mind—attempting to remake reality according to its own most extreme desires, rather than seeking rationally to grasp the structure of the real as something fixed and given—Breton was convinced of the truth of Freud's psychoanalytic position.

This, then, accounts for the difference between the surrealist view of chance and Duchamp's. Duchamp had seen chance as a way of enforcing the depersonalization of the object. Chance was one of many strategies used to disconnect the personality of the maker from the structure of the made thing. The systematic use of the readymade was another. Although the readymades were in fact selected by Duchamp, he saw this act of choice not as a projection of his own taste—stamping the object with the imprint of the finder's personality—but, instead, as a registration of "the beauty of indifference." But Breton spoke of "objective" chance, which was something else again.

The notion of "objective" chance proceeds from the energies of the unconscious operating at cross-purposes with reality. It predicts that the libido, working from within the subject, will shape reality according to its own needs by finding in reality the object of its desire. So Breton writes in *Nadja*, "not more than three days will pass without seeing me come and go, late in the after-

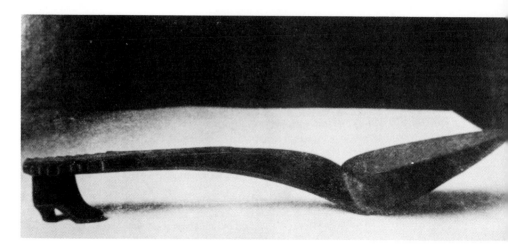

noon, through the boulevard *Bonne-Nouvelle*, between
the printing office of the *Matin* and the *Boulevard de
Strasbourg*. I do not know why it is my steps carry me
there, that nearly always I find myself going without
definite aim, with nothing decisive except that obscure
premise, namely that it will happen there."[5] The "it"
Breton contemplates is something unknown but expected,
the encounter with a piece of the world which will compose itself for him into a sign, both revealing and con-
firming the forces of his own will. The encounter Breton
expects may be with a person or with an object; the
character of the encounter will be the same in either
case. It will appear entirely gratuitous and at the same
time wholly meaningful. It will seem to Breton like a
revelation prepared for himself by his own unconscious
desires. The revelatory product of objective chance will
thus resemble those desires—and in this chance and
mysterious occurrence one will experience "the marvel-
ous."

It must be realized that with this resemblance between
desire and its product—between the viewer and the object
that appears to have been waiting just for him—one is
not returning to the constructivist resemblance between
the rational object and the constituting consciousness.
Because the constructivist relationship is predicated on
the notion that there is a fundamental identity between
the structure of subjective consciousness and the structure of objective reality. Furthermore, this identity, as
the condition of all experience, is obviously given prior

to experience and is impervious to human will. The surrealist resemblance, on the other hand, is between irrational, unconscious desire and the strange manifestation of it in the outer world—a manifestation which serves as proof that the outer world is itself transformable, that there is a possibility concealed within it of an alternate reality, or as Breton insisted, a surreality.[6]

In his novel, *L'Amour fou* (Mad Love), Breton gives many examples of the working of objective chance. One of these occurred while Breton and Alberto Giacometti were walking in the Flea Market. In one of the stalls Giacometti saw an antique "slipper spoon" (fig. 79) and realized suddenly that he had been troubled about a sculpture he was then working on. The spoon was exactly the shape that Giacometti had been trying to create in his work and he felt that, unconsciously, he had been calling for a pattern on which to model the sculpture (fig. 80). The chance encounter with it in the Flea Market was, for him and for Breton, a result of this unconscious demand.[7]

During the 1930s Giacometti insisted that the sculptural object he made bear no evidence of his own manipulation—either of his physical touch or his formal aesthetic calculation. It was to be a projection of desire rather than a product of something wrought or painstakingly fashioned. As with his encounter with the slipper spoon, "the sculptures," he wrote, "presented themselves

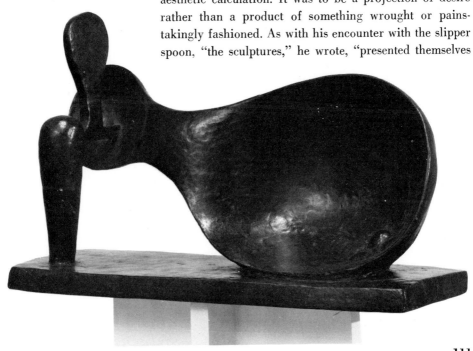

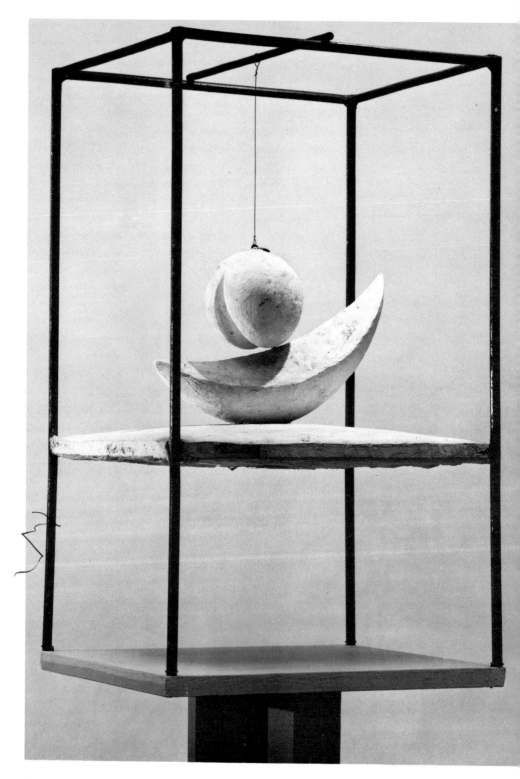

to my mind entirely accomplished." And so, with regard to the working of the material, "it was almost a bore to do it. I had to see them realized, but realization itself was irritating. It was essential that [with] the sketch having been made in plaster, they would be realized by a cabinetmaker (I retouched them afterward if it was necessary) so I could see them all done, like a projection."[8] This is the case with *Suspended Ball* (fig. 81), a sculpture of 1930–31, in which the wooden parts of the work are sanded to the smooth and impersonal finish of furniture.

Suspended Ball, with its erotic implications, was greatly admired by the surrealists, for it had the quality of objectifying the libidinal energy of the unconscious. The work is composed of three simple elements: an open cage with a platform inside it, on which rests a crescent-shaped wedge and a ball with a wedge-shaped slot cut out of its underside, the last element hung from a strut at the top of the cage. The pendular motion of the ball and the relation of slot to crescent implies the possible caress of one form by the other—a possibility thwarted by the fact that the string supporting the ball form is slightly too short to allow the two members of the work actually to touch. "Everyone who saw this object functioning," wrote Maurice Nadeau, "experienced a strong but indefinable sexual emotion relating to unconscious desires. The emotion was in no sense one of satisfaction, but one of disturbance, like that imparted by the irritating awareness of failure."[9]

Aside from its explicit eroticism, there are two features of *Suspended Ball* that make it a central object of surrealist sculpture. The first of these has to do with the kind of motion it incorporates, for unlike Boccioni's *Development of a Bottle in Space* (fig. 36), which projects an *illusion* of movement around the work through the agency of the corkscrew spiral, *Suspended Ball* engages in movement that is real. As Giacometti explained, "Despite all my efforts, it was impossible for me then to endure a sculpture that gave an illusion of movement, a leg advancing, a raised arm, a head looking sideways. I could only create such movement if it was real and actual. I also wanted to give the sensation of motion that could be induced."[10] Because the motion in *Sus-*

pended Ball is real, the temporal medium in which it engages is, correspondingly, literal. It is not the pregnant moment of Hildebrand and Rude, or the analytic time of Boccioni and Gabo—the compacted instant in which a sequence of moments before and after are contained and mentally projected. It is, instead, the real time of experience, open-ended and specifically incomplete. This recourse to real movement and literal time is a function of the meaning of surreality as taking its place alongside and within the world at large, sharing the temporary conditions of that world—but being shaped by an interior need.

And this shaping by desire accounts for the second feature of the sculpture, one that makes it quintessentially surrealist: by placing the suspended ball and the crescent within the cubic volume of the cage, Giacometti is able to hedge his bet on the situation of the object within literal space. He is able to make it an ambivalent participant in the space of the world, in that, while its movement is obviously literal, its place in that world is confined to the special theater of a cage—it is boxed off from the things around it. The cage functions, then, to proclaim the specialness of its situation, to transform it into a kind of impenetrable glass bubble floating within the spatial reservoir of the real world.

By being part of real space and yet somehow sectioned off from it, the suspended ball and crescent attempt to open up a fissure in the continuous surface of reality. The sculpture thus rehearses an experience that we sometimes have in waking life, an experience of discontinuity between various pieces of the world. Many examples come to mind. One of them occurred to me as I was standing with some friends in a small vestibule, about to enter a larger room where there was a concert of electronic music in progress. We had all paused a moment at the door, adjusting our eyes to the half-light of the space as we looked for seats. During that pause, I noticed a young man holding a trombone to his mouth, his cheeks expanding and contracting with air and his left hand moving the side of the instrument. Completely rapt in concentration, the man was soundlessly playing his trombone. My friends did not see him. They and everyone else were

82. BELOW *Max Ernst (1891–1976):* Femme 100 Têtes, *"Onset of day- evening- and nightgames." Plate from* La Femme 100 Têtes *(The 100 Headed Woman) (Paris: Editions du Carrefour, 1929).*
83. RIGHT *Giacometti:* The Palace at 4 A.M., *1932–33. Wood, glass, wire, and string, 25" x 28¼" x 15¾". Collection, The Museum of Modern Art, New York.*

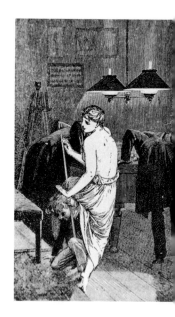

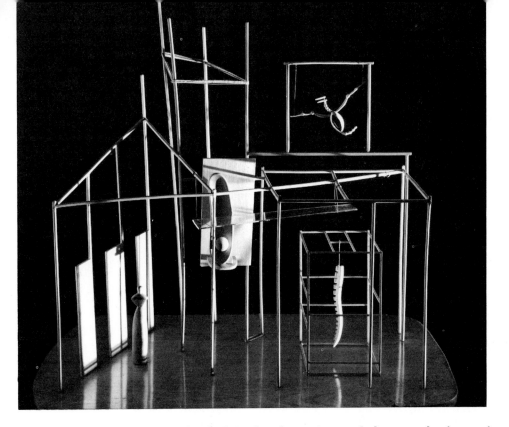

absorbed in the electronic sound that was the focus of attention for the occupants of the room, their purpose for being there. A moment earlier I had been joined to them in that intentional shared space, but now I was fixed by the trombonist's silent playing, which sectioned him off utterly from the rest of the space, as his body swayed to a different rhythm. Disconnected from everything else around him, he opened up a gap in the continuous reality of my space.

In the novels *Nadja* and *L'Amour fou*, Breton tells of many such incidents from his own experience. "At the end of one afternoon, last year," he writes, "in the side aisles of the 'Electric Palace,' a naked woman, who must have come in wearing only her coat, strolled, dead white, from one row to the next."[11] His image is of a silent disruption of the customary space of the movie theater—with his consciousness suddenly siphoned off from the flow of his fellow viewers' attention toward the screen. In the strange pictorial narrative *La Femme 100 Têtes* (The 100 Headed Woman), Max Ernst projects a chain of collage illustrations (fig. 82) directed at the

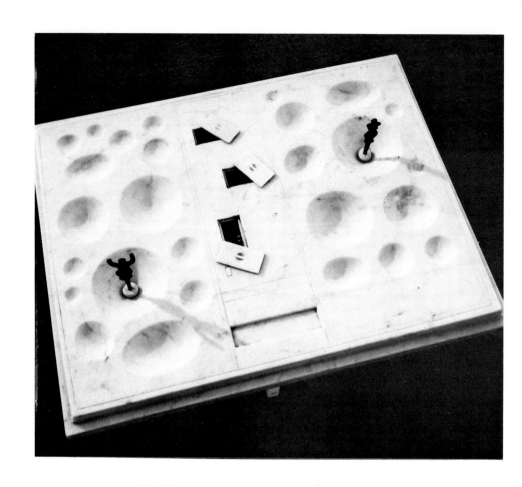

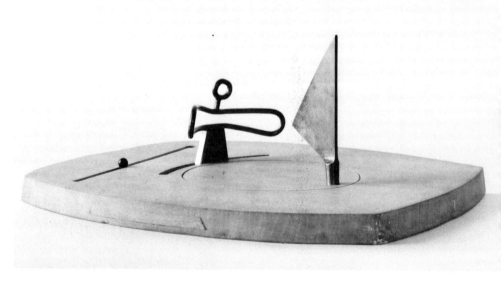

same sensation. Made from nineteenth-century engravings, these collages present the viewer with an overall sense of spatial continuity as a traditionally drawn perspective sets forth the simple coordinates of a landscape space or a domestic interior. With extreme stealth, Ernst then insinuates into these scenes materials foreign to them, sometimes objects from engineering manuals, or details from fashion catalogues—objects of a texture and scale separate from the background space of the collage, objects to which the occupants of that space are completely oblivious. The result is the transformation of the context of, say, a normal room into the psychically fractured space of Breton's cinema. In so doing, Ernst disrupts the space's metaphysical continuity without flattening or dispelling its depth.

There is, of course, a much more frequent experience of that disruption of a shared world: an experience which has the currency and feel of reality yet is at the same time utterly private. And that is the experience of dreaming. To Breton, the dream was the touchstone of surreality, for the surreal was like a waking dream—a fragment of real space altered, because it is created, by the desire of the dreamer, yet appears to him simultaneously as something independent of his own will, something he merely happened upon by chance.

84. ABOVE LEFT *Giacometti: No More Play, 1933. Marble, 15¾" x 11¾" x 2". Collection, Julien Levy, Connecticut. (Photo, The Solomon R. Guggenheim Museum, New York)*

85. BELOW LEFT *Giacometti: Man, Woman, and Child, ca. 1931. Wood and metal, 6⅜" x 14⅝" x 6¼". Kunstmuseum, Basel. (Photo, Oeffentliche Kunstsammlung Basel)*

86. BELOW *Giacometti: Circuit for a Square, 1931. Wood, 4.5 x 47 x 4 cm. Collection, Henriette Gomez, Paris.*

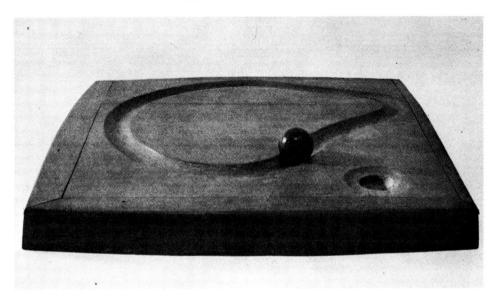

It is for this reason that Giacometti spoke of his works as "projections" he wished to see realized—out there in the world—but which he did not really want to fabricate himself.[12] It is for this reason that he encapsulates them in a separate little theater of their own even while trying to insure that they will appear continuous with the space of the real. One of the generic types Giacometti invested for this purpose is the sculpture-as-board-game. *No More Play* (1932), *Man, Woman, and Child* (1931) and *Circuit for a Square* (1931) all fall into this category (figs. 84–86). There is, in these works, that same physically continuous relationship between them and the viewer of *Suspended Ball*—except in the board games the pendular swing of the ball is replaced by the "moves" that the viewer can make with the separate pieces of the sculpture —relocating them back and forth along tracks in the ground plane of the board. In speaking of the literal movement he demanded for these works, Giacometti added, "I wanted one to be able to sit, walk, and lean on the sculpture."[13] Setting up the sculpture as though it were a game of chess is obviously an invitation to that kind of physical immediacy.

Yet, simultaneously, there is evoked by the board itself a sense of a strange landscape separated from continuous reality, with cause-and-effect relationships implicitly suspended, as in the case of *Man, Woman, and Child* (fig. 85), where the distinct tracks along which the three "pieces" move prevent them ever from meeting. With customary ambivalence, this work seems to situate itself *alongside* material reality.

Although Giacometti sets off most of his sculpture from space in general by a simulating "projected" reality— using cages or the strategy of the board-game—a few works were inserted more directly into the flow of ambient space. The *Woman with Her Throat Cut* of 1932 (fig. 87) was a work placed squarely on the floor, the human form fashioned from a disarray of sheathings, resembling a pile of old rags which the viewer might trip over. The 1931 *Disagreeable Object* (fig. 88), a phallic-shaped wooden form with little spikes protruding from the end, was to be placed on a table, like some kind of household implement which one might pick up by mistake. The

87. ABOVE *Giacometti:* Woman with Her Throat Cut, *1932. Bronze (cast 1949), 34½". Collection, The Museum of Modern Art, New York.*
88. BELOW *Giacometti:* Disagreeable Object (to be disposed of), *1931. Wood, 8⅞" x 19". Private collection. (Photo, The Solomon R. Guggenheim Museum, New York)*

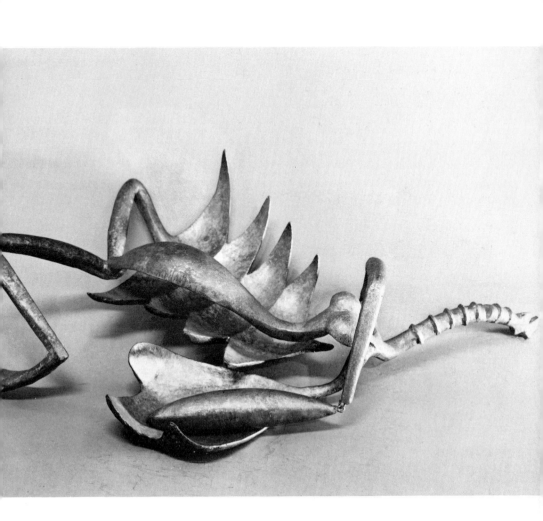

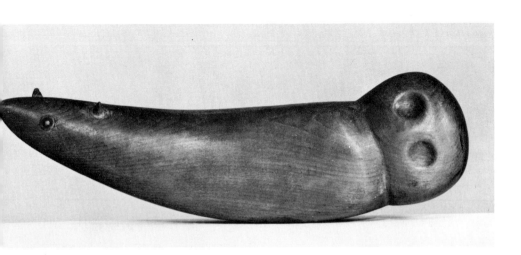

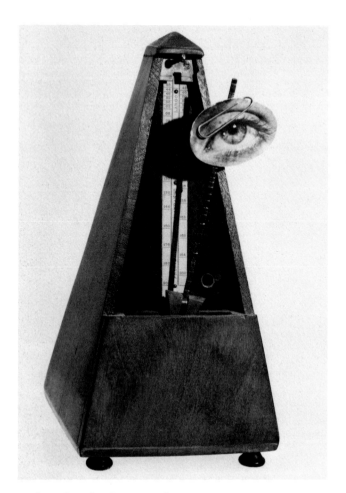

quality that the latter work projects is of some almost
ordinary object rendered disquieting by an unaccountable
deformation. In this sense, the work falls into a special
category of surrealist production in which many members
of the group participated—the category of "surrealist
objects," or as Salvador Dali called them, "Objects of
Symbolic Function."

Growing out of Duchamp's notion of the "assisted
readymade," these works were created by grafting a disparate skin, or strange detail, onto the body of an ordinary object. As in Giacometti's *Suspended Ball*, there is
often a literal temporality to these objects—real movement which synchronizes their existence with that of the
viewer's experience. Dali's *Venus de Milo with Drawers*
of 1936 (fig. 89) is one example, and Man Ray's
Object to Be Destroyed of 1923 (fig. 90) is another, the

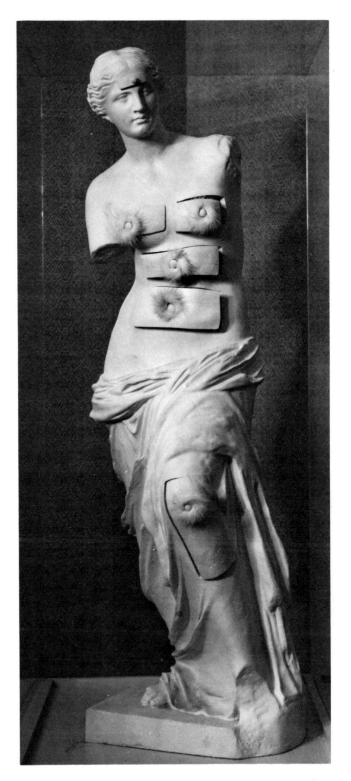

89. *Salvador Dali (1904–):*
Venus de Milo with Drawers,
1936. Painted bronze, 39⅜".
Gallerie du Dragon, Paris.
(Photo, Peter A. Juley & Son,
New York)

90. LEFT *Man Ray:*
Object to Be Destroyed, *1958*
replica of 1923 original.
Metronome and photograph,
9¼". Collection, Morton G.
Neumann, Chicago. (Photo,
Jonas Dovydenas)

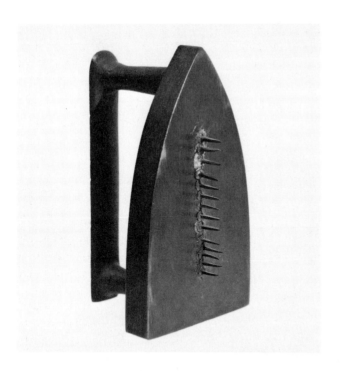

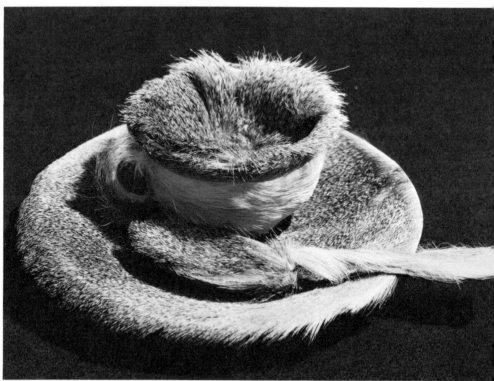

first a plaster statuette with the shell of the body sliced so that patches of the surface are made into drawer-fronts that can be pulled out by little tufted knobs, the second a metronome with a cut out photograph of an eye attached to the end of the pendular arm, slicing, disembodied, through space to the rhythm of real time.

Real movement was not always in question but, rather, what one might call the burgeoning significance of metaphor. In these cases, a simple conjunction would set off trains of narrative association—as in the sense of violence or pain dramatically implied by the row of nails fixed, spikes out, to the smooth underbelly of an iron in Man Ray's 1921 *Gift* (fig. 91), or the oral eroticism suggested by Meret Oppenheim's *Fur-Lined Teacup* of 1936 (fig. 92). Because of this coupling of two disparate entities, the object is shrouded in the temporality of fantasy. It can be the recipient of the extended experience of the viewer who projects his own associations onto its surface. The metaphoric connections supported by the object solicit the viewer's unconscious projections— invite him to call to consciousness an internal fantastic narrative he has not previously known. The time spent viewing the object is to be structured in terms of the temporal conditions peculiar to fantasy. The encounter provoked by the "surrealist object" is thus the meeting of two temporal arcs, which, while they are narrative in character, are (unlike traditional fiction) involved with effects that cannot be anticipated and causes that are previously unknown. Breton had explicitly said in the 1924 *Surrealist Manifesto* that the nineteenth-century novel was, for him, a repugnant genre. He saw it as positivist in kind and therefore as a function of "bourgeois rationalism." Yet, as one writer has pointed out, surrealist art "preserves in its own mode the circumstantiality of the novel."[14] Metaphor, which is the yoking of two separate ideas, had already been made explicitly dramatic, and thus temporal, in the phrase of Lautréamont that Breton and the other surrealists were fond of quoting: "beautiful as the chance encounter of an umbrella and a sewing machine on a dissecting table."[15] So that metaphor had been, for them, infected with the "circumstantiality" of time.

91. ABOVE *Man Ray: Gift, 1963 replica of 1921 original. Flat iron with nails, 6" x 3½". Collection, Morton G. Neumann, Chicago. (Photo, Jonas Dovydenas)*

92. BELOW *Meret Oppenheim (1913–   ): Fur-Lined Teacup (Lunch in Fur), 1936. Fur-covered cup, 2⅞", 4⅜" diameter; saucer 9⅜" diameter; spoon, 8" long. Collection, The Museum of Modern Art, New York.*

In looking at the analytic objects of Boccioni and Gabo, one sees the important function of the "core" of the sculptures—the static, ideal shape or principle lying at the heart of the various works. With the "surrealist objects," one finds in case after case the twofold trans-mutation of this notion of the core. For one thing, the metaphor is produced on the surfaces of the objects, as though metaphor supplied a protective coating that can be grafted onto their bodies. This more than anything reinforces one's sense of them as hollow volumes and, as such, without a structural and static core. Dali's *Venus de Milo* (fig. 89), Marcel Jean's *Horoscope* (fig. 93), and Magritte's *The Woman* (fig. 94) are examples in which even a relatively realistic rendering of the human form is deprived of the capacity to articulate an internal struc-ture. Second, the metaphor is substituted for the struc-tural element of the object—but instead of acting as a static support, it operates to wed the sculpture with the circumstantial flow of time.

93. Marcel Jean (1900–   ): Horoscope, 1937. Painted dressmaker's dummy with plaster ornaments, watch inserted on top, 33" x 17" x 12". Collection, Morton G. Neumann. (Photo courtesy of the artist)

Most of the fictions provoked and supported by sur-realist sculpture are slightly pornographic and sadistic in nature. A recurrent theme of violence runs through them, from Man Ray's *Gift* (fig. 91) and Giacometti's *Woman with Her Throat Cut* (fig. 87) to his 1932 *Caught Hand* (fig. 95), in which fingers are enmeshed in the gears of a little machine that can be turned by the viewer, and Hans Bellmer's series of dolls from the 1930s, in which the anatomical form of the toy is turned into various genital shapes both suggested and explicit. Yet the object, so psychologized, wears on its sleeve the badge of a formative irrationality. Through its distortions, the object becomes emblematic of a psychic process running counter to the rational contemplation elicited by the analytic object of constructivism.

This engagement on the part of the surrealists with psychological time as a "medium" for sculpture was given a slightly different cast in the work of the American artist Joseph Cornell. In his sculpture one finds a psycho-logical content based on nostalgic and adolescent fan-tasies, structured by a formal organization that is a striking variant on Giacometti's board-game strategy (fig. 96). Cornell's boxes with their shallow compart-

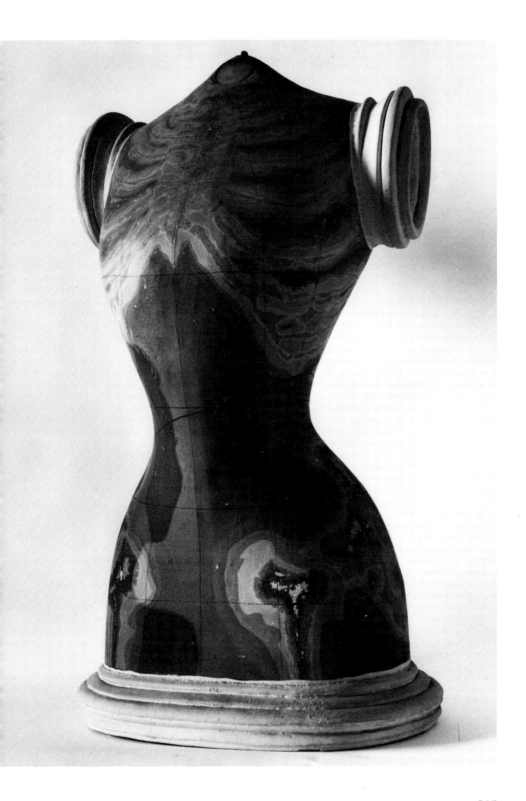

125

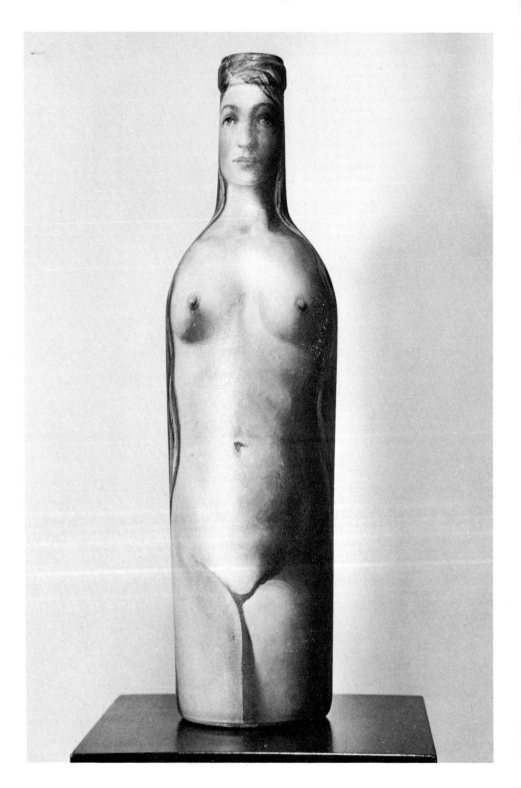

126

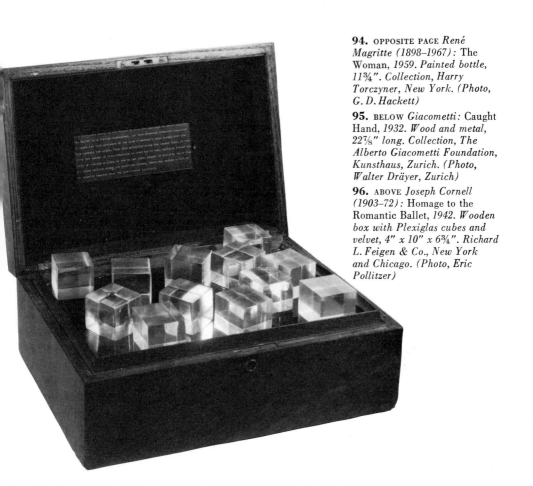

94. OPPOSITE PAGE *René Magritte (1898–1967):* The Woman, *1959. Painted bottle, 11¾". Collection, Harry Torczyner, New York. (Photo, G. D. Hackett)*

95. BELOW *Giacometti:* Caught Hand, *1932. Wood and metal, 22⅞" long. Collection, The Alberto Giacometti Foundation, Kunsthaus, Zurich. (Photo, Walter Dräyer, Zurich)*

96. ABOVE *Joseph Cornell (1903–72):* Homage to the Romantic Ballet, *1942. Wooden box with Plexiglas cubes and velvet, 4" x 10" x 6¾". Richard L. Feigen & Co., New York and Chicago. (Photo, Eric Pollitzer)*

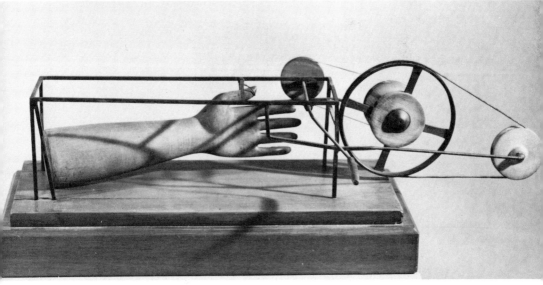

ments through which wooden balls are meant to roll, or with their parallel metal tracks along which rings are meant to slide, consort with the viewer in a way that is similar to Giacometti's work: they ask to be directly handled or manipulated. The designation Cornell gave to a series of these boxes—"slot machine" as in *Medici Slot Machine* (fig. 97)—openly admits to the way that the sculpture functions in real time and in immediate response to the viewer's touch. Yet the space through which these elements move is, like the space of Giacometti's sculpture, declared as not wholly continuous with the space of the viewer. Cornell's image/objects are given a tiny space all their own which they occupy as though it were a miniature stage, so that the slot machine's components are suspended within their own environment, like biological specimens placed in a bell jar.

Within that environment a strange equalization takes place among objects of extremely different types. A real compass and a real jack are juxtaposed with a map of the Palatine Hill and a reproduction of a painting by the Renaissance artist Moroni. Although, on the one hand, the map and reproduction are real objects, as are the compass and ball, they are, on the other, objects of a special kind. They are also *representations* of a distant reality—distant both in space and time. This quality of difference between the represented boy and schematic map and the compass and jack operates to distinguish the jack and compass from each other as well. For those two objects, while not being representations, are still unlike one another in that the compass measures a reality it can only fractionally occupy. Yet whatever the divergence in scale, function, and level of actual presence of the things it contains, the nature of the Cornell box is that it is a magical equalizer of all these differences. That is, within the space of the box, or stage, all these object/images acquire the same degree of presence or density—they all seem equally "real."

To create this sense of equalization Cornell depends on the temporal character of the board-game or slot machine structure as his chosen medium. For this allows him to imply that the spatial environment of the box is an objectification of a kind of psychological process that acts

97. *Cornell:* Medici Slot Machine, *1942. Construction, 13½" x 12" x 4¼". Collection, Mr. and Mrs. Bernard J. Reis, New York. (Photo, The Solomon R. Guggenheim Museum, New York)*

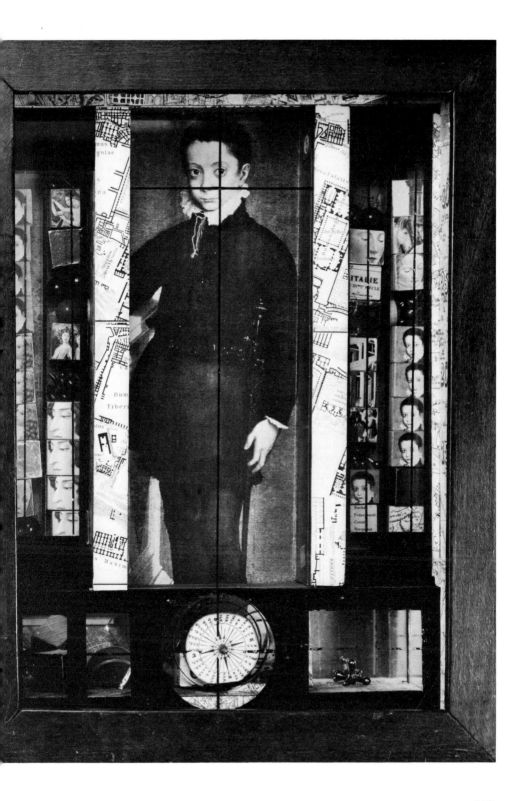

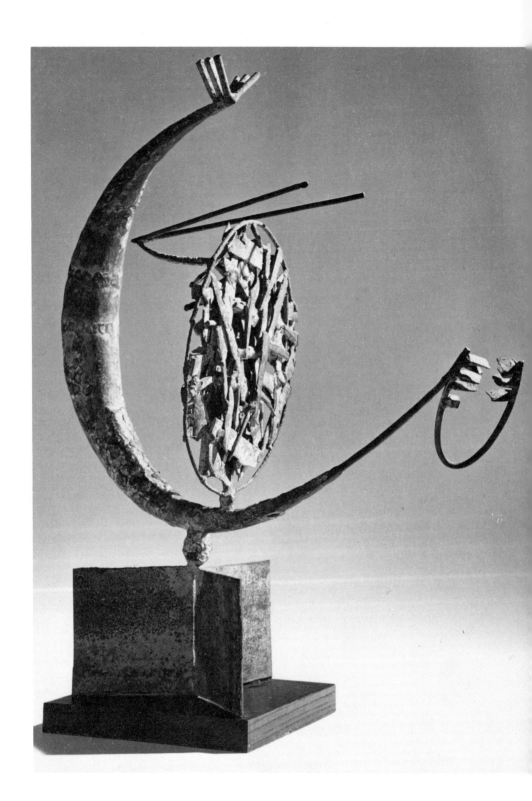

sequentially—through time—to bring about that illusion of equivalence between wildly different experiences. Specifically, the climate of the box seems to be an analogue with the process of human memory—a medium through which experiences of different degrees of realization (such as the remembered faces of friends, scenes from books, or from the conversations of others, or from dreams) can achieve an equal sense of expressive presence and importance. In this sense Cornell takes the surrealist medium of temporality and uses it to explore not the dream but the access to the past achieved by memory. Like the board-games or the "Objects of Symbolic Function," the box is an attempt to project the structure of a psychological process outward into the space of reality.

Working in self-imposed isolation in Flushing, New York, Cornell developed the basic structure of his art during the 1930s. The most important sources of his conception of the sealed box as a spatio-temporal medium were the work of Duchamp and the collage novels—such as *La Femme 100 Têtes*—of Max Ernst.

By the 1930s, then, the surrealists had established a kind of sculptural object that seemed to incorporate psychological qualities by bearing on its surface the imprint of sexuality, or, more often, of pain. This expressionist aspect infected much of the work of that decade, even sculpture produced by artists who had little or no connection with the surrealist group. Julio Gonzalez' 1935 *Head* (fig. 98) is a case in point. Here one sees the physiognomy of the face racked by a kind of hideous grimace, organized around stalklike eyes and clenched jaws fashioned like pincers. Yet while Gonzalez' *Head* shares some of the affect of the surrealist object, it is much more crucially influenced by the structure of Gabo's stereometry. For, like Gabo's early torsos or his later *Column* (fig. 46), the work establishes a sense of virtual volume, which is created by the right-angled intersection of two invisible major planes. A large, open crescent, bearing spiky tufts of hair at one tip and a pincerlike mouth at the other, sketches the cranium in profile. Inside the crescent, a ragged, circular disk, set at a ninety-degree angle to that profile, establishes the breadth of the face. The volume of the head, however, is created mostly out

98. *Julio Gonzalez (1876–1942)*: Head, *ca. 1935. Wrought iron, 17¾". Collection, The Museum of Modern Art, New York.*

of thin air, directed and shaped by the vectors of the implied planes that compose it. But the literal transparency of the object is, as in Gabo's practice of stereometry, simply a manifestation of the conceptual transparency that underlies it. For the absence of mass or enclosing volume insures that the relationship between the parts of the work will be completely open to inspection from any angle, and it is by grasping the abstract significance of that relationship that one re-creates the anatomical volume.

In Gonzalez' *Head* there is a marriage of surrealist affect and stereometric structure in which the original meaning of each prototype is lost. Stereometry endows the *Head* with a rational and immediately perceivable "core"; yet the psychological and expressionist cast of the object strips it of the mechanistic aura of constructivism. Surrealism had been Breton's weapon against positivism, his way of attacking "bourgeois rationality." Because Gabo's constructivism is in total sympathy with rationalism, the two movements are clearly ideological enemies. It might be said that Gonzalez' *Head*, suspended between the two of them, does not encompass the logical consequences of either one.

Originally trained as a stone carver, Gonzalez had learned about welding metal while working in one of the Renault factories in France during World War I. Prior to the 1920s, metal sculpture had been confined to the procedure of casting molten materials, like bronze, so that the finished work was always several steps away from the original creation of the plaster model, and was forced by technical limitations to a certain density of form.[16] By the late 1920s Gonzalez had perfected a technique of making stable and permanent sculpture by directly welding together metal sheets and rods, thereby short-circuiting the casting process and making possible a much more linear and fragile style. "To project and design in space with the help of new methods," Gonzalez wrote, "to utilize this space, and to construct with it, as though one were dealing with a newly acquired material —that is all I attempt."[17] And in Gonzalez' hands, the technical innovation of "direct-metal" sculpture contained within it a directive to make transparent or open sculpture, or as Gonzalez put it, "to draw in space."

99. *Picasso:* Construction in Metal Wire, *1929–30. Iron, 19⅝". Estate of the artist.*

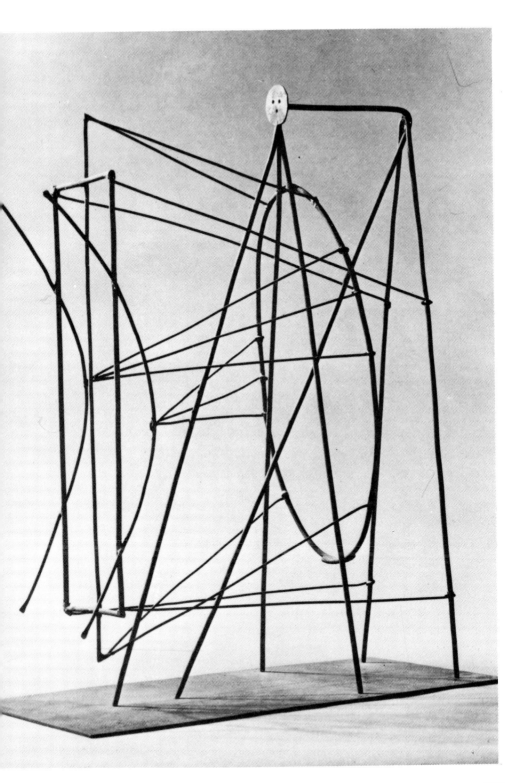

A Spaniard, Gonzalez was a friend of Picasso's, for whom he briefly worked as an assistant. It was Gonzalez who, in 1930, actually welded the gridlike *Construction in Metal Wire* (fig. 99) that Picasso had conceived in 1929. Like Gonzalez' later *Head* (fig. 98), Picasso's *Construction* is an exercise in Gabo-like virtual volume, a variation on the constructivist method of transparency.

A three-dimensional lattice of metal rods, the work suggests the presence of a volume, the external shape of which is a triangular prism with a rectangular base. Yet this resultant form also seems to be the outward projection of a core shape that has generated, from the inside out, the other components of the work. For at the interior of the sculpture is an elongated, bisected triangle which serves as the spine and legs of a figure whose arms, reaching forward from that establishment of its body, are triangular repetitions of that anatomical premise. These arms, manifesting the two parallel sides of the prism, extend toward the front face of the volume where they attach to two bluntly curved rods. The obvious suggestion is that the figure is actually holding reins and that the work as a whole is a kind of stick-figure parody of classical sculpture, specifically the *Charioteer of Delphi*. Not only do the "reins" promote that association but so does Picasso's use of primary geometrical shapes on which to construct the sculpture, and his formal statement about the reciprocity between the skeletal underpinnings of the body and the symmetry of the blocklike volume in which it surfaces. The sculpture functions, therefore, as a direct and witty critique of transparency as a sculptural medium. It shows the actual transparency of the three-dimensional grid to be essentially the same as the conceptual transparency of the classical figure, which, though massive rather than open to visual penetration, though monolithic rather than constructed from a network of line, is also premised on the ultimate understanding of the rational relationship between structure and surface.

At the same time as Picasso was making this critical parody of classical structure, he was experimenting with the surrealist notion of structure-by-metaphor, through which the sculpture is joined to the flow of time. As early as 1914 Picasso had introduced a common object

100. NEAR RIGHT *Picasso: Glass of Absinthe, 1914. Bronze, 8⅜". A. E. Gallatin Collection, Philadelphia Museum of Art. (Photo, A. J. Wyatt, staff photographer)*

101. FAR RIGHT *Picasso:* Head of a Woman, *1931. Painted iron, 39⅜". Tate Gallery, London.*

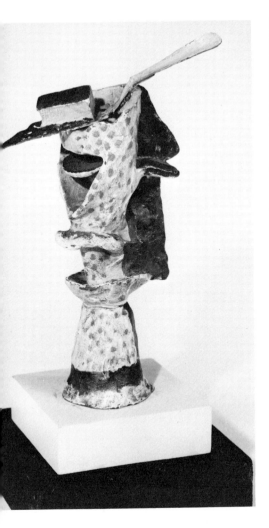

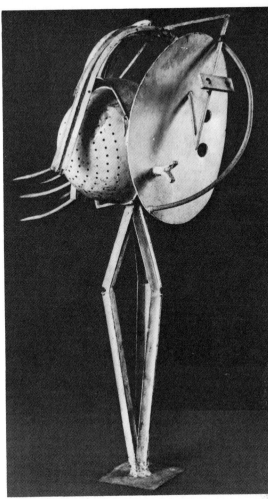

into his sculptural composition. *The Glass of Absinthe* (fig. 100), a tiny bronze maquette, supported a real sugar spoon on the lip of the fractured planes of the represented object, and the strangeness imparted to the work by the invasion of the actual into the orbit of the illusionary prompted Breton to include this work in the 1936 exhibition of surrealist objects.[18]

Head of a Woman (fig. 101), a standing figure that Picasso made in 1931, exploits the natural hollowness of a found object to deprive the human form of a sense of underlying structure. By connecting the hemispheres of two metal colanders to form the skull of the figure, Picasso reinforces the importance of surface by using a flat oval

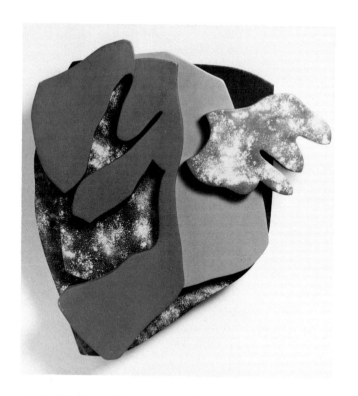

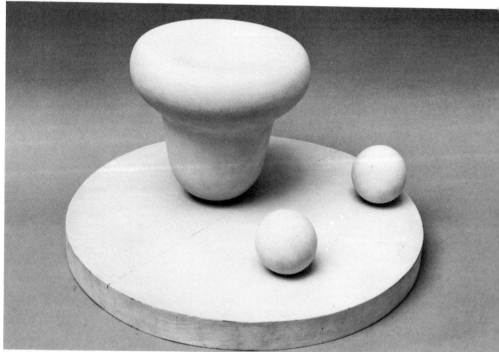

plane of metal to suggest the face as something detached or detachable from the rest of the head—like a mask. Because of its actual disjunction from the body that lies behind it, the mask functions in this sculpture as a denial of the classical principle which holds that the surface of a form is the external effect of an underlying cause. Arbitrarily applied, the mask has no logical connection to the form of its support; it is a demonstration of the opacity of surfaces. Picasso's 1931 figure expresses the detachment of the mask on two levels: the plane of the face disconnects from and opposes itself to the volume of the head lying behind it; and the perforated colanders, by forming a hollow bubble, seem to encapsulate the cranial volume while revealing nothing of its structure.

In dada's early celebrations of the irrational, masks had served as an important prop. At the early dada performances at the Café Voltaire in Zurich, the performers used masks both to allude to nonrational, primitivist thought and to celebrate an absurd present in which a distorted surface could cut off the perception of rational structure.[19]

Jean Arp initially formed his sculpture according to the principle of the mask in 1916, the same year as his association with the dada group at the Café Voltaire. Overlapping several layers of intricate shapes, cut out with a fretsaw, on the ovoid of a mask-shaped ground, he gave his reliefs the same unyielding frontality that had informed Picasso's early still-life constructions. And in 1917, the same year as his masklike *Some Shadows: Portrait of Tristan Tzara* (fig. 102), Arp also began to compose collages by means of the "laws of chance."

Unlike Tzara's attitude toward the way chance would cause the composition to resemble its maker, Arp saw chance as a strategy to disconnect the work from the personalization of his own control. "I further developed the collage," he wrote, "by arranging the pieces automatically, without will. I called this process 'according to the law of chance.' The 'law of chance,' which embraces all laws and is unfathomable, like the first cause from which all life arises, can only be experienced through complete devotion to the unconscious. I maintained that anyone who followed this law was creating pure life."[20] Though Arp's notion of chance differed from Tzara's,

102. ABOVE LEFT *Jean Arp (1887–1966)*: Some Shadows: Portrait of Tristan Tzara, *1916. Painted wood, 18⅞" x 18¼". Collection, Mme. Jean Arp. (Photo, Dietrich Widmer, Basel)*

103. BELOW LEFT *Arp*: Bell and Navels, *1931. Wood, 10" x 19⅜". Collection, The Museum of Modern Art, New York. Kay Sage Tanguy Fund.*

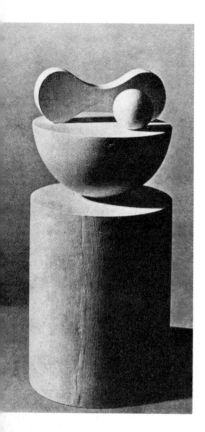

it was not, however, similar to Duchamp's. Arp's view of the artist as "creating pure life" had nothing in it of Duchamp's exploitation of the art object as a mode of posing questions about the nature of the work. Instead, Arp viewed the art object as a species of natural object— a unique addition to the inventory of natural forms. "Art is a fruit that grows in man, like a fruit on a plant, like a child in its mother's womb," he insisted. Or, speaking of the three-dimensional sculptures he began to make around 1930, calling them "Concretions": "Concretion designates solidification, the mass of the stone, the plant, the animal, the man. Concretion is something that has grown. I wanted my work to find its humble place in the woods, the mountains, in nature."[21]

The earliest of Arp's free-standing sculptures attest to his association with the surrealists during the decade of the 1920s, when, along with Tzara, Arp left Switzerland for France. As Giacometti does with his board-game strategy, Arp places sculptural components on a horizontal surface that invites the viewer's approach; like the "surrealist objects," they seem to be only slightly modified occupants of the tablelike platforms upon which they rest, like quiescent members of a still life. Both *Bell and Navels* (fig. 103) and *Necktie and Navel* (fig. 105) of 1931 possess this kind of plausibility, for the elements of these sculptures appear within the situation of a suggested activity, as though they were pieces of fruit placed on a tray and brought to the table. Yet, as in the case of the "surrealist objects," the surfaces of these components seem shaped by the projected fantasy of viewer or maker. They seem smoothed down until, like the parts of Giacometti's *Suspended Ball*, they approach resemblance to or analogy with human organs. And they are animated or given psychological qualities by this analogy. In the case of the 1930 *Head with Annoying Objects* (fig. 104), this exploitation of smooth visceral forms combines with a type of composition in which the ordering of the shapes is left to the contingencies of real time. This last is because the two "annoying objects" can be placed at will by the viewer, thereby making the sculpture responsive to the whim of someone other than the artist. Arp's attitude to composition in this work parallels Giaco-

104. OPPOSITE *Arp:* Head with Annoying Objects, *1930. Bronze, 14⅛" x 10¼" x 7½". Private collection, Paris. (Photo, Etienne Bertrand Weill)*

105. ABOVE *Arp:* Necktie and Navel, *1931. Painted wood. (Present whereabouts unknown.)*

metti's ambition for "the sensation of motion that could be induced."

Yet, in *Necktie and Navel* (fig. 105), for all its apparent continuity with the situation of an actual encounter, something foreign to surrealism is introduced. Unlike the "surrealist object," which is truly thrust into the unprogramed context of real space, this still-life assemblage is constructed to be seen from only one point of view. It is, then, frontal; and unlike the frontality of the dada-inspired mask—which implies nothing about the reality that lies behind or beyond it—this frontality is inferential, a little like Boccioni's or Gabo's. There seems to be a generating principle that expands outward from the smallest integer of the work to the largest, running through all of them like the formula for an algebraic

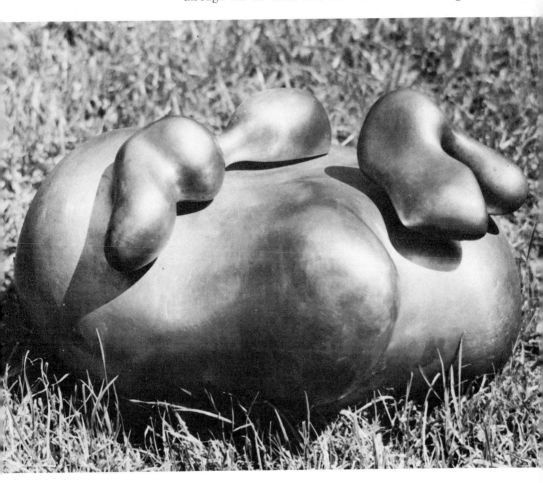

series, guaranteeing from the view of the front knowledge about the formal interconnections of all the parts. The entire work develops as a set of variations on a circle: the innermost object is a sphere (which Arp designates as a navel or umbilicus); the necktie form is two fused circles; the bowl that contains them is a hemisphere; and the pedestal on which the still life sits is a column. As in the surrealist metaphorical core or thread of fantasy, this theme of circularity imparts a certain degree of temporality to the work. For each part of the still life seems to be metamorphically derived from its neighbor. But unlike surrealist temporality, Arp's metamorphosis carries with it a sense of rational connection between each given cause and its effect. It suggests a kind of unfolding through time which we associate with the phenomenon of growth—like a plant progressing through the morphological stages of its life cycle, changing its shape from seed, to sprout, and to bud, holding within itself the essential unity of its own organic life. Thus in two years of working on free-standing sculpture, Arp had passed from surrealism into a position based on the idea of organic development which his "concretions" maintained from then on.

From that point, although Arp never formally broke with Breton and continued to exhibit occasionally with the surrealists, he moved closer to other circles of artists in Paris. He began to show his work with such groups as Abstraction-Création and Cercle et Carré, both of which were adamant in thinking of abstraction as the means to evolve new forms. The sculptor was likened to a creator, to the original Creator, who did not replicate given objects, but added new ones to the repertory of nature. In so doing, the sculptor was performing an act which accorded with the vitalist position held by certain nineteenth-century biologists, by which life itself was understood to be inert matter impregnated with a vital essence that rendered it organic, explaining the capacity of living cells to maintain themselves, to subdivide, to fecundate. Although modern biology, through electrochemical research, has developed the mechanistic view of living organisms, discarding the vitalists' belief in a mysterious "life force," vitalism continued to be a powerful

106. *Arp:* Growth, *1938. Marble, 39½" x 9⅞" x 12⅝". The Solomon R. Guggenheim Museum, New York. (Photo, The Solomon R. Guggenheim Museum)*

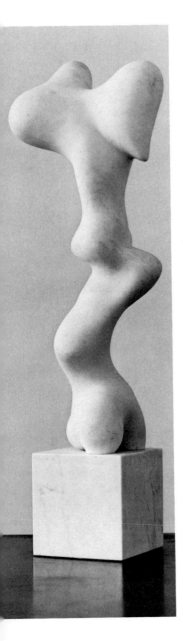

metaphor to describe the act of creation as the moment in which inert matter is suddenly impregnated with the animate properties of living form. At the beginning of the century, Henri Bergson had explored the meaning of the vitalist message for university audiences in Paris. And the essay "Creative Evolution" (1907) is an extended argument for the assumptions contained in the phrase *élan vital*.[22]

As Arp's work developed throughout the 1930s it continued to build on the ideas of growth and transformation as a double metaphor (fig. 106). The gentle bulges and twists in the smooth surfaces of the objects suggest that inorganic substance, such as marble or bronze, is possessed from within by an animate force; and at the same time, this soft pulse seems to beat inside a container that is itself in flux—changing from vegetable to animal life, or from bony matter to organic tissue. It suggests a certain kind of instability or flexibility of surface, a conformation of the exterior membrane of the sculptural volume that is disconnected from the notion of a rigid core. Projecting a sense of fluid pressure from within the volumetric container, Arp's stressed surfaces become images of variability and change.

When the English sculptor Barbara Hepworth visited Paris in 1932 she was struck by Arp's work. "The idea— the imaginative concept—actually is the giving of life and vitality to material," she wrote. "When we say that a great sculpture has vision, power, vitality, scale, poise, form or beauty, we are not speaking of physical attributes. Vitality is not a physical, organic attribute of sculpture— it is a spiritual inner life."[23]

During the later 1930s and the 1940s, both Hepworth and Henry Moore formed the English wing of vitalist sculpture. Yet, unlike Arp, their work seems to push the organic metaphor toward some kind of understanding with the constructivist aesthetic. For instead of composing an absolutely fluid surface, Moore and Hepworth carved volumes with far more structured and faceted surfaces, so that each section of the external form could be read as explicitly related to a rigid central core. Also, both sculptors were concerned with endowing their works with actual transparency, using planes built from scrims of

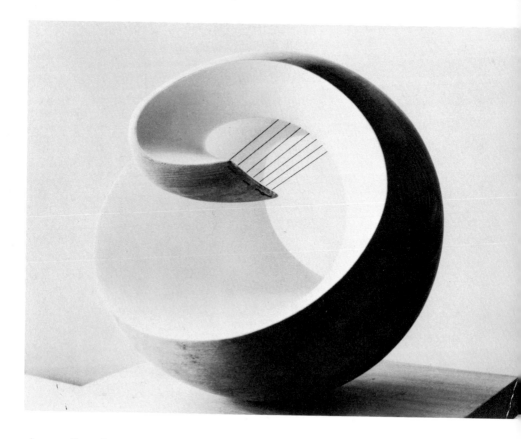

wire to allow the viewer access to the internal structure
of the object, forcing a sense that external surface and
internal skeleton were correlatives of one another. There
is, then, a rationalizing of the metaphor of growth into a
kind of constructivist, structural analysis of images of
living matter.

Arp had begun with free-standing sculpture that was
sympathetic to the surrealist attempt to place the object
within the flow of real time. He had moved from there
to creating an image that would project an illusion of
temporality through the concept of organic change. In
the hands of Moore and Hepworth, this notion of time
underwent yet a further modification when they returned
it once more to the classical mode of temporality. Again
the point of the sculpture seemed to be focused on the
development of volume, addressed to a rationalized three-
dimensionality, every facet of which was seen as a
variation on an internally held structural premise, with

all facets resolving into a single, synthetic conception from any one fixed vantage on the work.

Unlike Gabo and Pevsner, Moore worked with a carver's instincts rather than those of a constructor of volume from delicate geometric planes. The extremities of Moore's reclining figures (fig. 108) terminate explicitly within the limits of the original mass of material from which the figures were hewn. With outward edges of arms, legs, back, and head conforming to the primitive geometry of the initial block, and the midsection of the figure eroded away to a block-shaped void located at the interior of the figure on an axis perpendicular to the direction of its major mass, the work makes visible a contrapuntal relationship between the shape of the hollow core and the shape of the resultant figure. The sculptural forms appear to have developed from the geometric premise of the hollow core. The result is a sense of voluptuous reciprocity between the form of the container and that of the contained—the exterior mass cradling the void set at its center like a vital organ, and the shape of the void appearing as the key to the developed form of the whole (fig. 109).

107. *Barbara Hepworth (1903–75)*: Pelagos, 1946. *Wood with strings, 16″. The Tate Gallery, London.*

The two ideas that were generated by Moore's practice of sculpture seem at first to be antagonistic to the mechanistic ideology of constructivism. The first of these was a credo of "truth to material"—by which the organic form of the sculpted object and the organic development of the material from which it was carved would be shown to be interdependent. The veining of marble, the striation of limestone, or the grain of wood as it forms in nature, became the maps that Moore's carving instruments followed as he worked directly on the solid block, probing toward its center. Because of this kind of alert responsiveness, the figurative result was "true" to its material basis. "Every material," Moore declared, "has its own individual qualities. It is only when the sculptor works direct, when there is an active relationship with his material, that the material can take its part in the shaping of an idea."[24] But the fact remains that the "idea," no matter what material embodies it, whether the curvilinear geometry of the wood's annual rings or the rigid corrugations of the rock's stratification, was an analytic idea at heart. It was a similar kind of conceptual transparency that had guided the composition of Boccioni's *Bottle* (fig. 36) and Gabo's *Column* (fig. 46), only now this transparency demonstrates that the solid matter of nature is itself formed by the same geometric principles which a rational intelligence brings to its perception. At one stroke, the figure *and* the material can be brought within the same conceptual grasp.

The second notion provoked by Moore's work speaks to this possibility of rationalized volume being a mode of "grasping" the sculptural idea. This is a notion that returns to the ideal tactility which Hildebrand had described as "a unitary, all-inclusive judgment of depth," situating the viewer in relationship to the work so that he could "grasp it . . . in its entirety." Moore's concept of sculpture is directed at the viewer's sense of touch as the instinctual and sensuous extension of his capacity to conceptualize. As Sir Herbert Read expressed it, "Sculpture is an art of *palpation*—an art that gives satisfaction in the touching and handling of objects." For Read, Moore is the supreme sculptor who "gets the solid shape

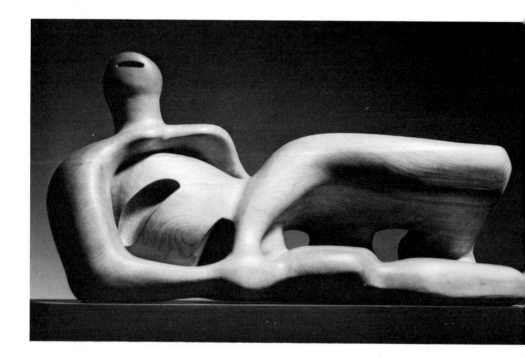

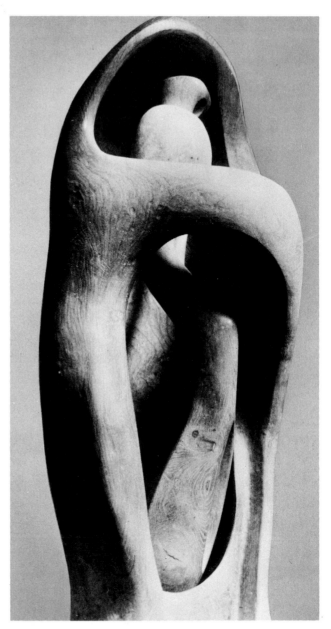

108. LEFT *Henry Moore (1898–ᅠᅠᅠ): Reclining Figure, 1945–46. Elm wood, 75" long. Private collection. (Photo, courtesy Henry Moore)*

109. RIGHT *Moore:* Internal and External Forms *(detail), 1953–54. Elm wood, 103" x 36". Albright-Knox Art Gallery, Buffalo, New York.*

as it were inside his head; he thinks of it, whatever its size, as if he were holding it completely enclosed in the hollow of his hand. He mentally visualizes a complex form *from all round itself*; he identifies himself with its center of gravity, its mass, its weight; he realizes its volume as the space that the shape displaces in the air."[25] Just as "truth to material" is about the revelation of geometry in the formation of matter, Read's ideas about "the sensation of volume" are similarly an extension of the satisfactions of a constructivist conceptual possession into an imagined tactile possession. There is nothing in Read's statement about shape that could not be applied with equal accuracy to the *Development of a Bottle in Space.*

The major difference between Moore's reclining figures and Giacometti's *Suspended Ball* comes down to a difference in the kind of time each one occupies, and the relationship each one bears to the space around it. Moore's figures exist in the pregnant moment of rational sequential, causal time. Further, they are shaped as if they came to being at intersecting points in a continuous axial grid. In this sense they seem to be orchestrations of geometrically conceived space, whereas the surrealist work is about another order of perception. It is a foreign body intruding itself into the fabric of real space—making a weird island of experience which disrupts a rational sense of causality—a peculiar pocket of subjectivity, about which the apparition of the naked somnambulist in the movie theater informed Breton. And its time, unlike the time of rational inference from a given cause, is the slow unfolding of unprogrammed experience. So it is the projection of lived time outward—the imposition of that time on the material context of the world.

Tanktotem: 5
welded images

In 1950 David Smith constructed *Tanktotem I* (fig. 110).
As it knifes across one's line of sight, the sculpture's
bladelike assemblage displays an almost aggressive flatness—an insistent planar quality which struck its first
viewers with an immediate sense of strangeness. Against
the background of an obsessive concern with volume
(whether real or virtual) which forms the twentieth-
century sculptural tradition, *Tanktotem I* appears with
the insubstantiality of a paper cutout (fig. 110).

Suspending two disklike elements on a tall, vertical stem,
Tanktotem I earns its title by conjuring up the image of
the human figure. The lower disk, fashioned from a tank
top or boiler head, serves as the bottom part of the
figure's torso, while the upper disk caps the sculpture with
a flange-like representation of the totemic head. Yet, in

the very way that the image is brought into existence, one feels confronted not so much by a surrogate for figural presence as by an abstract sign for it. This emblematic quality arises less from the economy of form with which the figure is stated—or from the way the steel rods that form the stem establish themselves as linear, or drawn —than from an extreme two-dimensionality that gives to the work an insistent aspect of something like a signpost randomly set up within one's space. *Tanktotem I* was the first of a long series to which Smith gave the designation "totem." As is true of every object in the series, the work locates itself at a strange border halfway between the human figure and the abstract sign.

In these two respects—the interest in the totem and the treatment of matter to create an emblem or sign—Smith's work is intimately tied into the concerns of the generation of American artists of which he was a part—the abstract-expressionists. At some time in their careers, generally early on, most of Smith's contemporaries, sculptors and painters alike, made objects which they either labeled "totem" or gave titles that indirectly indicated a concern with totem practice. One thinks of the sculptors Louise Nevelson (fig. 111), David Hare (fig. 112), Seymour Lipton (fig. 113), Isamu Noguchi (fig. 114), and Louise Bourgeois (fig. 115) in this connection and of the painters Jackson Pollock (fig. 116), Adolph Gottlieb (fig. 117), Mark Rothko, Clyfford Still, and Barnett Newman. Especially among the painters one finds an abiding concern with the emblem; for Rothko and Gottlieb, the emblem as such became a basis for their mature painting —in that they composed their works by suspending a simple, frontalized shape in a neutral, undifferentiated space. Like other more familiar emblems—the red cross, for example, or hazard indicators along a highway—the emblem in their work makes no direct formal contact with the edges of the field on which it occurs. Furthermore, the emblem is understood as resting on the surface of that field, and unlike representational images, which may depict real objects at a scale that is larger or smaller than the one they actually have, the emblem stubbornly exists at the scale in which it literally manifests itself and in the material of which it is made.

110. NEAR RIGHT *David Smith (1906–65):* Tanktotem I, *1952. Steel, 90" x 39". Art Institute of Chicago.*

111. FAR RIGHT *Louise Nevelson (1900–   ):* Two Hanging Columns (from "Dawn's Wedding Feast"), *1959. Wood, painted white, 72" x 6⅝" and 72" x 10⅛". Collection, The Museum of Modern Art, New York. Blanchette Rockefeller Fund.*

148

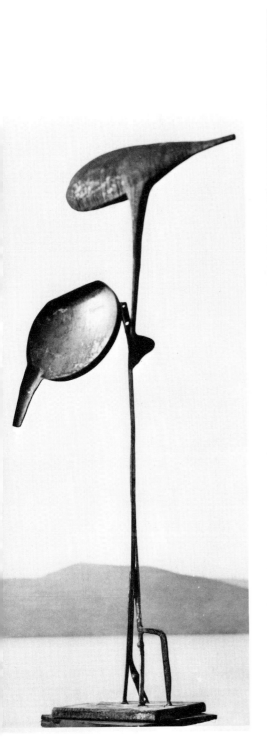

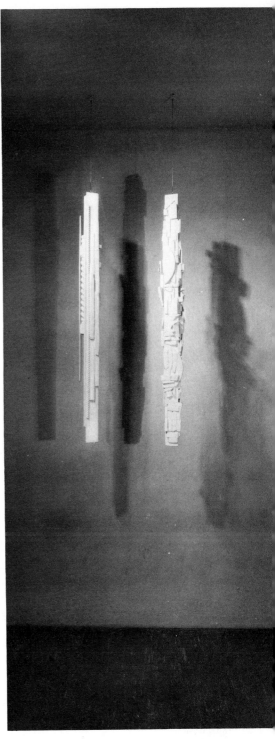

149

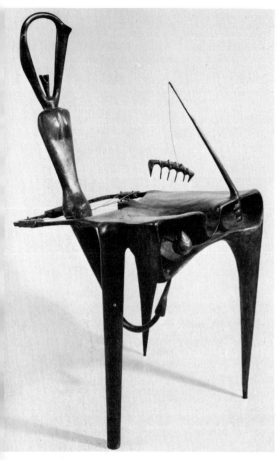

112. ABOVE LEFT *David Hare*
(1917–   ): Magician's Game,
1944. Bronze, 40¼" x 18½" x
25¼". Collection, The Museum
of Modern Art, New York.
Gift of the artist. (Photo,
Geoffrey Clements)

113. ABOVE *Seymour Lipton*
(1903–   ): Imprisoned Figure,
1948. Wood and sheet lead,
85" x 27" x 22". Collection,
The Museum of Modern Art,
New York. Gift of the artist.
(Photo, Geoffrey Clements)

All these qualities—frontality, centralization, and literal size and surface—characterize the developed work of most of the abstract-expressionist painters; even those who, like Pollock and Newman, eventually dropped some of these emblematic features continued to work with the most central aspect of the sign or emblem. And that is its mode of address. For while we can think of a traditional picture or a photograph as creating a relationship between author and object that exists independent of an audience, addressing no one in particular, we must think

114. NEAR RIGHT *Isamu*
Noguchi (1904–   ):
Monument to Heros, 1943.
Paper, wood, bones, string, 30".
Collection of the artist. (Photo,
Rudolph Burckhardt)

115. FAR RIGHT *Louise*
Bourgeois (1911–   ):
Sleeping Figure, 1950. Balsa
wood, 74½". Collection, The
Museum of Modern Art, New
York. Katharine Cornell Fund.

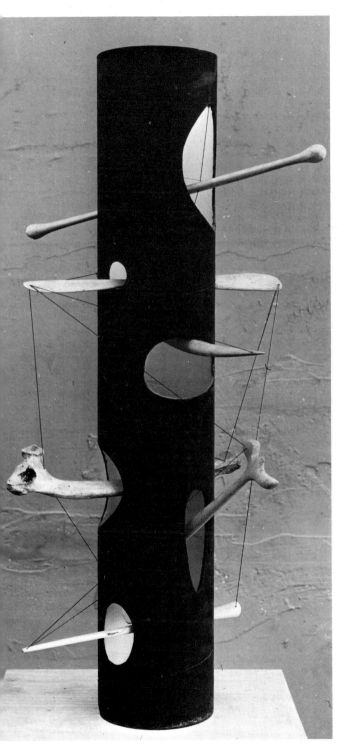

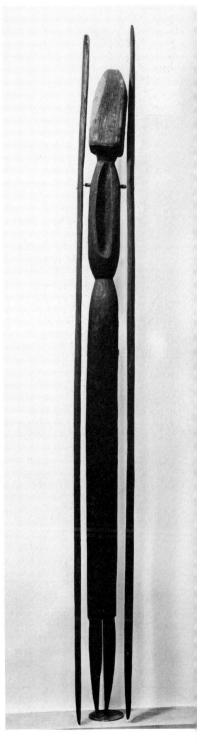

151

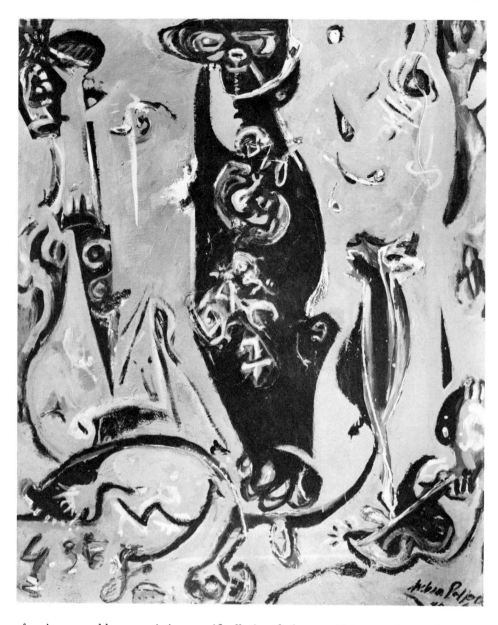

of a sign or emblem as existing specifically in relation to a receiver. It takes the form of a directive addressed *to* someone, a directive that exists, so to speak, in the space of confrontation between the sign or emblem and the one who views it.

David Smith's exposure to surrealism in the 1930s and 1940s called his attention both to a sculpture concerned

116. ABOVE *Jackson Pollock (1912–56):* The Totem: Lesson II. *Oil on canvas, 70⅛" x 62". (Photo, Otto E. Nelson)*

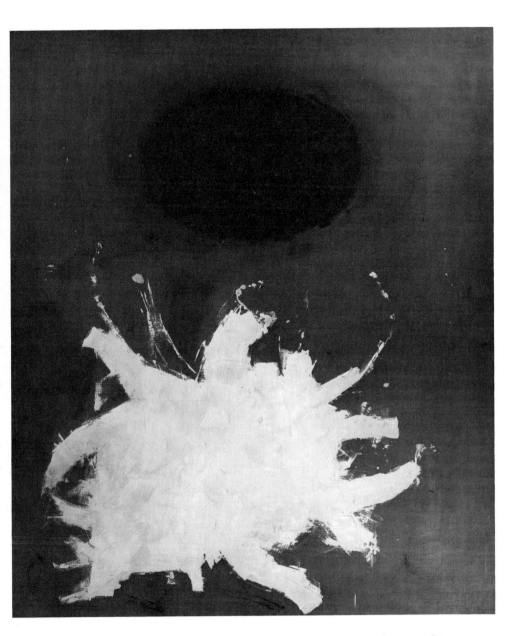

117. ABOVE *Adolph Gottlieb (1903–74): The Crest, 1959. Oil on canvas, 108¼" x 99¼". Collection of The Whitney Museum of American Art, New York. Gift of the Chase Manhattan Bank. (Photo, Geoffrey Clements)*

with a strategy of confrontation and to a subject matter involving such magical objects as fetishes and totems. Confrontation is a major resource for Giacometti's *Woman with Her Throat Cut* (fig. 87); fetishism is omnipresent in the work of Bellmer or Dali. But like his painter contemporaries, Smith entirely reworked these sources. Out of them he fashioned a sculptural statement that became a *formal* counterpart to what Smith saw as the essence of totemism itself. Thus the form of his work and the notion of the totem became two interlocking and reciprocal metaphors which pointed to the same thing: a statement about how the work could not be possessed.[1] To see how this operated one must turn first to what Smith understood as the structure of totemism, and then to the kind of formal expression with which it unfolded in his work.

In the sketchbooks from the 1940s, into which Smith entered notations for sculpture and cryptic expressions of the ideas which interested him, one finds drawings of objects labeled "totem" and references to psychoanalytic texts. Given Smith's interest in the work of Freud, it is probable that his view of totemism was drawn primarily from *Totem and Taboo*, a text that insistently tied primitive practices into the modern structure of relationships as they were described by psychoanalysis. For Smith, then, the totem was not an archaic object. Rather, it was a powerfully abbreviated expression of a complex of feelings and desires which he felt to be operative in himself and within society as a whole.

Briefly, Freud described the way totemism operated within primitive cultures as a system to outlaw incest, by insuring that members of a given tribe or clan would not marry or cohabitate with each other, but would be forced to seek partners outside their own tribal families. Each tribe would identify itself with a particular totem object—usually an animal—and each tribe member would take on the name of that object so that man and totem were one. Once that identification was made, the laws that applied to the totem animal logically applied to the human bearer of its name. And these laws, the taboos, were mostly prohibitory, protecting the totem and making it inviolate. The totem was not only established as a sacred or venerated object; it was also set apart from all other objects that could be physically appropriated. Usually the chosen animal could not be killed or eaten, or even touched. For some tribes, the taboo extended as far as prohibiting a tribesman's approaching or even looking at the totem. Since the tribesmen and women carried the name of the totem as well, the laws of taboo,

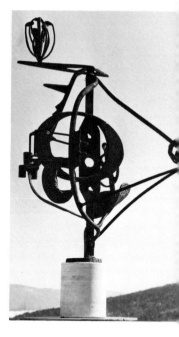

118a and **118b.** *Smith: Blackburn: Song of an Irish Blacksmith (two views), 1949–50. Steel and bronze, 46¼" x 49¾" x 24". Wilhelm Lehmbruck Museum, Duisburg.*

by extension, applied to themselves, making incestuous union a direct violation of the tribal law. Freud saw in totemism the manifestation of a particular desire coupled with a system of preventing its consummation.

In Smith's eyes, this structuring of the relationship between two members of a set so that the appropriation or violation of the one by the other is outlawed became important during the 1940s for both personal and political reasons. World War II was raging, and Smith identified its carnage in the sexual and cannibalistic terms that made totemism suddenly relevant. What then began to take place within Smith's art was the formulation of a sculptural strategy to translate the taboos of totemism into a language of form. And the goal of this formal endeavor seems to have been to contravert the by-then established transactions between viewer and sculptural object, which, as we have seen, had developed into a system of either

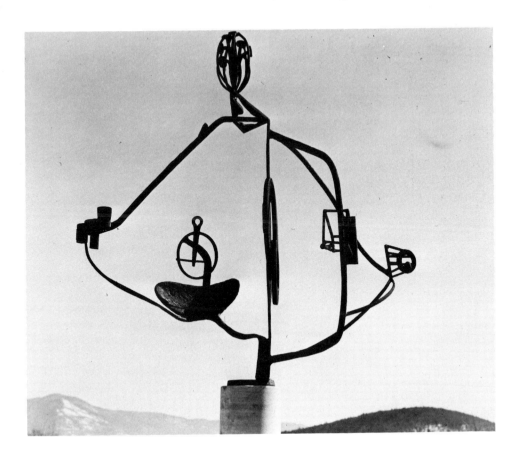

intellectual appropriation as in constructivism or sensuous possession as in the work of Henry Moore.

By 1949–50 Smith had consolidated this formal language. In a work called *Blackburn: Song of an Irish Blacksmith*, he describes the human figure in a sculptural

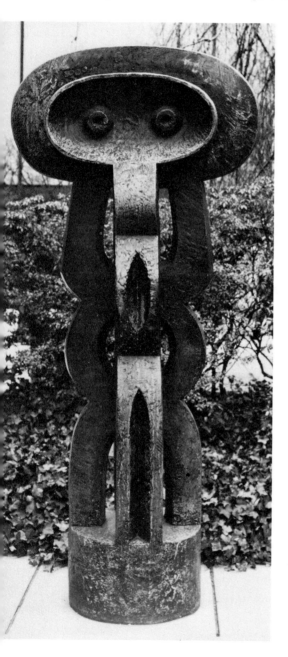
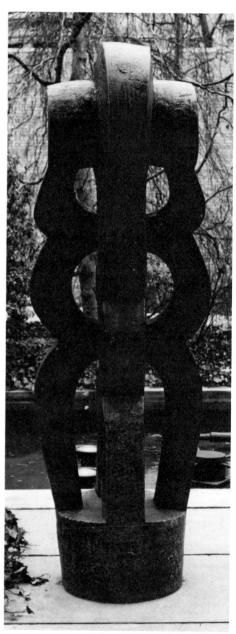

syntax that one might call a grammar of extreme visual disjunction. This disjunction depends on the fact that the two major views of the work—full-front (fig. 118a) and profile (fig. 118b)—cannot be related to each other through the constructivist mode of internal transparency that had become the major resource for abstract sculptural composition over the preceding four decades.

The kind of transparency that *Blackburn* avoids is to be found, for instance, in a 1926 *Figure* (figs. 119a and 119b), by Jacques Lipchitz. In it the principle of construction is to intersect two nearly identical silhouettes at right angles, so that a similar set of forms occurs in all views of the work. These profiles, which look like the linked circles of a chain, read as the external manifestation of an internal string of spherical hollows. Thus, just as all views of a sphere are the same, since all views are generated by the repetition of a single geometrical form, the visible interior voids of Lipchitz's *Totem* seem to open out equally onto all faces of the work. Visually, the work is an interlock system in which the profile views can be read off the front view and the front can be fully determined by simply inspecting the work from the side. In this sense his *Figure* meets the demand for conceptual understanding and organization that we have already seen operating in futurist and constructivist sculpture.

In comparison to this, *Blackburn* projects its front image of the human torso as a kind of open frame, in which all sculptural detail appears to be pushed to the peripheries of the work, leaving its interior an open void through which the eye easily passes to the space beyond. From this view the work reads as a hieratic image of the human figure, frontalized, nearly symmetrical, noncorporeal—the body reduced to a silhouette of bent steel rod. The open space, or absence of its interior, contrasts with the mechanistic steel elements (cotter pins, hinge sections) that meet at points along its exterior rim. Unlike the frontality of Gabo's *Head* (fig. 44), Boccioni's *Bottle* (fig. 36), or Lipchitz's *Figure*, the full-face view of *Blackburn* is completely unrevealing. It does not prepare the viewer to experience the object's other perspectives, its other sides. Prediction about those other views simply cannot occur in *Blackburn*. The sculptor seems to have

119a and **119b.** *Lipchitz: Figure (two views), 1926–30. Bronze, 85½". Collection, The Museum of Modern Art, New York.*

turned his back on the obsessive concern with information we have seen in other constructed sculpture.

If the side view of *Blackburn* cannot be calculated from the front, this is because the side view contains a whole complex of expression which the front face of the work has both negated and disdained. From the side, the interior of the torso is noisy with figurative incident; it is filled with a clutter of metal shape, like a shelf in a machine shop heaped with old tools and new parts. Densely packed with a jagged overlay of forms, the side view gives the effect of agitated confusion, whereas from the front the torso had appeared serene and uncluttered. The relationship of head to body is different on each side as well. Instead of the frontal declaration of symmetry, there is on the side an eccentric displacement of the head that underscores the rich tension generated by the profile of the work. Confronted by the profile of *Blackburn* one feels that one is not so much seeing another *view* of the work, as that one is almost seeing another work.

If Smith has accepted the totemic statement of the human presence as the subject of *Blackburn*, he has also rejected that definition of presence which underlies not only Lipchitz's *Figure* but also the whole of constructivist sculpture: in those works presence rested upon the establishment of a thematic center or core which guarantees to all the facets of the work the appearance of logical derivations. Moving around those works is to experience a continuity through time and is something like hearing the development of a musical theme. In *Blackburn*, Smith rejects that quality of formal continuity, substituting for it a sensation of schismatic break between one facet and the next, depending on the principle of radical *discontinuity*.

It is by insisting upon this discontinuity that Smith captures and incorporates into *Blackburn* the fundamental law of totemism, rather than merely resuscitating the surface primitivism of its original forms. Totemism worked to establish laws of distance between the object and its viewer, to create taboos against the possible appropriation of both totem and its human counterpart, to maintain the tabooed object as something apart. By

120. *Ibram Lassaw (1913–): Star Cradle, 1949. Plastic and steel, 12" x 10" x 14". Collection of the artist.*

refusing to endow the work with the inevitability of formal relationships we saw in constructivism—by which sculpture was delivered over to the spectator's intellectual grasp—Smith announces his own aesthetic separateness. In this sense his work is removed from that parental umbrella of constructivism, under which many of his fellow sculptors worked; for his American contemporaries, such as Seymour Lipton and Ibram Lassaw, continued the procedures of the virtual volume and Gabo's stereo-metric construction. Lassaw's *Star Cradle* (fig. 120), made in 1949, the same year as *Blackburn*, is separated from Smith's arbitrariness and premeditated incoherence by its own strict concern for unity. In *Star Cradle*, the

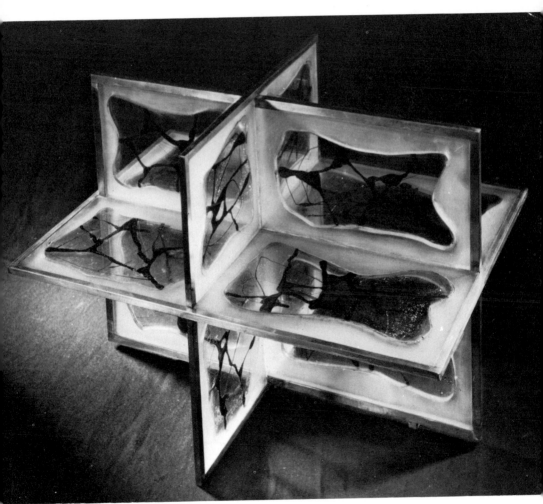

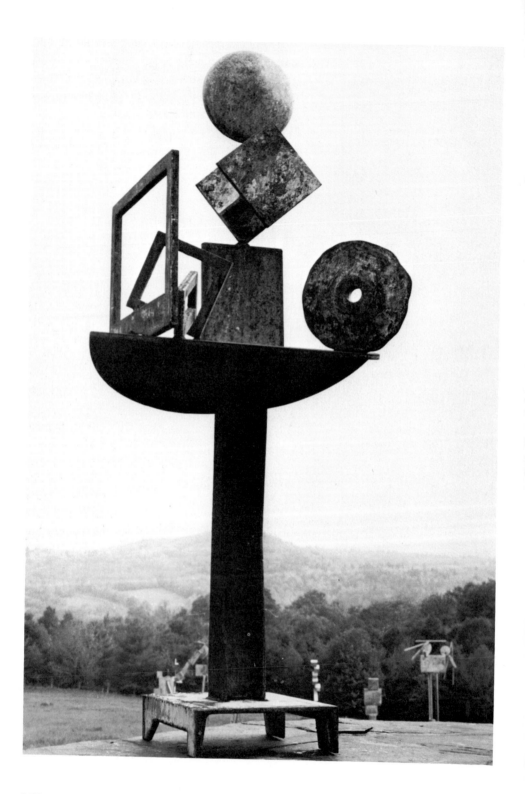

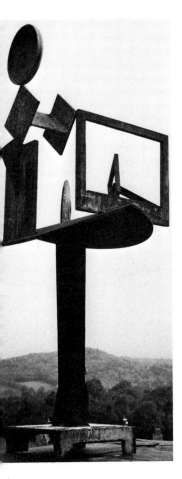

121a and **121b.** *Smith: V-B XXIII (two views), 1963. Steel, 69¼" x 74" x 25½". Collection, Miss Sarah Greenberg, New York.*

principle of intersection operates as the core for the planes that radiate from it. Looking at *Star Cradle* from its "front," we are aware that if the work were to rotate on either its X- or its Y-axis, it would continue to display the same information about this structure. Its obedient stereometry makes it the legitimate child of Gabo's diagram of 1937 (fig. 42). By contrast, Smith's lack of obedience was expressed not only formally, through his rejection of the principles of geometric organization, but thematically as well. For, by using the theme of totemism, Smith puts distance between himself and the kind of technological content that characterized orthodox constructivism.

From the time of *Blackburn* to the last years of Smith's career, the same formal and thematic concerns continued to shape his work. *V-B XXIII* (1963), for example, has that same avoidance of a predictable relationship between front (fig. 121a) and profile view (fig. 121b). From the front it assumes a quality of hieratic verticality and flatness similar to *Blackburn*, while from the side it opens out into eccentric relationships of precarious balance where its parts fail to cohere in terms of a fixed center.

Thematically, *V-B XXIII* also carries forward Smith's concerns with totemism and the protection of the object from violation or appropriation. For the image in *V-B XXIII* has as long and enduring a history within Smith's work as the totem figure. It is an image of the human form—or at least a fragment of it—set on a kind of altar table, its effect having both the neutrality of a still-life assemblage and the aura of mutilation attached to a sacrificial object. From the front, the vertical stacking of a rectangular plate, the diamond-shaped face of an I-beam section, and the circular disk of a boiler head suggest the torso of a figure, which is placed on a table-like pedestal.

This image of torso-as-still-life not only relates to other works of the 1960s, such as *Cubi XIX*, but also reaches back to the early 1940s in several of the versions of *Head as Still Life* (fig. 122) and the explicit *Table Torso* (fig. 123) of 1942.[2] As a metaphor, the image of the sacrificial object operates like the totem image in that its content concerns primitive rituals which express physical violation. As in the case of the totem image, Smith uses the image of sacrificial victim both to acknowledge unconscious desires for physical possession and to construct a formal prohibition against the possibilities of that action. And, like the totem, this sacrificial image *minus* the strategy of formal prohibition was fully part of Smith's artistic heritage, having emerged as a major theme of

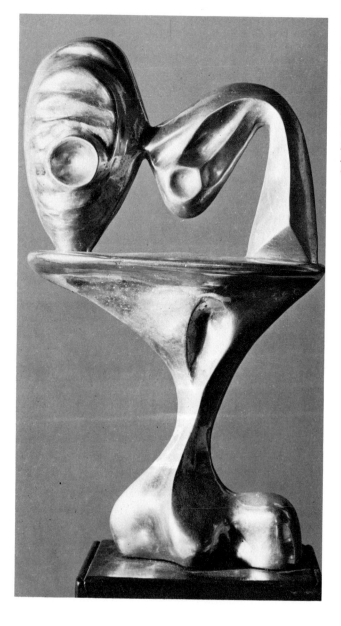

122. LEFT *Smith:* Head as a Still Life II, *1942. Cast aluminum, 14" x 8½" x 4". Estate of the artist.*

123. RIGHT *Smith:* Table Torso, *1942. Bronze, 10" x 4¼" x 5⅝". Rose Art Museum, Brandeis University Art Collection, Waltham, Mass. Gift of Mr. and Mrs. Stephen Stone, in memory of Charna Stone Cowan. (Photo: Mike O'Neil)*

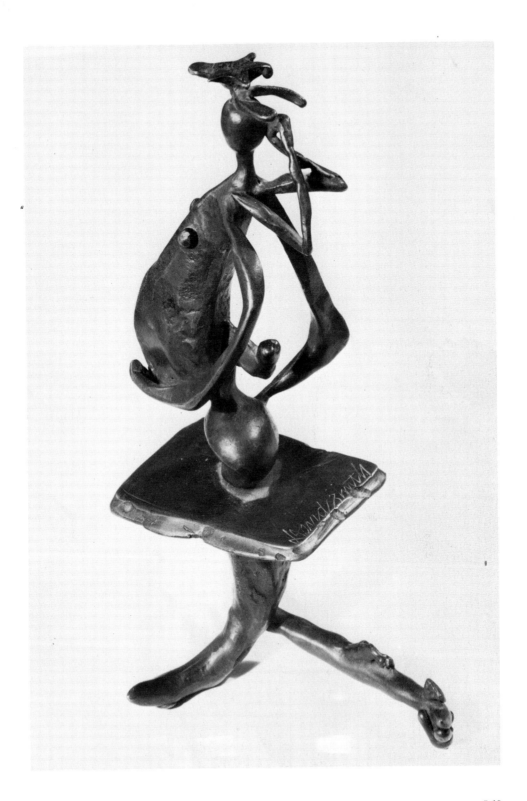

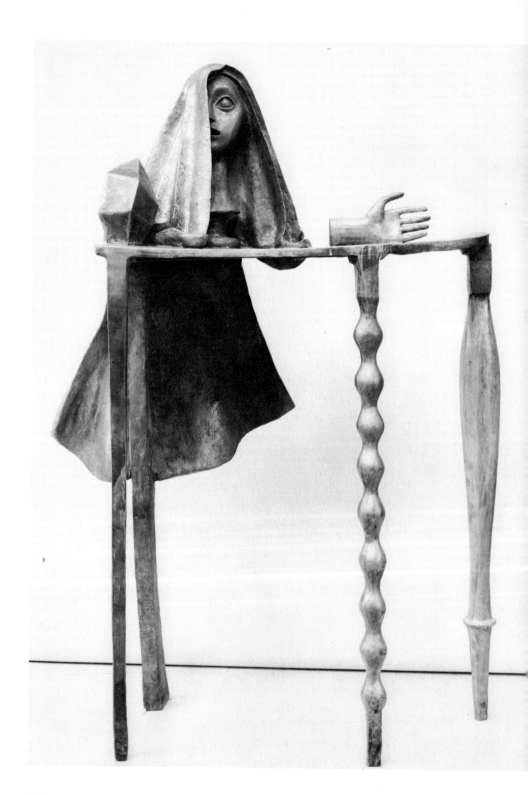

surrealist sculpture. But there, as in Giacometti's 1932 *Table* (fig. 124) or his 1930–31 *Suspended Ball* (fig. 81), the human object/table assembly was used as a goad to, rather than an embargo on, possession. As we saw earlier, Giacometti's work is couched within the very terms of sexual possession—as a narrative prolongation of those fantasies of desire—that *V-B XXIII* is determined to reject.

The sign, perhaps even the success, of Smith's creation of a formal language that would act to thwart the surrealist impulses toward possession, was that Smith's mature work was for so long understood as purely abstract sculpture. Throughout the 1950s and 1960s his major pieces appeared, to others, to be nonrepresentational,[3] which seems to have been caused by a heightening of the principle of discontinuity. The discontinuity that exists between the separate views of *Blackburn* began to work within any given view, to disrupt the coherence between separate elements, to prevent the viewer from seeing them coalesce into a recognizable image. For a long time this is the way the *Cubis* were read—that last series in which Smith assembled monumental sculpture from building blocks which he fabricated of gleaming stainless steel. The broad, planar surfaces of these sculptures glinted with the meandering tracks of a carborundum wheel, and radiated a world of optical defraction, a sense of the image submerged and lost beneath a web of burnished line. Critics were tempted to draw an analogy between the surfaces of the *Cubis* and the imageless painting of Jackson Pollock. But *Cubi VI* (fig. 125) is not abstract. It clearly continues the theme of the upright totem figure, using the glitter of the burnished surface as one more resource to insure a sense of formal distance between viewer and object. Similarly, *Cubi XIX* (fig. 126) carries forward into the later work the image of the altar table/still life.

Despite the spareness and noncommittal geometry of their parts, these late sculptures *do* maintain Smith's earlier thematic allegiances. The work's formal impact continues to act within the arena of an imagery devoted to violent possession and its abjuration. In *Zig IV* (fig. 127), the repertory of curved sheet steel geometries

124. *Giacometti:* The Table, *1932. Plaster, 56¼". Musée National d'Art Moderne, Paris. (Photo, Musées Nationaux) (The bronze one is from the Giacometti Foundation, Kunsthaus, Zurich.)*

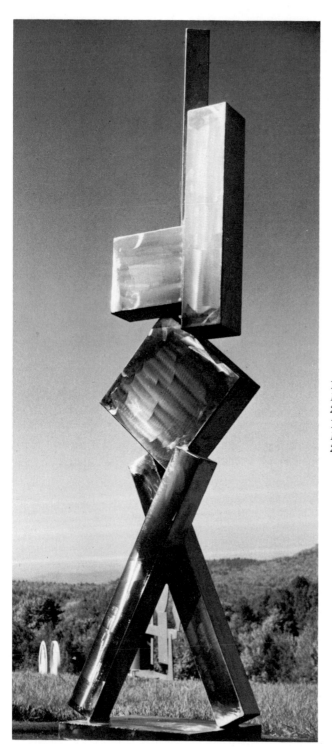

125. LEFT *Smith:* Cubi VI,
*1963. Stainless steel, 118⅛" x
29½". Estate of the artist.*
126. RIGHT *Smith:* Cubi XIX,
*1964. Stainless steel, 113⅛" x
21¾". Tate Gallery, London.*

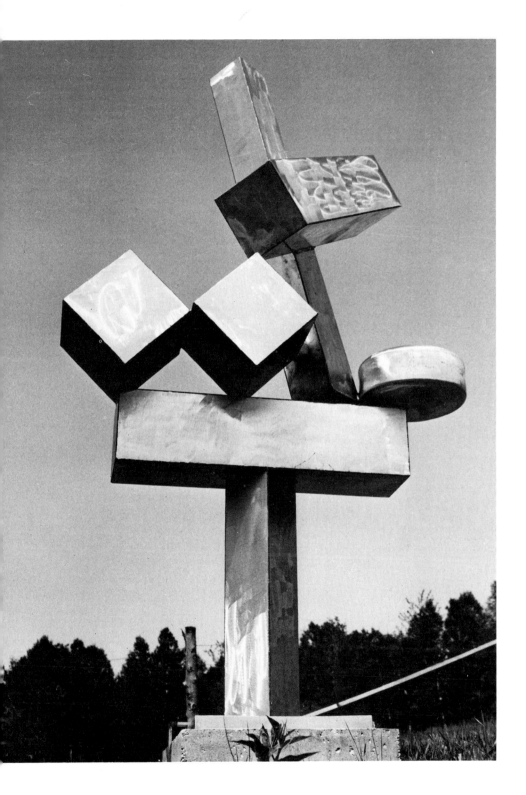

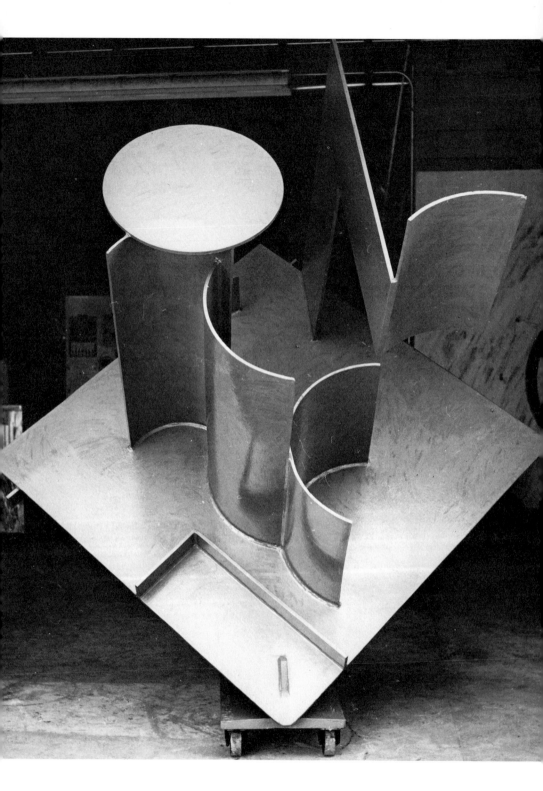

appears at first to resist any reading but that of pure abstraction; yet here as well one finds Smith turning to the limited group of images that had shaped his work since the early 1940s. But in this instance one confronts a work from which the human element has been banished; in its stead one finds a schematic reference to a cannon—an image that had long stood directly for Smith's personal and political relationship to violence.

In *Zig IV*, the curved steel parts, which form separate tubular sections, project from a diamond-shaped, angled platform, which is supported by a section of steel beam mounted on wheels. The artillery-like character of this assemblage, seen also in *Zigs VII* and *VIII* (1963), has its genesis in works from the 1940s which expressed quite directly Smith's horror of war. In sculptures such as *The Rape* (fig. 128), *War Landscape, Jurassic Bird*, and *Specter of War* (all 1945), Smith makes the cannon a symbol of military power and casts it into the role of mutilator.

In these strangely obsessive sculptures of the 1940s, Smith transforms the cannon from object into actor, a machine imbued with peculiarly animistic features. Always endowing it with wings, Smith often mounts the cannon's muzzle on wheels, but sometimes he gives it human legs and feet. In each case the muzzle is portrayed as phallic, so that the public violence of warfare is staged as the more private violation of rape. This winged, sexualized cannon first appeared in a series of fifteen medallions entitled *Medals for Dishonor* (1939–40) (fig. 129). The bronze-caster with whom Smith worked on this series had once given Smith a strange memento of their working relationship: a small replica in silver of a classical winged phallus, an object Smith had seen in Pompeii in the 1920s and one that continued to fascinate him. Smith took this form of antique origin and made it the basis for his cannons.

Because these early cannon sculptures are throwbacks to a naturalistic nineteenth-century tradition of modeled miniature statuary, they hold litle formal interest for us. Rather, their importance is thematic because they give us a glimpse into the sources of Smith's concern with the question of violence. The evidence in Smith's private

127. *Smith:* Zig IV, *1961. Steel, 95⅛" x 84¼" x 76". Lincoln Center for the Performing Arts, New York. (Photo, David Smith)*

notebooks and sketches (fig. 130) suggests that he identified strongly with this image of freewheeling and violent masculinity, that it objectified what terrified him most in his own world of fantasy, and in his relationships with other human beings. Thus, in this weirdly composite image, one finds both an accusing finger pointed outward toward society and an inwardly directed assumption of personal guilt. Which is to say that the cannon was made an actor on the stage of public violence at the same time that it was accepted by Smith as a personification of his own urges toward destructiveness. This destructiveness Smith read even into the seeming neutrality of his choice of medium: "Possibly steel is so beautiful," he wrote, "because of all the movement associated with it, its strength and functions. . . . Yet it is also brutal: the rapist, the murderer and death-dealing giants are also its offspring."[4]

Somehow one feels that it was this personal identification with brutality that gave Smith's mature work its deepest expressive power. His development of a formal language seems to be aimed at rejecting and defeating, on the most basic structural level, the politics of posses-

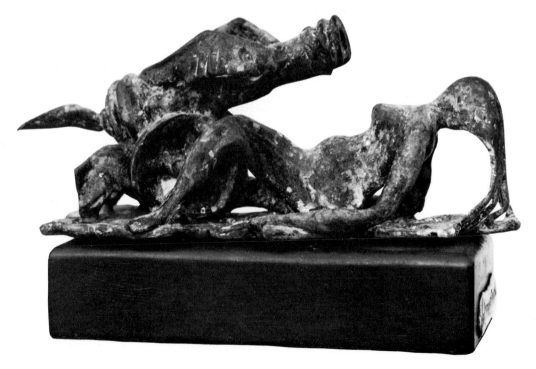

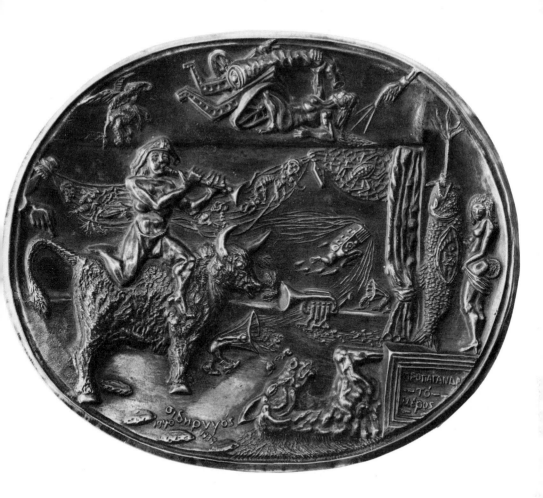

128. LEFT *Smith:* The Rape,
1945. Bronze, 9" x 5⅜" x 3½".
Collection, Mr. and Mrs.
Stephen Paine, Boston. (Photo,
David Smith)

129. ABOVE *Smith:* Propaganda
for War (Medals for
Dishonor Series), *1939–40.*
Bronze relief, 9½" x 11½".
The Museum of Modern Art,
New York. (Photo, Rudolph
Burckhardt)

sion that came out of his own private cycle of desire and
remorse. The formal and ethical commands his work tries
to encode are thus interrelated; their effectiveness *as
sculpture* depends on their simultaneous maturation (figs.
131a and 131b). By the beginning of the 1950s, the
comparative realism of these first works with the cannon/
phallus is absorbed into the characteristic assemblage of
machine parts that makes up the *Tanktotem* figures.

As I have said, it is the *relationship* between the dis-
junctive syntax of this assemblage and the thematic
material that constitutes Smith's originality—and sets
him apart from his American contemporaries. For it is
in this relationship that he is able to qualify the meaning
that such images as the totem or the sacrificial object
have within his work.

In the hands of Lipton, Ferber, and Hare, very similar
themes were elaborated into sculpture, but in a way that

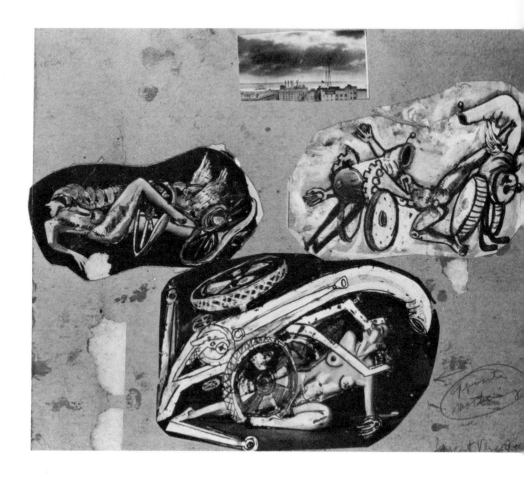

was still dependent on the aesthetic forces that shaped
their original surrealist formulation. Ferber's 1947 *Surrational Zeus II* (fig. 132) not only asks, by means of
its name, to be understood within the context of the
European movement but it has also absorbed the formal
language for entrapment and containment that characterizes Giacometti's sculpture of the 1930s. With its pro-
tracted central spine encircled by the open, podlike forms
of the outer flesh, the *Zeus* looks like a version of Giacometti's *Woman with Her Throat Cut* (fig. 87) lifted
off the floor to become vertical. Throughout the 1950s
Ferber worked with a sculptural format consisting of an
openwork container with the writhing bands of metal
that make up its interior explicitly set into tension against
the exterior shape of the volume that encloses them. As
the interior bands of metal become increasingly supple,
their texture softened with applied coats of softened nickel

and lead, they come to evoke ribbons of flesh. The encaged and struggling expressionism of *Calligraph in Cage with Cluster No. 2* (fig. 133), and similar works of the early 1960s, re-enacts the surrealist drama of possession. Ferber's content and the formal language used to express it are visible in the work of Hare and Lipton as well. Hare's *Lady-of-Waiting* (1944) conceives the human body in precisely those terms of ominous enclosure that one has seen in the object fetishes of Magritte, Dali, and Giacometti, and the same is true for Lipton's *The Cloak* (1952).

In *The Cloak* (fig. 134) the totem figure is built of a vertical assemblage of podlike forms, some of them partially split open to reveal an interior shaft at their center. The whole figure is itself sheathed by two half-cylinders, which seem to constrict or contain the figure and which call to mind the surrealist image of the cage. Yet in the work there is also a dialogue between what is contained and what is revealed, and in this sense *The Cloak* comes close to being an American reworking of the totemic 1925 *Figure* (figs. 119a and 119b) by Lipchitz; for it has an unselfconscious combination of both surrealist imagery and the constructivist insistence that the revealed core can be understood as having generated the external shape of the work.

This merging of constructivism and surrealism produced in the work of Lassaw and Lippold objects that draw an analogy between technology and magic. Geometries that radiate from a core or center are made out of wire—Lippold spinning in air a membranous, three-dimensional interlacing of shapes, and Lassaw contriving volumes out of intersecting grids thickened with brazed ligaments. The two men share a fascination with cosmos (Lippold's *Sun* and Lassaw's *Milky Way*), both as a transparent presence and as an unrationalizable mystery.

Smith had looked for sources of meaning in the formal condition of disjunction. For the American sculptors who followed him, in the early 1960s, the notion of disjunctiveness became a powerful generative tool. Like Smith, they tended to treat the sculpture as an irrational volume: a set of peripheral elements deprived of the

130. *Smith:* Uncatalogued Page in the Archive, *early 1940s. Archives of American Art, New York.*

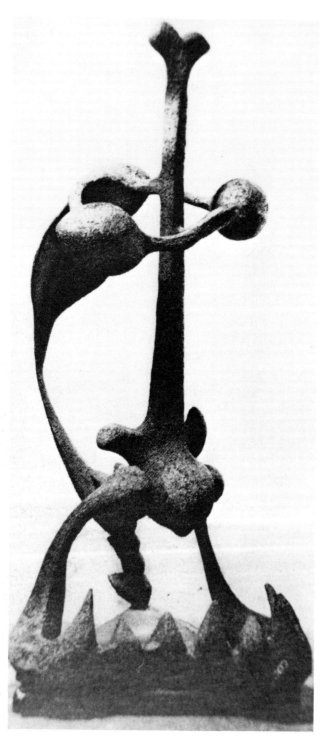

131a NEAR RIGHT and 131b
FAR RIGHT *Smith:* Voltri XVII
*(two views), 1962. Steel, 95" x
31⅜" x 29¾". Private
collection.*
132. LEFT *Herbert Ferber
(1906–): Surrational Zeus
II, 1947. Lead 48" x 30".
Collection of the artist.*

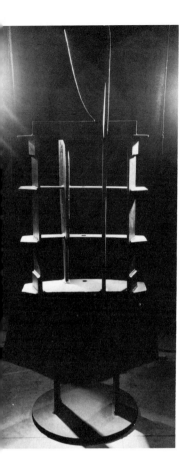

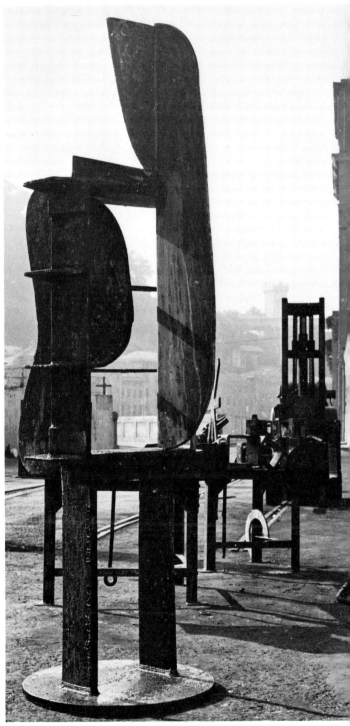

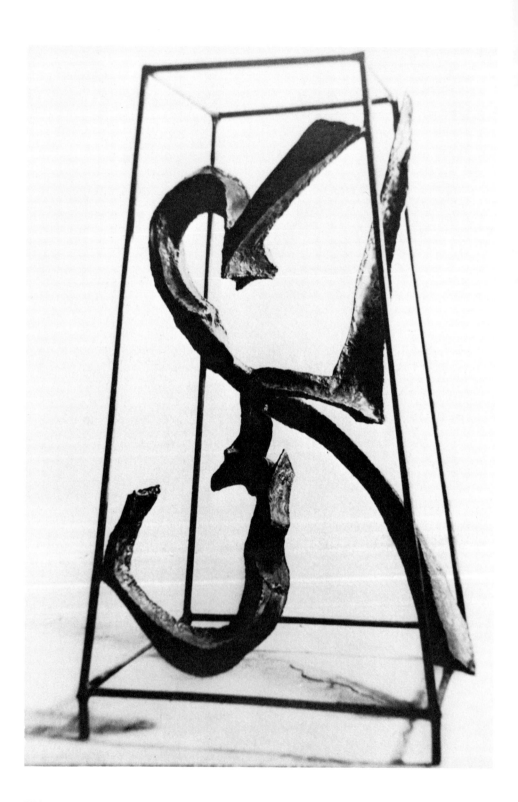

176

133. LEFT *Ferber:* Calligraph
in Cage with Cluster No. 2
(with Two Heads), *1962.
Copper and brass, ca. 46" x
32" x 36".*

134. RIGHT *Lipton:* The Cloak,
*1952. Bronze and steel, 96".
Collection, Nelson A.
Rockefeller, New York.
(Photo, Geoffrey Clements)*

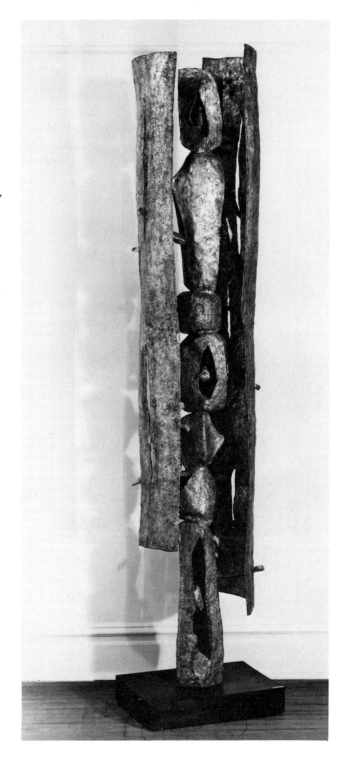

logic of a constructive core. Mark di Suvero's *Che Farò Senza Eurydice* (fig. 135) of 1959, for example, is an agglomeration of heavy timbers that lean outward along three diverging axes to loom high above the viewer's head. Had di Suvero stressed the geometrical under-pinnings of this structure—its form as an inverted pyramid—*Che Farò* would have taken on the quality of being the model of an idea about volume that conditions constructivist art. The particular size of the work and its specific materials would have been absorbed by the geometric rationale for which it would appear to be only one of many possible expressions. As it is, however, *Che Farò*'s center seems less a point of connection between its three arms than a visual barrier or disruption, so that each of the sections appears to be disengaged and falling away from the others. One is forced, therefore, to experience the actual weight and size of the timbers and the precariousness of their relationships.

Like di Suvero, David von Schlegell followed that direction within Smith's art that leads toward expressive gesture (fig. 136). But other sculptors responded more to the possibility—also prefigured in Smith—of a shifting and illusive relationship between the surface of a volume and its center. Beverly Pepper writes, for example, "The works I made of highly polished stainless steel in the later 1960s achieved this kind of dualism primarily through the mirror-like finish of their surfaces. Those surfaces acted to emphasize the actual density and weight of the steel, and at the same time they made the physical bulk of the sculpture withdraw behind a smoke-screen of reflections. Under certain light conditions and from certain angles this reflectivity picks up the sculpture's environment . . . and this causes the work almost to disappear; so that all that remains visible is the network of blue enamel line that indicates the interior faces of the forms. From other angles the surfaces reflect into one another, causing geometries to appear which are not part of the physical format of the work."[5] Thus the point of a sculpture like *Venezia Blu* (fig. 137), 1968, is not its selection of material from the vocabulary of an advanced metal technology but the formal language that vocabulary is made to serve.

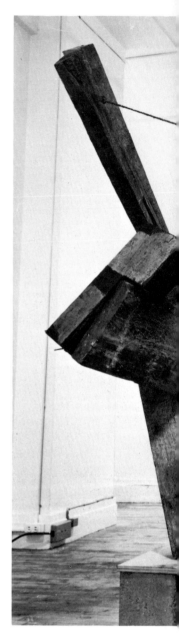

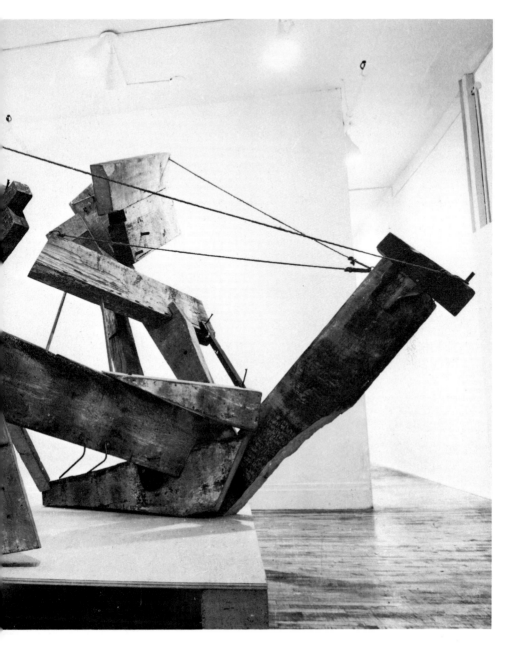

135. *Mark di Suvero (1933–
) :* Che Farò Senza
Eurydice, *1959. Wood and
iron, 84″ x 104″ x 91″. Scull
Collection, New York. (Photo,
Rudolph Burckhardt)*

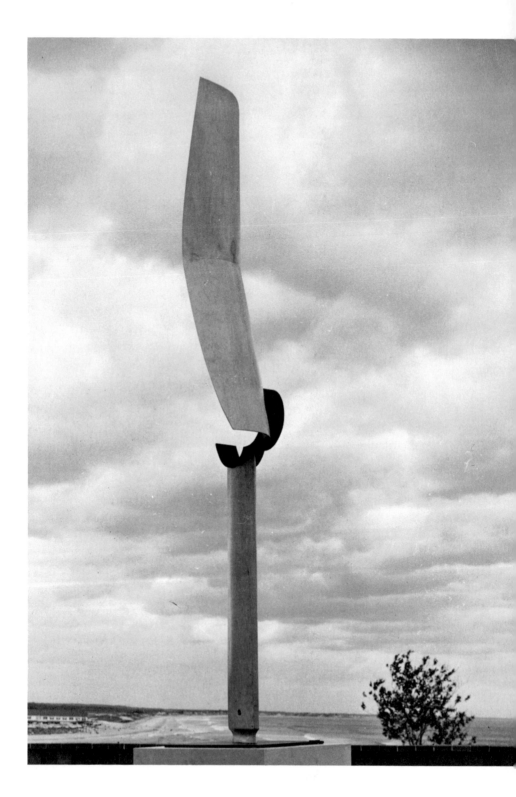

John Chamberlain's 1962 *Velvet White* (fig. 138) creates a sense of irrational volume not through the agency of disorienting reflection but by ballooning surfaces of crumpled steel into massive, three-dimensional shells. The obvious hollowness of the sculpture insures that one will not see its material surface as the outward manifestation of an internal armature or core. Donald Judd described this effect as "something about the volume exceeding the structure. . . . The structure sort of rattles around in this big space." Thus, like di Suvero's timbers, Chamberlain's ripped sheets of steel are not supplied with a constructive rationale. They are not provided with the aesthetic justification of an object made lucid through the visual procedures of analysis.

It is this evident disdain for the analytical that connects Chamberlain's sculpture with that of Smith's, but *Velvet White* has other qualities that separate the work of the two men. The sense one has of it as a massive and nearly unarticulated volume allies it with that sensibility that was becoming more and more apparent in the early 1960s, both in this country and in England. The early work of Philip King, for example, also possesses this quality of a wholistic, unitary volume which dispenses with an internal armature, forcing all attention on the elaboration of its surface (fig. 139). The kind of sculpture Chamberlain and King were creating had thus entered the aesthetic territory that later came to be known as minimal art. If Judd, a major practitioner of and spokesman for minimalism, was responsive to Chamberlain's work, this was because he saw in it the possibility for an entire realignment of sculptural practice. That reorganization was to have profound effects on the scale, placement, and materials of sculpture and on the procedures of its making as well. Most importantly, it was to change our notions of what a sculpture means. But before discussing the terms of this change, it is necessary to look at one more example of Smith's continuing influence during the 1960s.

In the late autumn of 1959 David Smith met a young British sculptor whose work seemed, on the surface, to exist in an aesthetic space far removed from Smith's own.

136. *David von Schlegell (1920–   ): Sentinel, 1963. Maple, oak, and steel, 72". Collection, Mrs. J. S. Smart, Ogunquit, Me.*

Anthony Caro had apprenticed as an assistant to Henry Moore and throughout the mid and late 1950s had worked within Moore's tradition of figurative bronze casting. Yet, despite Caro's technical distance from the structural idiom of Smith's welded-steel sculpture, with its piecemeal construction and its conjoining of disparate elements and shapes, Caro seemed to be prepared to grasp the fundamental property of Smith's work—its formal strategy of discontinuity. When Caro returned to England in the spring of 1960 he began to experiment with welding,

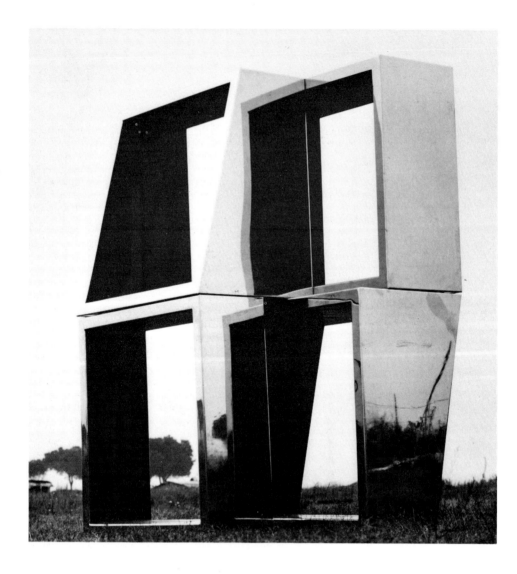

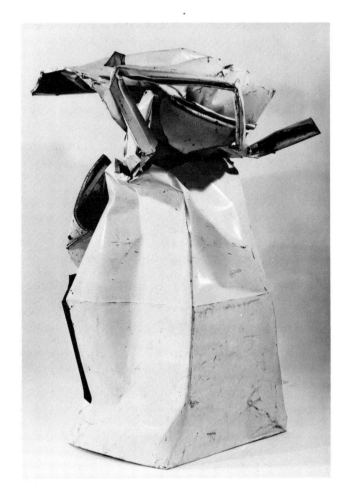

137. LEFT *Beverly Pepper
(1924–): Venezia Blu,
1968. Stainless steel, 100" x
55" x 90". Collection of the
artist.*

138. RIGHT *John Chamberlain
(1927): Velvet White,
1962. Welded automobile
metals, 81½" x 61" x 54½".
Collection of The Whitney
Museum of America Art, New
York. Gift of the Albert A.
List Family. (Photo, Geoffrey
Clements)*

trying to absorb the formal lesson Smith's work had
taught him.

His first constructed sculpture, though somewhat crude,
is surprisingly direct in capturing the formal essence of
Smith's art. Entitled *Twenty-four Hours*, it is an assemblage of simple geometric planes cut from sheet steel and
grouped to form an aggressively frontal, unitary image,
which gives the work the simultaneous character of
strong physical presence and of insubstantial sign. As in
Smith's work, the simplicity and seeming fixity of the
relationships between the elements of the sculpture when
seen from the front (fig. 140a) change when one views
it from the side (fig. 140b). The planes angle away from
each other, opening up the compact abstract image formed

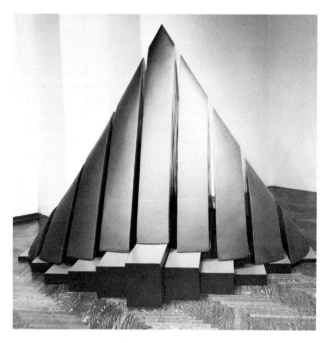

139. ABOVE *Philip King (1934–):* Through, *1966. Fiberglas, 84" x 108" x 132". Richard Feigen Gallery, New York. (Photo, Geoffrey Clements)*

140a and **140b.** *Anthony Caro (1924–):* Twenty-four Hours *(two views), 1960. Painted steel, 54½" x 88" x 35". André Emmerich Gallery, New York. (Photos, André Emmerich)*

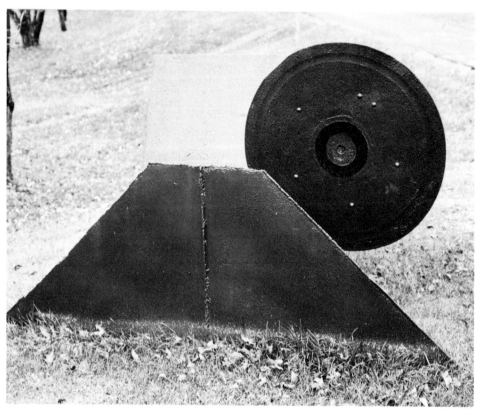

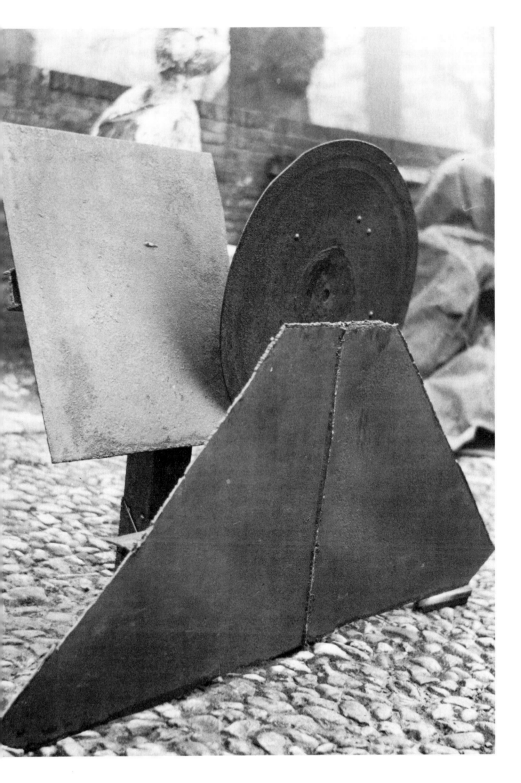

by the front view to include lateral slices of space.

The speed and decisiveness with which Caro grasped the formal meaning of Smith's sculpture seems to have depended on the younger man's own experience of discontinuity which he had been trying to express through more traditional plastic means. Critic Michael Fried has pointed out that Caro's early figures were bent on expressing an experience of the body in which a particular action forces the separate parts to be perceived unequally (fig. 141). "In *Man Taking Off His Shirt*, for example, the disproportion between the small head and the heavy arms seems to have been intended as an equivalent for the figure's concentration upon an action in which the arms do all the work and the head is mostly in the way."[6] This is to say that Caro rendered the human form not as it looked from the outside, with its proportions objectively fixed, but as it *felt* from the inside, with its relationships subjectively conditioned. This subjective sense could be likened to the experience one has with an injured limb which completely usurps one's attention, making the rest of the body seem to vanish in the enormity of the pain that blots out all other sensations.

In the sculptures that followed *Twenty-four Hours*, Caro began to discover areas where his sensibility diverged from Smith's. He began to sense, for example, that while Smith's art established or maintained an enforced distance between viewer and sculpture, a distance whose *point* depended on the felt relationship between the sculpture and the human form (the sculpture being experienced as something like a surrogate for the human body), his own feelings did not demand that same totemic presence. The discontinuity that Caro wished to project was more in relation to his own body—recapitulating the kind of subjective experience of inequality between parts of the body expressed in the earlier bronzes. That is, instead of acknowledging a distance between the self and others, the distance projected was between different aspects of the single self. The earlier bronzes had pointed to the way one's own body, engaged in its various actions or its separate feelings, creates an image that exists somehow apart from the solid physical fact of that body. "For example," Caro has explained, "when you're lying down, you feel heavy; your weight causes you to feel flattened and pressed down."[7] At an abstract level this becomes a question of expressing the lack of connection between the lived image and its factual or literal support, and it was on this abstract level that Caro began to proceed.

Early One Morning (fig. 142a) is a monumental sculpture (it extends front-to-back more than twenty feet) that Caro made in 1962. With three exceptions, every element in the work is experienced as physical structure. Its beams, poles, and channel-sections are placed at widely spaced intervals along a twenty-foot horizontal element, which they support much the way a table's legs support its top. This analogy with a table is further suggested by the

141. *Caro:* Man Taking Off His Shirt, *1955–56. Bronze, 31".* *Collection, Philip King, London.*

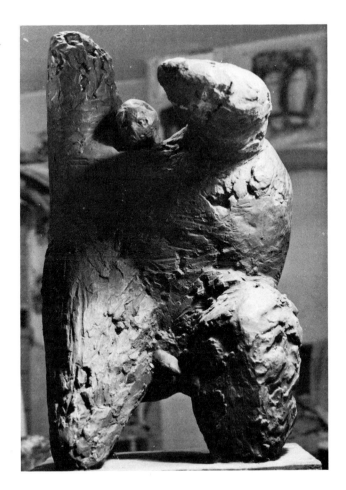

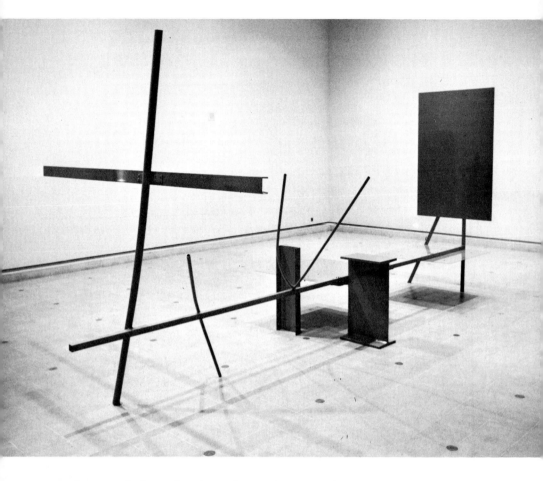

two large steel plates that form the work's major horizontal plane, also supported by the vertical posts and resting about twenty-four inches off the ground. The attachments among all of the work's steel members involve a system of bolts that adds to one's experience of the sculpture as a rational, physical object. Through this experience of structure, one has a firm sense of what it means for an object made of discrete parts to achieve verticality—to stand upright. Displayed before one is the kind of post-and-beam system that is common to most of our built environment.

But as I mentioned, there are three elements in *Early One Morning* that are superfluous to its structure as a physical object. One of these is a large vertical plate that rides the two "legs" at one end of the work like a fixed

142a and **142b.** *Caro:* Early One Morning *(two views)*, *1962. Painted aluminum and steel, 114" x 244" x 131". The Tate Gallery, London.*

sail. Another is a spar-like elevated beam that crosses the vertical support at the opposite end of the sculpture. And the third is a pair of thin, bent tubes that jut off the "table plane" at something like a forty-five-degree angle midway down the course of that plane. It is with these three nonstructural elements that Caro addresses the issue of verticality—but addresses it in a way that is very different from the reality of posts and beams.

The kind of verticality to which I am referring—one that is quite different from that achieved by systems of physical weight and support—is the verticality of painting. Because what one confronts in a painting is a system of graphic display by which *all* elements in real space, including horizontal ones, are made into shapes borne by the vertical surface of the canvas. In a picture, every

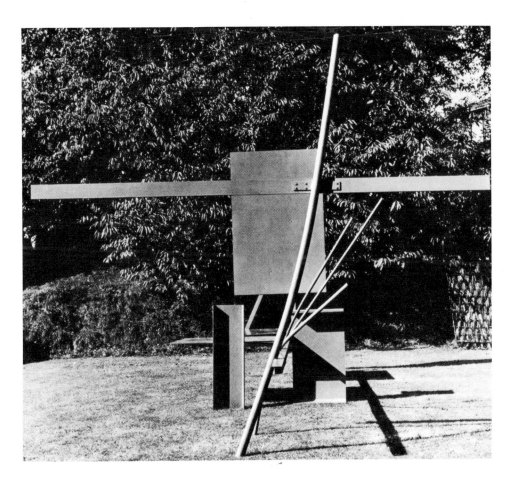

dimension of real space must be collapsed onto a flattened, vertically oriented plane; and in *Early One Morning* Caro constructs a model of this experience of a world compressed into the uprightness of painting. If the viewer stands at one end of the work, so that the sail-like plane is the element farthest from him, he does indeed experience the space that the work occupies as enormously collapsed or contracted (fig. 142b). The back-most surface appears as a picture plane against which the horizontal line and the slender projecting tubes become major linear elements.

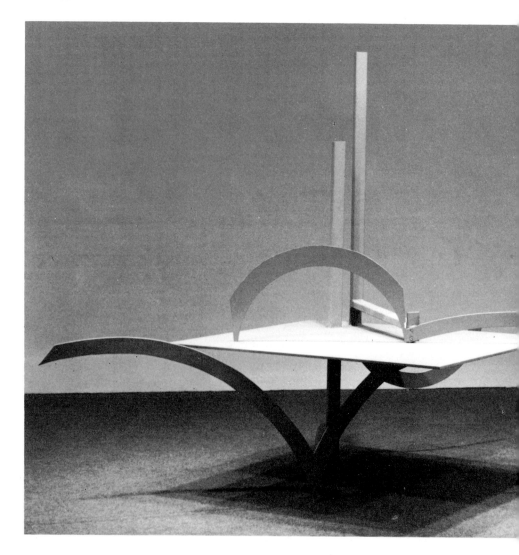

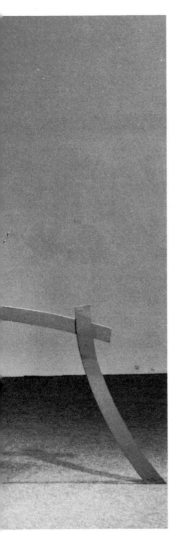

143. *Caro:* Trefoil, *1968. Painted steel, 83" x 123" x 74". The David Mirvish Gallery, Toronto.*

There are, then, two ways of relating to *Early One Morning.* The first is to experience it as a physical construction, and any position one takes in relation to it but the one described above yields this experience. The second alternative arises from standing directly in front of the work and thereby experiencing it pictorially. The achievement of *Early One Morning* is not only that it provides these two possibilities but that it shows them to be mutually incompatible. From the "side" the viewer looks down on the construction, much the way he would look down onto a table or any other article of furniture. He senses the work in terms of its mass because it shares the same space that he does and clearly relates to a ground that is the same as his own. From the "front" this orientation to a horizontal ground changes completely. The work becomes a vertical assembly, and thus its space is no longer occupied by the viewer. Just as there is a gulf between a viewer's space and the space of a painting— a break between his own ground, which he sees as he looks down at his feet, and the beginning of the ground of the picture's space, which he can only see by raising his head—so the pictorialized space of *Early One Morning* is not only sensed as flattened but as irrevocably distanced as well. The thin tubular elements become the major visual factors within this view of the work, partly because their fanlike configuration seems to enact that transposition of horizontals into vertical, which I mentioned before as the fact of picture-making.

This linear gesture of the piece follows logically from the meaning of the work, which centers on a sense of the mutual incompatibility of the two conditions of a constructed sculptural object. What it implies is that pictorial organization is now incompatible with an experience of three-dimensional physical mass. I say "now," because for other forms of sculpture this incompatibility is not the case. In carved reliefs, for example, the two experiences are the fruition of one another. The shallow shapes that are organized on the surface of the stone are given "body," or mass, as expressions of the dense, physical matrix from which they are partially released. As Adrian Stokes writes in *The Stones of Rimini:* "Carving shape, however abstract, is seen as belonging essentially to a particular substance . . . a figure carved in stone is fine carving when one feels that not the figure, but the stone, through the medium of the figure, has come to life." The physical experience of substance and the intelligence expressed through drawing or composition are thus aspects of the *same* view of the work. But this effect of carved relief depends on representation and illusion, and *Early One Morning* dismantles this kind of illusion. The axis along which one relates to the work as a physical object is turned ninety degrees to the axis which establishes its meaning as image. The change from horizontal to vertical is expressed as a change in condition, or being.

Caro's use of color in this work heightens one's sense of the separation between its two ways of existing for a viewer. The bright red paint covering its surface reinforces the material coherence of the sculpture seen as physical object; the color unifies the work's somewhat dispersed elements, declaring that they are all parts of the same *thing*. But, at the same time, the color serves the aspect of the work that functions as image. For the compressed, pictorial view of the work, the color addresses a different kind of coherence from the one that whole, physical objects simply have. This is the coherence of the configurative image in which separate elements are juxtaposed or interconnected on a plane surface in order to produce meaning.

One of Caro's later sculptures in which this use of color is most effective is the 1966 *Red Splash* (fig. 144), where the effulgence of the painted surface couples with a structure of inverse perspective that serves to drive a wedge between the imagistic sense of the work and its actual components.

In the later 1960s Caro became increasingly extreme in forcing the material substance of his work into a kind of pictorialism. In the 1966 *Carriage* (fig. 145), for example, a long, gently curved pole that connects the two separate planes of the work functions explicitly as a drawn line, while the wire-mesh rectangles that fill in the two planar halves take on the quality of crosshatching or shading, irresistibly suggesting the presence of an invisible picture surface to which they might adhere, and recalling a similar device in the Picasso construction, *Violin* of 1914 (fig. 38).

144. ABOVE *Caro:* Red Splash, *1966. Painted steel, 45½" x 69" x 41". Collection, Robert Mirvish, New York. (Photo, Geoffrey Clements)*

145. BELOW *Caro:* Carriage, *1966. Painted steel, 77" x 80" x 84". Collection, Henry and Maria Feiwel, New York.*

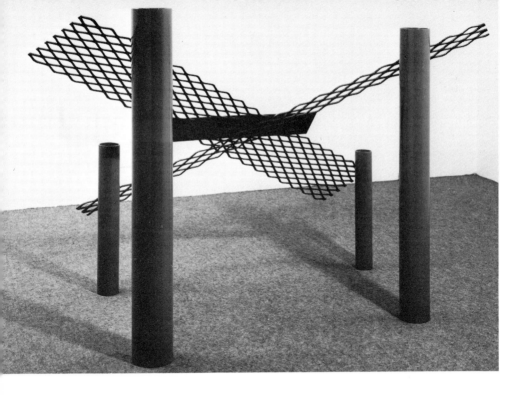

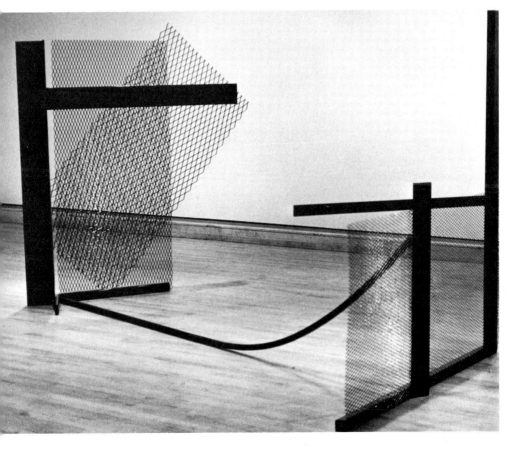

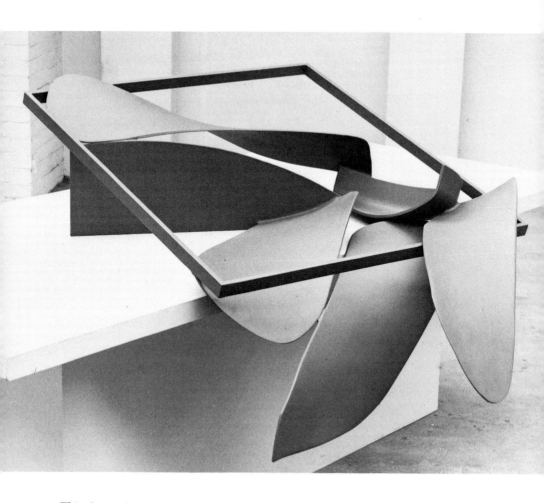

This demand for a two-dimensional plane on which the image of the sculpture could stabilize itself begins to be met in an increasingly material way in the table sculptures that Caro started to make in 1967. The curved elements of the work are constructed on the top surface of a table (fig. 146), so that they extend over its edge and drop to a point somewhat below it, as if they were organized around something like a horizon-line. That is, the edge of the table establishes a rigidly frontal aspect within which the image is organized, and because this frontality contains within itself a horizontal midpoint, it calls to mind the specific composition of landscapes or still lifes in paintings. In this kind of pictorialism, the connection to the space of the viewer's own body and the resulting tension begin to disappear from the works. And with the diminishing of that tension, the cursive elements—the curved tubes, the thin crescents of metal sheet, the small areas of mesh—take on a quality of decorativeness that they did not have in the earlier work.

This decorative pictorialism was a risk that was run by the younger generation of English sculptors who followed Caro into the medium of constructed and painted sculpture, a generation including Tim Scott, Michael Bolus, William Tucker, and David Annesley (fig. 147). And Philip King has increasingly shifted from an earlier concern with large, inert sculptural volume (as in *Through* [fig. 139]) to this pictorial mode (fig. 148).

Tim Scott's 1965 *Quantic of Sakkara* (fig. 149) might stand as a general example of the preoccupations of this group of sculptors. Standing seven and a half feet tall and extending across fifteen feet of ground, it is a work that constantly juxtaposes the massive amount of space it displaces with the insistent pictorialism of the relationship between its parts. The work's quadrafoil or ziggurat structure is undercut by a set of illusionistic properties built into the forms. For example, at the work's center, the flat edge of a crowning element possesses a mirrorlike finish. This creates a surface onto which another planar edge, set at right angles to the first, is reflected, so that the second element appears to continue into a space that does not in fact exist, jumping the gap of the open space formed by the work's central armature, which is itself shaped like a stepped-pyramidal contour made of steel tubing. One is forced to see the deep negative of open space as a flat, positive shape silhouetted by the dark plane of the rectangular edge and its reflection. Since both appear to pass *behind* this space, the way a fence passes and continues behind a tree that stands in front of it, the space itself is read as an opaque shape blotting out one's vision of the continuous plane.

The aesthetic of visual ambiguity being pursued here is closely allied to the strategies of cubist collage in which a plane seems to shift in space as the viewer chooses between a number of possible readings or interpretations of its placement. Scott's work maintains this seeming open-endedness of interpretation about what plane is in front of or behind another, about what part of the work

146. *Caro:* Table Piece, *1970. Painted steel, 29" x 45½" x 40". André Emmerich Gallery, New York. (Photo, Guy Martin)*

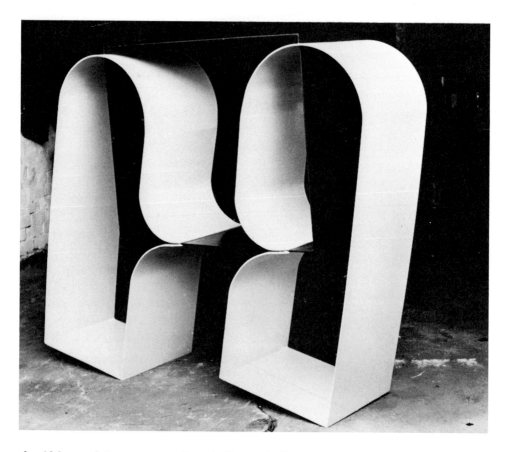

should be read in a context of verticality and what part in reference to the horizontal of the floor, about what is neutral "background" and what is positive shape. This is accomplished through the use of mirror reflection which causes the overlap described above and the transmutation of horizontal planes into the illusionistic bearers of vertical shapes. The use of color, which converts structural elements into the flat profiles of relational shapes, is another means of producing this ambivalence. These transformations work, in short, to turn physical masses into picture planes and tubular armatures into swathes of drawn line.

The goals of Scott's pictorialism, arising out of and continuous with that of Caro's, are centered on detaching one's reading of the work's relationships from one's experience of its structure, its physical being. If the reasons for this detachment had begun in Caro's work for the reasons given above—namely, a sense of discontinuity between the subjective experience of one's body and the comparative fixity of its external appearance—they carry forward into the sculpture of the younger men (Scott, Tucker, Bolus, Annesley, and the post-1965 King) on somewhat different grounds. For in pictorializing sculpture these artists are attempting a more general distinction: they are working to establish the difference between a sculptural object and any other ordinary object. Before the 1960s there had quite simply been no problem about distinguishing between these two classes of things. The material of sculpture, its mode of transformation, its isolation from ordinary space, all guaranteed that it would be neither apprehended nor treated like an ordinary object. As early as 1917 Duchamp had, of course, introduced the possibility of this confusion when he submitted *Fountain* (fig. 58), the signed urinal, for exhibition. But until the early 1960s that possibility had lain dormant, the cocoon of an idea waiting for a change in season before opening.

For a variety of reasons—which the following chapters will investigate—that change of climate had come. And

147. LEFT *David Annesley (1936–): Lonely Avenue, Edition 1973. 50½" x 58". The Waddington Galleries, London.*
148. BELOW *King:* Slant, *1965. Armorite, 84" x 180" x 75". Richard Feigen Gallery, New York. (Photo, Geoffrey Clements)*

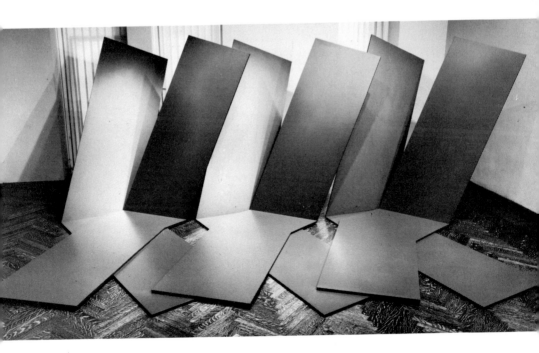

sculptors were coming forward to propose as their work objects in which the process of formal transformation had not taken place in any obvious way. In characterizing such work as "minimal art" Richard Wollheim had stated of these objects "that they have a minimal art content: in that either they are to an extreme degree undifferentiated in themselves and therefore possess very low content of any kind, or else the differentiation that they do exhibit, which may in some cases be very considerable, comes not from the artist but from a non-artistic source, like nature or the factory."[8]

The sculptors who fell heir to Wollheim's theoretical category of minimal art were Donald Judd, Robert Morris, Dan Flavin, Carl Andre, and Tony Smith. Not only did their work demonstrate a lack of differentiation but the constituent elements of the objects they made were drawn from the inventory of very ordinary stuffs: plywood panels, fluorescent tubes, fire bricks, rope, and industrial felt. In their seemingly obdurate refusal to transform the commonplace, the minimalist sculptors produced work that appeared to be aspiring toward the condition of nonart, to be breaking down any distinction between the world of art and the world of everyday objects. What their work seemed to share with those objects was a fundamental property that went deeper than the mere fact of the banality of the materials used. That property one might describe as the inarticulate existence of the object: the way the object seems merely to perpetuate itself in space and time in terms of the repeated occasions of its use. So that we might say of a chair or table that, beyond knowing its function, one has no other way to "get the meaning" of it. For the adult participant in cultural experience, there is no moment in which comprehension dawns about objects of that kind. They simply exist within the user's own time; their being consists in the temporal open-endedness of their use; they share in the extended flow of duration.

Given the apparent inarticulateness of a plywood cube by Robert Morris or a set of fluorescent tubes by Dan Flavin, one might extend the description of the chair or table to those sculptural objects as well and say that experience of them is a matter of repeated encounters, no

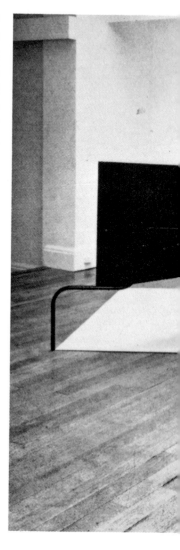

149. *Tim Scott (1937–): Quantic of Sakkara, 1965. Wood, steel tube, and aluminum, 84″ x 180″ x 108″. Collection of the artist.*

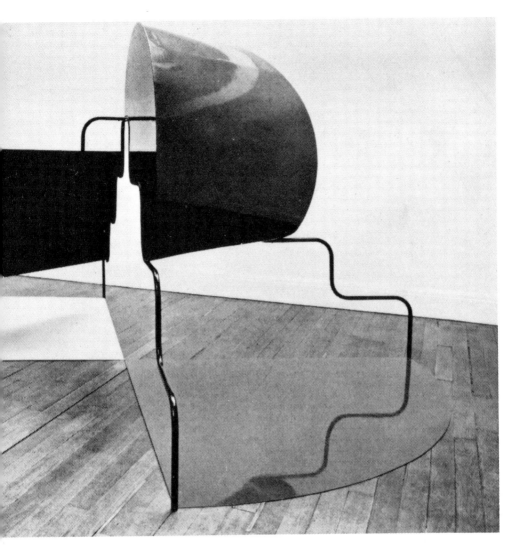

single encounter seeming to reveal anything more or significantly different from any other. So that, for them as for ordinary objects, there is no single moment, eclipsing all others, in which they are "understood."

In sculpture like Caro's there is an implicit criticism of the objectlike condition of minimal art. This criticism insists that there is an essential difference between the nature of art and that of objects, a difference which it is a sculptor's particular duty to preserve.[9] The crux of that difference involves, in this view, the withdrawal of the work from duration since, Caro would contend, with works of art there is *a* moment of understanding, *a* goal of apprehension in which all the relationships within the work participate in the single instant of clarity by which the elements are fused with their meaning. It is this condition that sets art objects outside the world of duration, a condition "of existing in, indeed of secreting or constituting, a continuous and perpetual present."[10]

If there is an art form that can serve as the model for this kind of presentness, it is painting; for essential to the two-dimensionality of painting is the fact that its contents are available at any one time to a viewer with an immediacy and a wholeness that no three-dimensional art can ever have. It is basically on these grounds that Caro and the sculptors who follow him defend the kind of pictorialism that came increasingly to the fore in their work. They seem to feel that only with highly inflected forms and the kind of openwork structure that creates a two-dimensional image can they articulate a sculpture that is more than a "mere" object—that is formed by, indeed suffused by, meaning.

Mechanical Ballets: light, motion, theater

The curtain parts. In the center of the stage is a column, standing upright, eight feet high, two feet on a side, plywood, painted gray. Nothing else is on the stage. For three and a half minutes nothing happens; no one enters or leaves.

Suddenly the column falls. Three and a half more minutes elapse. The curtain closes.

The author, in 1961, of both this performance and its "performer" was the sculptor Robert Morris.[1] Although the column was devised for an expressly theatrical setting, there is very little visual difference between it (fig. 150) and the subsequent work that Morris showed in gallery or museum contexts as sculpture (e.g., fig. 198). But, for certain critics, it was not only the column's monolithic

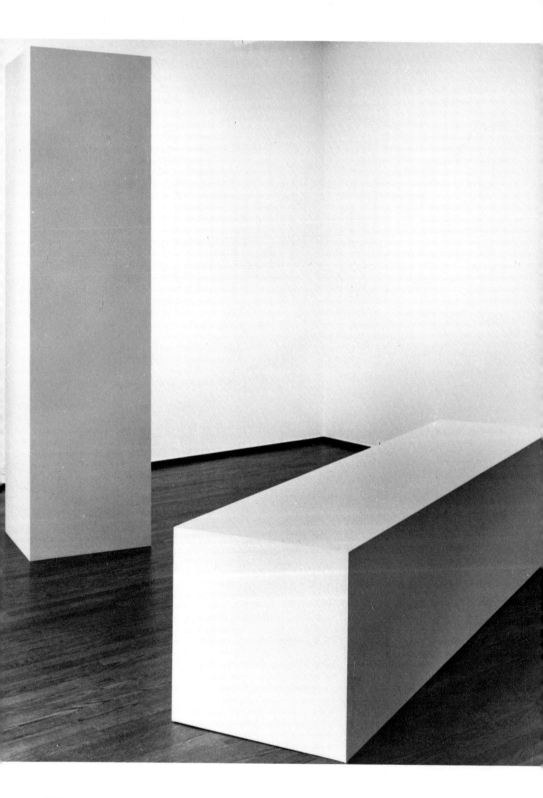

simplicity that carried over into Morris's later work; it was the set of implied theatrical components as well—a sense that the large obdurate forms that Morris went on to make possessed a kind of stage presence, like the column's. His later works did not withdraw themselves into an aesthetic space, separate from that of the spectator but, instead, were clearly dependent upon a situation in which the beholder of the works was actually their audience.

By 1967 this uneasy feeling that theatre had invaded the realm of sculpture was focused into a direct attack. At that time, Michael Fried wrote:

. . . I want to make a claim which I cannot hope to prove or substantiate but which nevertheless I believe to be true: viz., that theatre and theatricality are at war today, not simply with modernist painting (or modernist painting and sculpture), but with art as such—and to the extent that the different arts can be described as modernist, with modernist sensibility as such. . . . *The success, even the survival, of the arts has come increasingly to depend on their ability to defeat theater.*[2]

That is the central thesis of "Art and Objecthood," an essay on sculpture which has a long critical tradition stretching back to the nineteenth century, beginning with Matthew Arnold and extending through T. S. Eliot, a tradition that sees art essentially as a form of moral statement and assumes an absolute and clear-cut separation between the arts. Thus, only as a particular art form identifies itself to itself, by finding its own irreducible essence (the property that separates painting from music, say, or music from poetry),[3] can its practice and its perception become a model for the practice and perception of moral distinctions. Or as Michael Fried insists in his essay, *"The concepts of quality and value—and to the extent that these are central to art, the concept of art itself—are meaningful, or wholly meaningful, only* within *the individual arts. What lies* between *the arts is theatre."*[4]

With regard to sculpture, the point on which the distinction between itself and theater turns is, for Fried, the concept of time. It is an extended temporality, a merging of the temporal experience of sculpture with real time,

150. *Robert Morris (1931–): Columns, 1961–73. Painted aluminum, each column 96" x 24" x 24". Leo Castelli Gallery, New York. (Photo, Bruce C. Jones)*

that pushes the plastic arts into the modality of theater. While it is through the concepts of "presentness and instantaneousness that modernist painting and sculpture defeat theatre."[5]

Now it is beyond question that a large number of postwar European and American sculptors became interested both in theater and in the extended experience of time which seemed part of the conventions of the stage. From this interest came some sculpture to be used as props in productions of dance or theater (fig. 151), some to function as surrogate performers, and some to act as the on-stage generators of scenic effects. And if not functioning in a specifically theatrical context, certain sculpture was intended to theatricalize the space in which it was exhibited—by projecting a changing play of lights around that space, or by using such devices as audio speakers or video monitors to connect separate parts of a space into an arena contrapuntally shaped by performance. In the event that the work did not attempt to transform the whole of its ambient space into a theatrical or dramatic context, it would often internalize a sense of theatricality—by projecting, as its *raison d'être*, a sense of itself as an actor, as an agent of movement. In this sense, the entire range of kinetic sculpture can be seen as tied to the concept of theatricality.

So theatricality is an umbrella term, under which one could place both kinetic and light-art, as well as environmental and tableau sculpture, along with the more explicit performance art, such as "happenings" or the stage properties Robert Rauschenberg constructed for the dances of Merce Cunningham. But, because theatricality has become a polemical term in the criticism of modern sculpture—a term of condemnation as in the essay by Fried, or of praise, in the mouths of the supporters of these various enterprises—we should try to unpack the notion of theatricality. For it is too dense and too confusing. It is rife with internal contradiction, with conflicting intentions and motives. The question is not whether certain artists have wanted to seize the space of the stage or exploit the dramatic time projected by real motion; the question is why they would have wanted to seize or use those things, and to what aesthetic ends?

151. ABOVE *Noguchi: Set for a production of* Phaedra, *1960. Choreography by Martha Graham. Collection, Martha Graham Company. (Photo: Martha Swope)*

152. BELOW *Alex Hay (1935–): Grass Field, 1966. Performed by Alex Hay, Steve Paxton, and Robert Rauschenberg. (Photo, Peter Moore)*

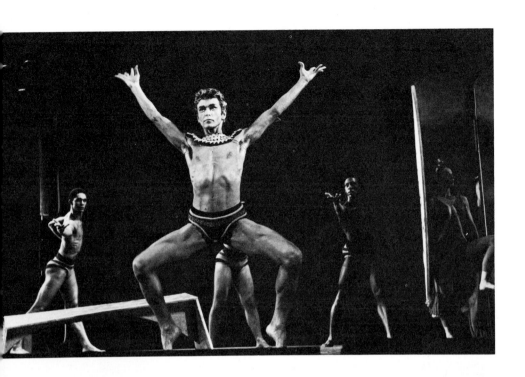

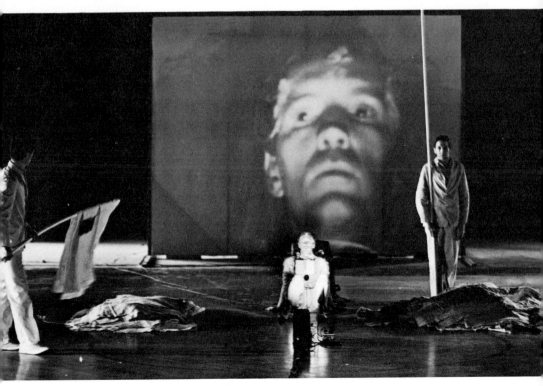

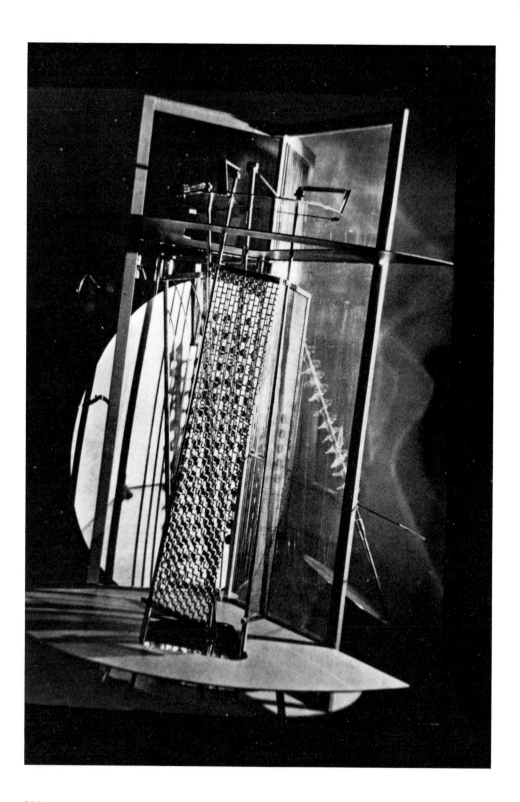

206

153. *Moholy-Nagy:* Light Prop for a Ballet, *model (also called* Light-Space Modulator*), 1923–30. Steel, plastics, and wood, 59½" (including base). Busch-Reisinger Museum of Germanic Culture, Harvard University, Cambridge, Mass. Gift of Sibyl Moholy-Nagy.*

In sorting through this confusion, one might turn to some of the prefigurations of "theatrical" sculpture in the early part of this century, to the early history of light-art, for example, as it grew out of considerations about the space of the stage. Two examples come to mind: Moholy-Nagy's *Light Prop* (fig. 153), finished in 1930, was intended to function during a performance by operating as an on-stage projector, weaving around its turning center a widening fabric of patterned light and shadow. Picabia's set for *Relâche* (fig. 154), produced by the Ballets Suédois, was a drop curtain constructed of 370 spotlights, each backed by a metal reflector. At the beginning of the second act the audience was nearly blinded when that arsenal of light was switched on.

Both artists created work expressly for the stage and thought about the function of this work as something fused with the unfolding temporal and dramatic events upon that stage; moreover, they both considered light as energy rather than static mass and therefore as a medium which is itself temporal. Thus we might be prompted to link together what they made. Because both the *Light Prop* and the décor for *Relâche* use the radiance of electric light to undermine the physicality of the object which is the source of that radiance, exploiting the fact that light projects away from its source and makes its way through space to rest at some distance from the object itself—a place shared by the spectator—we might be tempted to judge these works to have uncovered *in the same way* the formal possibilities of light as a medium for sculpture. But that would be wrong. Because the *Light Prop* is a surrogate person, an actor in technological disguise, and Picabia's bank of 370 spotlights is not.

In design, the *Light Prop* is an elaborate version of Gabo's *Column* (fig. 46). Its major structure depends on the conjunction of three vertical, transparent planes to create an apparent or virtual volume. Within the three resultant sections of this scaffolding, which rotates on a central axis, are various perforated disks and planes through which a play of light creates an environment of reflections and shadow. As the *Light Prop* turns, there are not one but two sets of external sheathings spun around the open skeleton of the revolving machine. The first is

207

that of the disks and wire-mesh planes, which pass in and out of view to become a changing but persistent skin completing the immediate cocoon of the work. The second is made from the projections thrown off by the *Prop* onto the walls of its stage, a shifting pattern that describes the volume of space in which the object sits, like a diaphanous enclosure maintained by the *Light Prop*'s energy and presence. Like a human figure, the *Light Prop* has an internal structure that affects its outward appearance, and, more crucially, an internal source of energy that allows it to move. And, like a human agent, the work is meant to affect its space through the gestures which it makes over a period of time. The fact that these gestures—the patterns of projected light and the shifting patterns that relate throughout its internal structure—change in time, and have a complex program, gives the object an even more human, because seemingly volitional, quality. Thus, no matter how abstract its forms and its function, the *Light Prop* is a kind of robot; the place it was meant to take on stage is that of a mechanical actor.

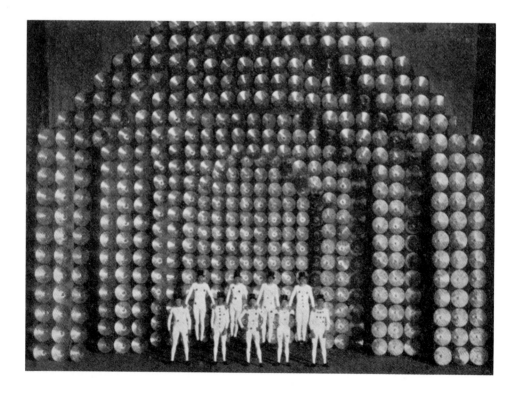

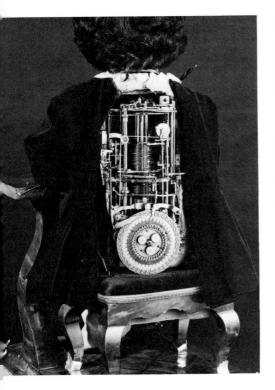

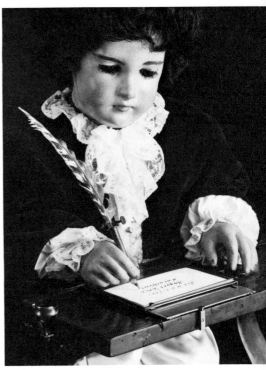

154. LEFT *Francis Picabia (1879–1953): Set for* Relâche, *1924. Cardboard stage model, 15½" x 20" x 8" Danse Museet, Stockholm. (Photo, L'Amour de l'Art, no. 12, December 1924)*

155a and **155b.** ABOVE *Pierre Jaquet-Droz, father (1721–90): The Clerk (two views), 1774. Mechanical doll. Musée d'Art et d'Histoire, Neuchâtel.*

As such, the *Light Prop* has a patrimony that extends back several hundred years into the history of automatons. Behind it stands a far-reaching mimetic impulse, a passion to imitate not simply the look of the living creature but to reproduce as well its animation, its discourse with the passage of time. In his book *Beyond Modern Sculpture*, Jack Burnham argues that the most fundamental ambition of sculpture, since its beginnings, is the replication of life. If until very recently this ambition has had to limit itself, within the practice of the high arts, to the lifelike but static representation of human or animal figures, there have been in the minor or popular arts early attempts to break out of the limits of this immobility. The extremely intricate clockwork automata created in the eighteenth century by Vaucanson arose from and satisfied the need to perfect the appearance of lifelikeness in the mechanical creature (figs. 155a and 155b).

In describing this branch of "subsculpture," Burnam says, "The history of automata has always run close to

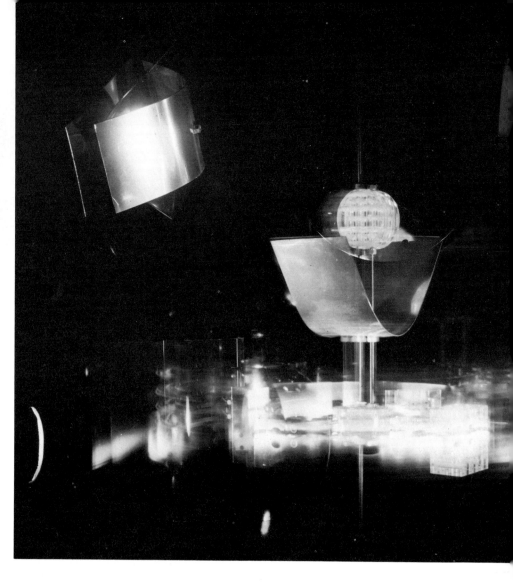

that of technology."[5] And so Burnham sees the aspirations change in the creation of the robot as technology itself develops. If the robot still clothes the mechanized performance of certain functions in a shell that bears some resemblance to a human agent, there are other machines that simulate human activity for which this kind of resemblance is completely beside the point. For example, for computers, "nonanthropomorphic automata," the simulation of the living organism has been centered in the artificialization of intelligence.

Burnham's thesis is that sculpture's "distant goal" is to assimilate itself into the complex technology of cyber-

156. *Nicolas Schöffer (1912–): Microtemps 16, 1966. Chrome-plated steel and Plexiglas, (Photo, Studio Yves Hervochon, courtesy of Nicolas Schöffer)*

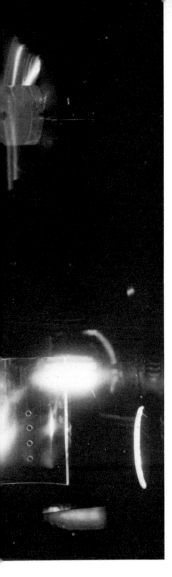

netics. Extrapolating from his idea of the present and past aspirations of sculpture—the ambition to imitate, simulate, and, finally, replace the human organism—he predicts a future in which the goals are "Faustian." He speaks of artists and scientists sharing "an unstoppable craving to wrest the secrets of natural order from God— with the unconscious aim of controlling human destiny, if not in fact becoming God itself. The machine, of course, is the key to this transference of power. If it constructs our destiny, it can do no less than become the medium through which our art is realized."[6]

But is sculpture fundamentally mimetic? Is it necessarily "about" the imitation, simulation, and nonbiological re-creation of life? And if it is not about that, what are we to think of Burnham's thesis?

Well, clearly, some sculpture has been about that, particularly the work that Burnham regards with most approbation. But much sculpture has not been about mimesis in any form. Of work that is more-or-less contemporary with *Light Prop*, we can point to Picasso's constructions (figs. 38, 39, 40), Duchamp's readymades (figs. 55, 56, 58), or Tatlin's tower (fig. 47) and say with certainty that they do not fit into Burnham's propositions about either the fundamental nature or the necessary goals of sculpture. And further, we can recall the analysis that Eisenstein made of sculpture through his film *October*, in which he pointed to the ideological role of all art. As a function of a given ideology, works of art project a particular picture of the world, or what it is like to be in the world; but "world" in this context is understood as being fundamentally different as viewed from different ideological vantages. And these vantages are themselves thoroughly structured or impregnated by systems of values, so that art is in this sense never morally neutral, but is involved, willfully or not, in upholding or maintaining those values, or—in certain extreme cases— challenging or subverting them. For Eisenstein, the golden automaton of the clockwork peacock was made in the service of an idealist position. Insofar as the peacock and Kerensky served as the images of one another, the bird symbolized a system of thought which the Russian Revolution viewed as its enemy. Eisenstein insisted that, no matter how much the peacock looked like a trivial toy, it was not value-free.

The technocratic premise of *Beyond Modern Sculpture* regards the aim of re-creating life, "of controlling human destiny," as natural to both science and art and therefore as morally neutral. But many liberal and Marxist historians and social philosophers have labored to show us that these technocratic goals are not value-free, but are products of a social and economic system for which "control" of that kind is the logical corollary.[8] Burnham's book is one of the most extensively and closely argued presentations of sculpture made in the service of a mechanistic view of the world. But that view—far from being necessary—is precisely what much of contemporary sculpture (and art in general) wishes to overturn.

The set for *Relâche* is an example. When that quiescent and decorative arrangement of crystal globes suddenly, and without warning, unleashes thousands of watts upon an unsuspecting audience, it participates in the kind of terrorism that Antonin Artaud was to speak of in "A Theatre of Cruelty," when he said, "The theatre, like dreams, must be bloody and inhuman."[9] The two essential qualities housed in Picabia's wall of light are those of abruptness and attack. The first of these shatters the audience's assumption that the spectacle is proceeding along expected, conventional lines. Unlike *Light Prop's* performance, which unwinds rhythmically and without surprise, the move made by the *Relâche* décor is completely unprepared for, dramatically or narratively; it is unmotivated and gratuitous. It disrupts the spectator's idea that he is to be given some measure of control over the events on stage by knowing how to anticipate the direction the action will take. The conventional drama locates the spectator outside the staged event, looking on, ignored by the actors. This removal from the physical flow of action on stage affords the viewer a kind of external perspective which promotes his independent analytic stance. *Light Prop* supports that removal; the business it attends to is its own. But *Relâche* strikes out at the audience directly—absorbing it, focusing on it— by lighting it. So the audience is blinded even while it is illuminated, and that double function demonstrates that once the watcher is physically incorporated into the spectacle, his dazzled vision is no longer capable of supervising its events.

Although the *Light Prop* and the *Relâche* set are both theatrical, they are vastly different kinds of objects. The first is a technological contribution to the conventional sense of dramatic space and time, while the second is involved in a movement to radicalize the relationship between theater and its audience. The mechanized *Light Prop* supports the constructivist analytic mode of sculpture, while *Relâche's* violence wishes to discredit those routines by which we think we understand the properties of objects.

In terms of the sophistication of its technology, *Light Prop* stands midway on a spectrum of the artist's use of movement to endow the sculptural object with the animate qualities of the human actor. At the more primitive end of this spectrum one would locate the work of Alexander Calder, an American contemporary of Moholy-Nagy's, with its mechanical simplicity reflecting the naïve and humorous direction of its content. On the other, more complex, end, one would place the work of someone such as Nicolas Schöffer, whose use of computers makes the sculptural ensemble visibly responsive to its environment (fig. 156)—to the point where a piece such as *CYSP 1* (cybernetic-spatiodynamic construction) utilizes control devices to allow the sculptural array to respond to changes in ambient sound and light. "Different colors make its blades turn rapidly or lie stationary, move the sculpture about the floor, turn sharp angles or stay still. Darkness and silence animate the sculpture, while brightness and noise make it still. Ambiguous stimuli . . . produce the unpredictability of an organism."[10]

Schöffer (along with Jean Tinguely, Takis, and the new tendency sculptors)[11] implants the sculpture with sophisticated devices to give one the sense that its animation has been motivated by some aspect of the sculpture's environment. Using a far less elaborate technology, Calder is able to produce a similar animation.

Calder's mobiles (which were begun in 1932) achieve in their developed form an equilibrium delicate enough to be disturbed and set in motion by the wind, or by air

157. BELOW *Otto Piene (1928–*
): Light Ballet from
"Fireflowers," *1964.*
Light environment. Berlin,
Studio Diogenes. (Photo,
Manfred Tischer)

158. RIGHT *Alexander Calder*
(1898–1976): Thirteen
Spines, 1940. Sheet steel, rods,
wire, and aluminum, 84".
Wallraf-Richartz Museum,
Cologne. (Photo, Herbert
Matter)

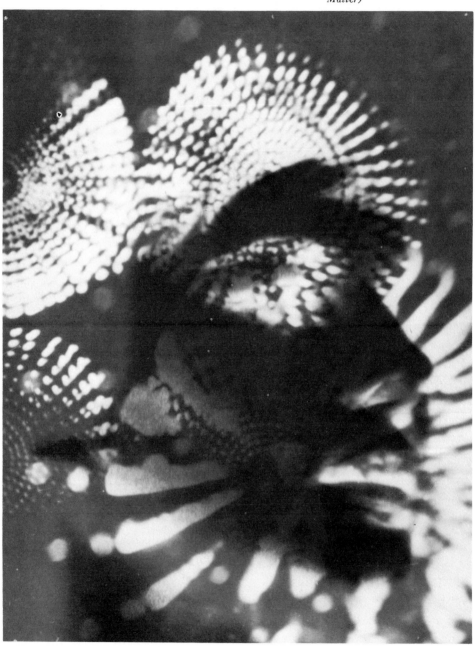

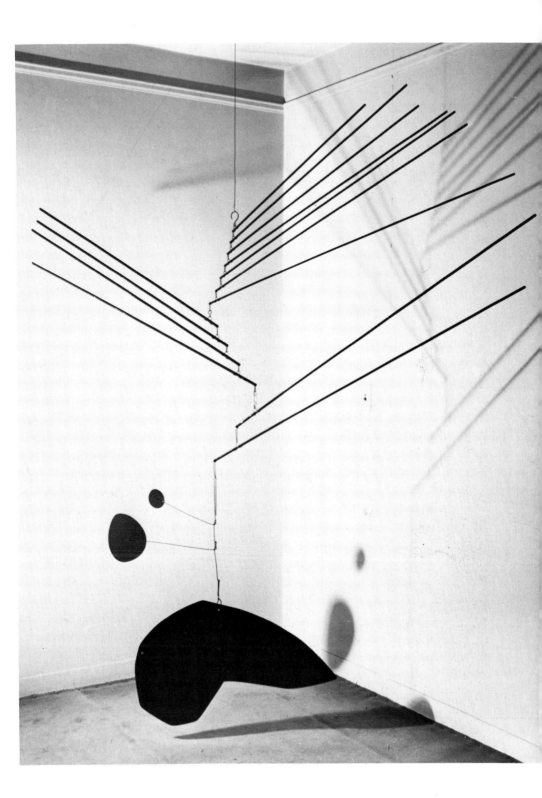

215

currents in the room in which they hang, or by the touch of one of their viewers. The filament-like backbone of their structure is composed of a cascade of wire canti-levers, attached at one point to the linear member above it and at another to the next lowest element of the chain (fig. 158). In calculating these double-point balances, Calder takes into consideration the weight of any given member—determined either by its actual length or by the additional leverage of a metal disk fixed to its free end—in order to achieve the set of counterbalances necessary to extend the construction to its full length. The viewer sees this extension of the mobile as a free reach through space, a breadth that is visibly due to its internal struc-tural logic rather than to the natural displacement and rigidity of a solid mass.

Further, Calder's design insures the capability of any of these linear arms to rotate in relation to the others, once the entire chain is made to move. For Calder is concerned that once in motion—spinning slowly around their points of connection—these single vectors will con-jure for the viewer a sense of virtual volume (figs. 159a, b, and c). That this creation of apparent volume is con-structivist at its roots is acknowledged by Calder's state-ment, "When I use two circles of wire intersecting at right angles, this to me is a sphere . . . what I produce is not precisely what I have in mind—but a sort of sketch, a man-made approximation."[12] And it is this generated sense of volume that makes the mobiles a metaphor for the body as it displaces space, but it is a body sketched now by the linear pen of constructivism in terms of a striking transparency. Through that transparency they also become images of the body's response to gravity, of the internal source of its opposition in its determination to move. In that sense they have traveled some distance from the purism of Gabo's 1920 *Kinetic Construction* (fig. 160), an experiment in virtual volume created by the motorized oscillation of a single, flexible rod to create the illusion of a diaphanous column set perpendicular to its solid base. The path of Calder's mobiles leads from Gabo's abstract geometries to the anthropomorphic con-tent of the body's intermittent action.

In that it is a description of aspects of the body, in

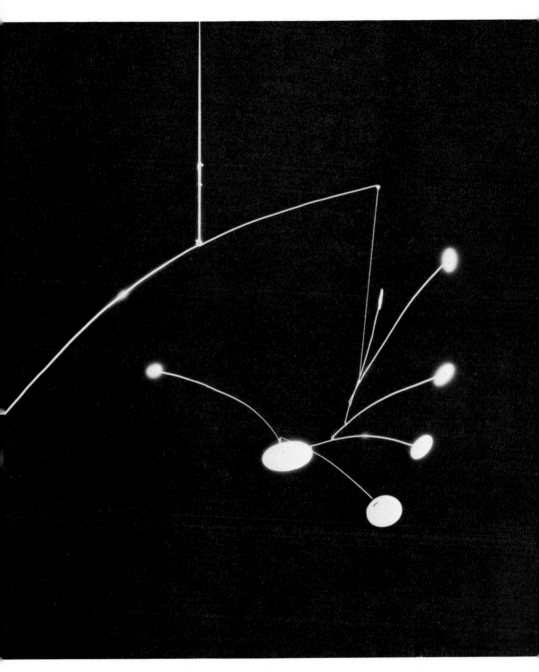

159a, ABOVE, **b** and **c**, OVER
Calder: Hanging Mobile *(three
views), 1936. Aluminum, steel
wire, 28″ wide. Collection, Mrs.
Merie Callery. (Photos,
Herbert Matter)*

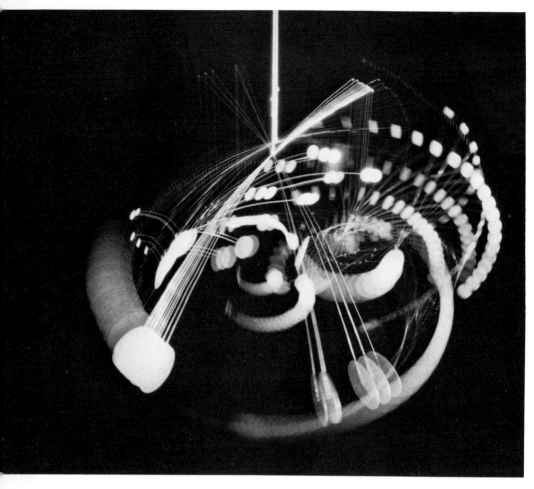

(Continued) **159 b** and **c.**
Calder: Hanging Mobile

that its motion is intermittent rather than mechanically continuous, in that one feels impelled to set it in motion in order for it to "perform" the role of filling out and inhabiting its own spatiality, the mobile locates its sculptural meaning as a kind of actor (fig. 161). Indeed its beginnings were in the little wire toys Calder built for his "circus" soon after arriving in Paris in 1927, the performances of which brought troops of artists and musicians to his room in Montparnasse. By the mid-1930s Martha Graham saw in the mobiles the innate drama of their performance and had several enlarged to function as "plastic interludes" during dance performances of her group. Also in the mid-1930s Calder designed a set for a

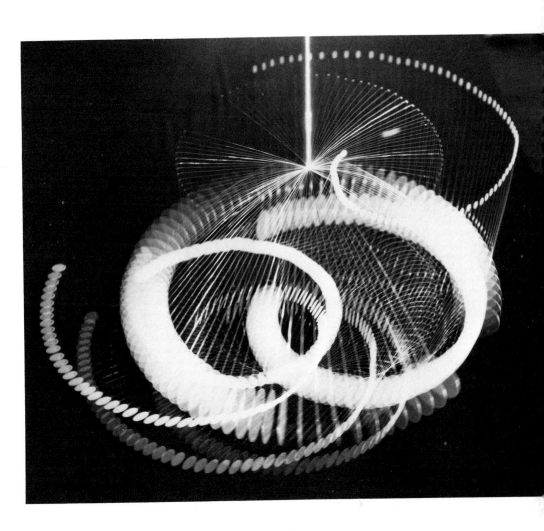

production of Eric Satie's *Socrate* when it was staged at the Wadsworth Atheneum in Hartford, Connecticut. Calder's sculpture dramatizes its motion in the same sense as *Light Prop*, for it spins out its tale of achieved volume through a slowly unfolding temporal sequence, satisfying in its logic and predictability. The drama is heightened by the flexibility and change it projects as it responds to the vagaries of its motivating force, which only fixes that movement more securely as a metaphor for volitional activity. As usual, Duchamp performed the role of the subtlest of critics. Recalling the source of their collective title, Calder described Duchamp's first encounter with these objects: "I asked him what sort of a name I could give these things and he at once produced 'mobile.' In addition to something that moves, in French it also means motive."[13]

But sculptors were to discover that no matter what the variation in the type of balance used, wind-driven objects tended to produce very similar types of rhythms and patterns of movement. Although George Rickey exploited the knife-edge fulcrum for his own kinetic work (fig. 162) and substituted plane geometry for the curvilinear vocabulary of the mobiles, the rotations and swings of these elements projected an expressive content very similar to Calder's. In the intensified production of kinetic sculpture that took place in the 1960s, internal mechanization was used to allow the performing object to locate itself at various points on the spectrum of emotion. Len Lye's work, for example, sometimes projects a feeling of violence and aggression as the dramatic by-product of the forms' snapping toward the boundaries of the volumes they weave through air. Automatically programed and specifically staged as performances, this sculpture is meant to "enact" itself. As Lye describes his 1963 Loop (fig. 163):

The Loop, a twenty-two foot strip of polished steel, is formed into a band, which rests on its back on a magnetized bed. The action starts when the charged magnets pull the loop of steel downwards, and then release it suddenly. As it struggles to resume its natural shape, the steel band bounds upwards and lurches from end to end with simultaneous leaping and rocking motions, orbiting powerful reflections at the viewer and emitting fanciful musical tones which pulsate in rhythm with The Loop. Occasionally, as the boundless Loop reaches its greatest height, it strikes a suspended ball, causing it to emit a different yet harmonious musical note, and so it dances to a weird quavering composition of its own making.[14]

160. *Gabo:* Kinetic Construction, *1920. Metal rod with electric vibrator, 24¼".* *Tate Gallery, London.*

In opposition to Lye's exuberant mechanical calisthenics, one can think of Jean Tinguely's self-deprecating gestures expressed through sculptural objects that look like little more than animated junk. Yet these works, too, were thought of as actors in specific performances, the most celebrated of which was staged in 1960 in the garden of The Museum of Modern Art by a sculpture that was programed to self-destruct (fig. 164). Pol Bury's work exem-

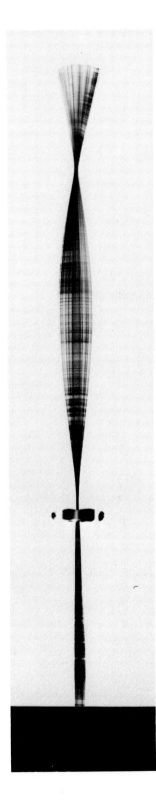

plifies a still different mood—repressed sensuous excitation. It exploits barely perceptible patterns of movement, as the surface of wall reliefs tremble with a kind of subliminal animation, or elements of free-standing sculpture slowly stir against one another (fig. 165). Bury speaks of the object's "journey" rather than its action, saying that "Journeys avoid 'programmization' in the degree that they are endowed with a quality of slowness; they finally achieve a real or fictional liberty, a liberty acting on its own account and for its own pleasure. . . ."[15]

Because the movement of Bury's sculpture hovers just above the threshold of perceptibility, Burnham wonders whether this work can really be classed with the rest of kinetic sculpture. He speaks of the lack of drama in any given object and the sense in which it stimulates the viewer's kinesthetic responses only peripherally. But he satisfies himself that it does qualify as kinetic when he reflects that "the experience of a whole roomful of Burys is something else. Through silence, one *feels* the creaking of cords, spools, and linked shapes from all directions. Out of the corners of the eye hundreds of multisensual movements take place imperceptibly. As in the hull of a sailing ship, wood strains against wood as the elements press against the live shell of doweled beams and planks. Without the interference of other human visitors, a room of Bury sculptures rocks with subliminal activity."[16]

One feels, within Burnham's description, a subtle shift of gears from the position of the sculpture as the explicit actor in a kinetic performance to a position of another kind. In this latter stage a roomful of Burys contrives a very special environment of sensuous alertness, one that theatricalizes the room to the point where it is the *viewer* who is the actor in question. The drama of motion is one that the spectator completes or bestows on the assembled work, his participation enacting in large scale or explicit gesture the "subliminal activity" which the work suggests. The sculpture makes the viewer complicit with the direction of its "journey" through time; in being its audience, he becomes, automatically, its performer.

In this sense, one can think of tableau sculpture—such as the work of George Segal (fig. 167) or Edward Kienholz—as theatrical, although no internal mechanization impels the sculptured actors to "perform" in time. It is,

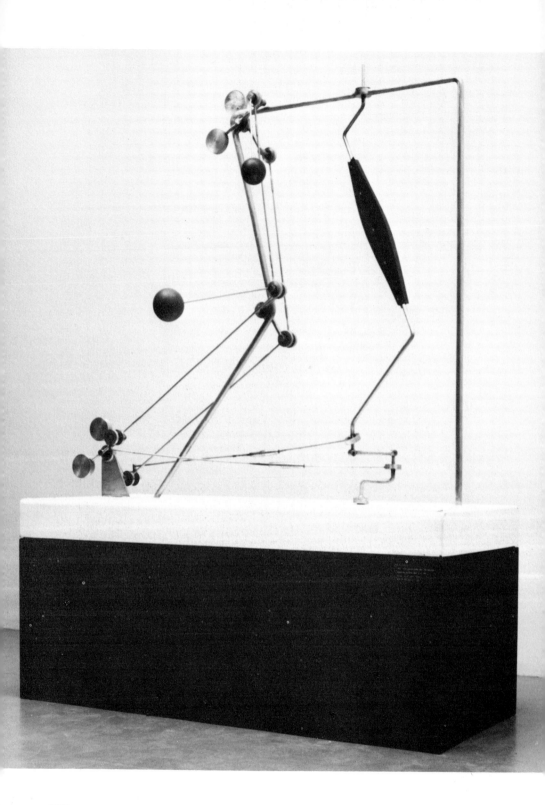

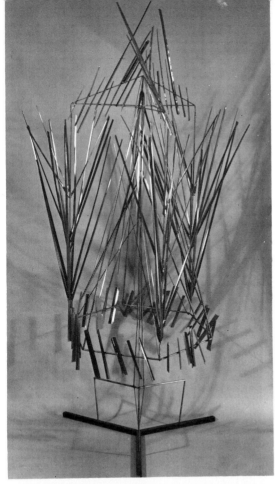

161. LEFT *Calder: The* Bicycle,
*1968. Wood, wire, pipe metal,
52". Collection, The Museum
of Modern Art, New York.
Gift of the artist.*

162. ABOVE *George Rickey
(1907–   ): Homage to*
Bernini, *1958. Stainless steel,
68½" x 36" x 36". Collection
of The Whitney Museum of
American Art, New York. Gift
of Mr. and Mrs. Patrick
McGinnis. (Photo, Geoffrey
Clements)*

163. BELOW *Len Lye (1901–
    ):* The Loop, *1963.
Stainless steel, 60" x 6".
Courtesy of The Art Institute
of Chicago.*

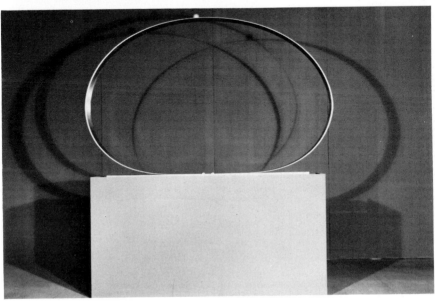

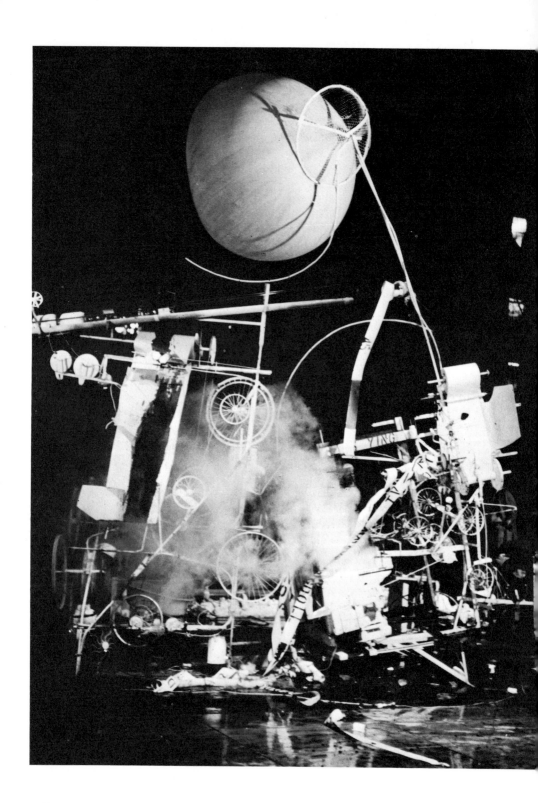

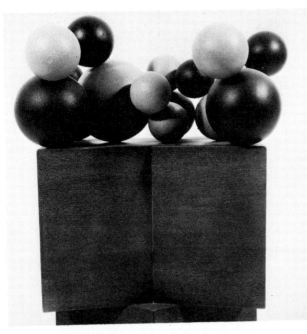

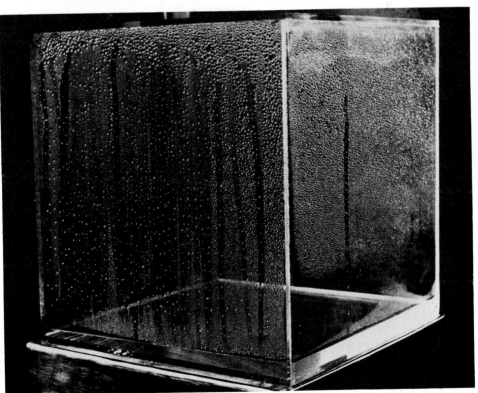

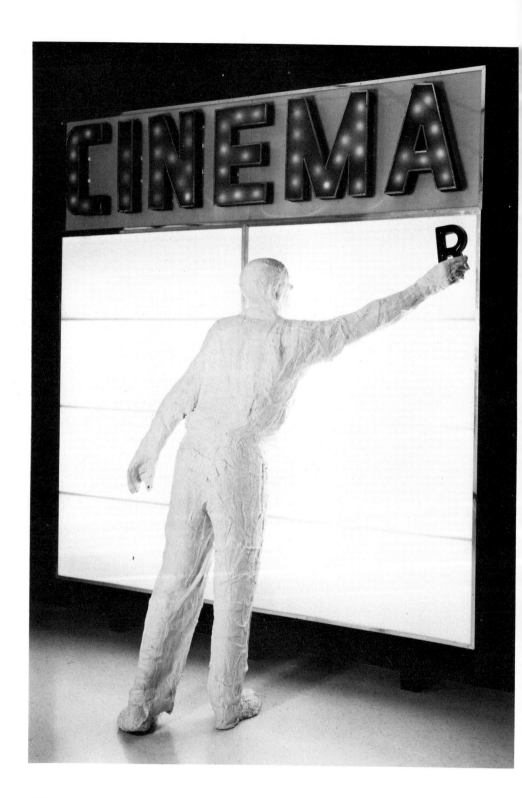

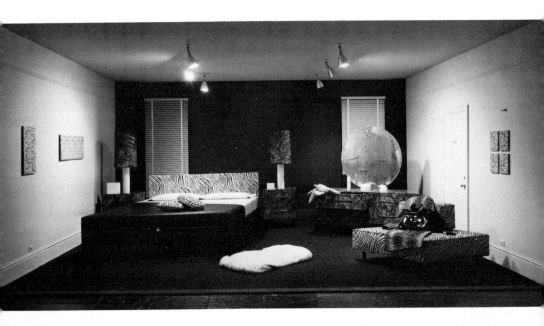

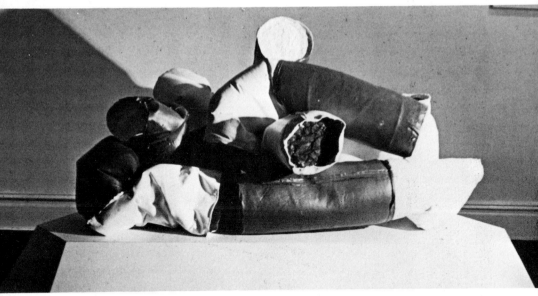

167. LEFT *George Segal (1924–
): Cinema, 1963. Plaster
statue, illuminated Plexiglas
and metal, 118″ x 96″ x 39″.
Albright-Knox Art Gallery,
Buffalo, N.Y. Gift of Seymour
H. Knox. (Photo, Sherwin
Greenberg, McGranahan and
May, Inc.)*

168. TOP *Claes Oldenburg
(1929–): Bedroom
Ensemble, 1963. Mixed media,
204″ x 252″. National Gallery
of Canada, Ottawa. (Photo,
Geoffrey Clements)*

169. BOTTOM *Oldenburg:
Giant Fag Ends, 1967. Canvas,
urethane foam, and wood,
52″ x 96″ x 96″. Collection
of The Whitney Museum of
American Art, New York.
Gift of the Friends of The
Whitney Museum of American
Art. (Photo, Geoffrey Clements)*

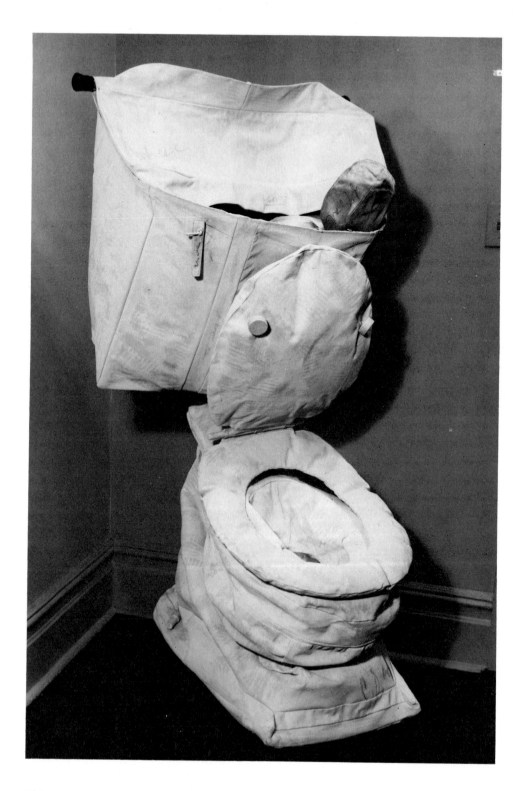

rather, the viewer's movement as he walks around the sculptural diorama, or takes time to interpret the narrative meaning of the various details of the tableau, that endows these works with dramatic time. The use of actual bathtubs or theater marquees or hospital beds on which plaster manikins are placed heightens the sense of continuity between the viewer's world and the ambience of the work. The sculpture of Claes Oldenburg also organizes itself into environments or tableaux and has recourse as well to imagery drawn from the unsterilized realm of popular culture. It traffics in "suites" of bedroom furniture (fig. 168), or toilets and telephones, or hamburgers and french fries, or cigarette butts.

But what are we to think of a cigarette butt that is over four feet long (fig. 169), or a toilet made of canvas stuffed with kapock (fig. 170)—constructed like an elaborate, exhausted pillow? These objects, staged like lugubrious obstructions in our space, do theatricalize their environment, do render us participants or actors in the drama of their presentation. But actors of what sort— and in a drama of what kind?

The two major formal devices Oldenburg uses to transform the ordinary object are the strategies of gigantism and/or softness. They are obstructions in the viewer's space because they have become colossal variants on their natural scale, and because they promote a sense of interaction in which the viewer is a participant, their mass being construed in terms that suggest his own body— pliant and soft, like flesh. The viewer is then forced into two simultaneous admissions: "They are *my* things—the objects I *use* everyday"; and "I resemble them."

Surrealism (particularly in painting) resorted to violent dislocations in scale in order to open a cleft in the continuous ground plane of reality, and Oldenburg's sense of scale obviously stands in relation to that source. Yet his terms are different and the balance between audience and object subtly shifted. Breton saw the dislocations in the external world as objective confirmations of some part of the author's self—his unconscious needs, his desires. The surrealist encounter was conceived of as a kind of proof that objects could be shaped by that aspect of the self. Objects were manifestations, then, of the self as it

170. *Oldenburg: "Ghost" Toilet, 1966. Painted canvas filled with Kapok, wood, 51" x 33" x 28". Collection, Albert A. List Family, Connecticut. (Photo, Geoffrey Clements)*

projected outward.[17] They were the realization of the Tzara prediction about the poem that "it will resemble you," where "you" is understood as the author. But the viewer's reaction to Oldenburg's work transposes these terms to, "I resemble them," where the "I" is the spectator and "they" are the banal objects that fill his space. With that reversal comes a realization that cuts much more deeply into an a priorist view of the self, by which the self is thought to be structured, in its most basic sense, prior to experience.

In discussing Rodin we talked about an alternative to that notion.[18] We spoke of a view by which the knowledge of some of the most private reaches of the self could be thought of as having been learned from the behavior of others—from their gestures of pain, for example, or of love. We spoke of Rodin's conversion of the source of *significance* of the gesture, transferring its meaning from the center of the figure to its skin, rendering it, if one can speak in this way, profoundly superficial. One feels a certain terror if one thinks of the self as constructed *in* experience rather than prior to it. Terror because some notions of control have to be given up, because some certainties about the source or functions of knowledge have to be shifted or restructured. Yet the optimism in Rodin's work stems from the fact that, after all, the experience shaping the gestures is still human. With Oldenburg the tone becomes sardonic and the intellectual surgery more radical, because the image of influence on the self is made up of objects.

Though softened and veiled by irony, the relationship Oldenburg's work has with its audience is one of attack. The softness of the sculptures undermines the conventions of rational structure, and its associations for the viewer strike at his assumptions that he is the conceptual agent of the temporal unfolding of the event. When Picabia turned the spotlights on the audience of *Relâche*, his act of incorporation was simultaneously an act of terrorism. If Oldenburg's work is theatrical, it is so in the sense of *Relâche* rather than in the terms of conventional theater, whether those terms are realized by the movement of Moholy-Nagy's *Light Prop* or the static nature of the sculptural tableau.

171. *Oldenburg:* The Store, *1961. Environment. New York. (Photo, Robert R. McElvoy)*

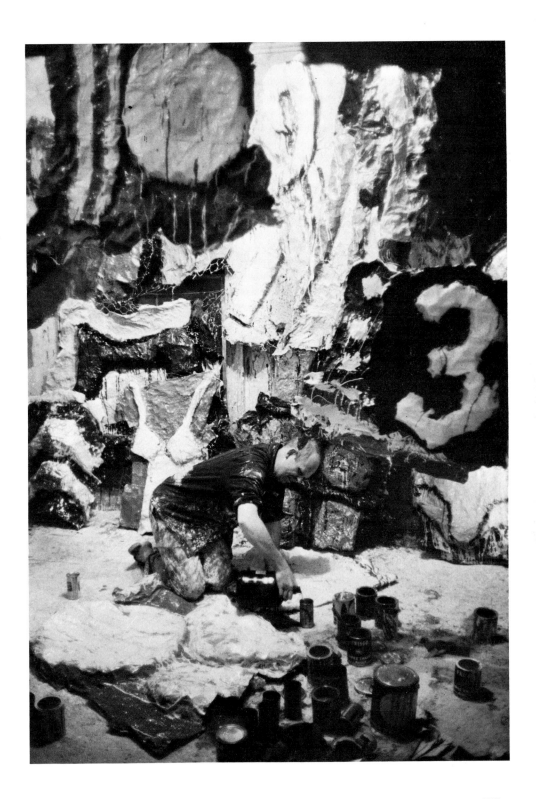

The link between Oldenburg's work and the notions of a "theatre of cruelty" was forged in the late 1950s and early 1960s through the sculptor's participation in the theatrical manifestation of "happenings."[19] Happenings were dramatic events staged for the most part in New York by artists and their friends, who performed in lofts, galleries, or, as in Oldenburg's case, storefronts (fig. 171). As Susan Sontag has pointed out, three typical features of the happening connect it to Artaud's notion of theater: "first, its supra-personal or impersonal treatment of persons; second, its emphasis on spectacle and sound, and disregard for the word; and third, its professed aim to assault the audience."[20] In describing this last aspect Sontag writes:

Perhaps the most striking feature of the happening is its treatment (this is the only word for it) of the audience. The performers may sprinkle water on the audience, or fling pennies or sneeze-producing detergent powder at it. Someone may be making near-deafening noises on an oil drum, or waving an acetylene torch in the direction of the spectators. Several radios may be playing simultaneously. The audience may be made to stand uncomfortably in a crowded room, or fight for space to stand on boards laid in a few inches of water. There is no attempt to cater to the audience's desire to see everything. In fact this is often deliberately frustrated, by performing some of the events in semi-darkness or by having events go on in different rooms simultaneously. In Allan Kaprow's *A Spring Happening*, presented in March 1961, at the Reuben Gallery, the spectators were confined inside a long boxlike structure resembling a cattle car; peepholes had been bored in the wooden wall of this enclosure through which the spectators could strain to see the events taking place outside; when the *Happening* was over, the walls collapsed, and the spectators were driven out by someone operating a power lawnmower.[21]

If the attack with the lawnmower in *A Spring Happening* signaled the end of the event, many happenings gave their audiences no such clues as to when they were over. Lacking any kind of narrative or dramatic arc, and lacking suspense or structure, they often left their audiences standing and waiting for some time after they were in fact ended. "The Happening operates by creating an asymmetrical network of surprises, without climax or consummation; this is the alogic of dreams rather than the logic of most art. Dreams have no sense of time; neither do the Happenings. Lacking a plot and continuous rational discourse, they have no past."[22] And this with-holding of a sense of structure is, if sublimated, as much an attack on the audience as the physical menace of the power mower.

Another aspect of the happening, "its supra-personal or impersonal treatment of persons," is clearly important to Oldenburg's sculptural thinking. In the happenings, performers were often shrouded in burlap sacks or wrapped in paper to resemble objects; or they were rendered inanimate props (fig. 173);[23] or acted upon as though they were depersonalized instruments—lifted, thrown, pushed, stroked. "Another way in which people are employed is in the discovery or the impassioned repetitive use of materials for their sensuous properties rather than their conventional uses: dropping pieces of bread into a bucket of water, setting a table for a meal, rolling a huge paper-screen hoop along the floor, hanging up laundry."[24]

In this last respect, happenings joined themselves to a dance tradition that was simultaneously developing out of the choreography of Merce Cunningham, in which there was growing insistence on the objectification of movement. Describing the goals of the "new dance," and correlating them with those of the sculpture of the mid-1960s, Annette Michelson declares, "Central to those considerations was the distinction between a time one might call synthetic as against a time that is operational, the time of experience, of our actions in the world."[25] She goes on to say that the common aim of the dancers associated with the Judson Theatre[26] "was the establish-ment of a radically new economy of movement. This required a systematic critique of the rhetoric, conven-tions, the esthetic hierarchies imposed by traditional or classical dance forms. That rhetoric was, in fact, reversed, destroyed, in what came to be known as the dance of 'ordinary language' and of 'task performance.'" The tasks that constituted the fabric of this dance—like moving mattresses or carrying bricks or following the rules of a game—serve a double strategy: to exchange

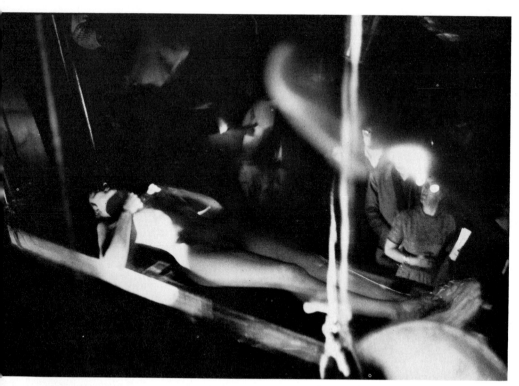

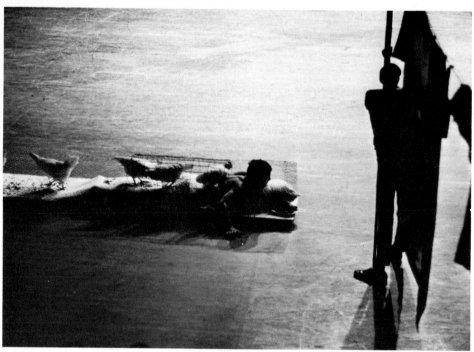

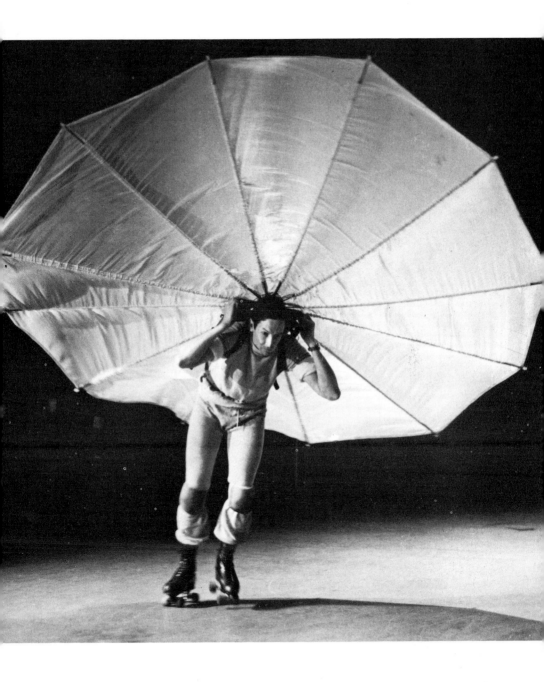

172. ABOVE LEFT *Allan Kaprow
(1927–   )*: A Service for the
Dead *(1), 1962. Happening.
New York. (Photo, Robert R.
McElvoy)*

173. BELOW LEFT *Robert
Rauschenberg (1925–   )*:
Linoleum, *performed at the
"New Festival," April 26, 1966,
Washington, D.C. (Photo,
Peter Moore)*

174. ABOVE *Rauschenberg:*
Pelican, *May 25, 1965. (Photo,
Peter Moore)*

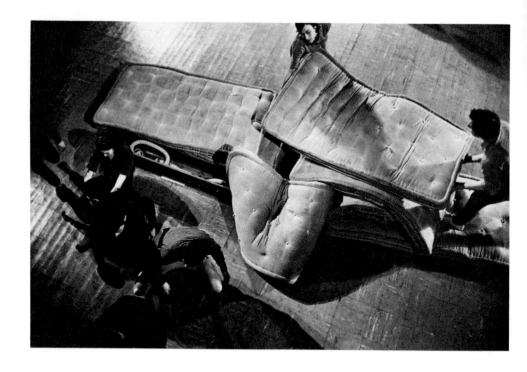

illusionism for real-time[27] and to de-psychologize the performer.[28]

In writing about her own work, Yvonne Rainer insisted on the parallels between the sensibility of the new dance and that of minimalist sculpture (fig. 175).[29] And, indeed, just as Oldenburg's work began to flourish in the theatrical ambience of the happening, a concern with performance in the context of the new dance shaped some of the initiating attitudes in the work of Robert Morris. As described at the beginning of this chapter, Morris was allocated seven minutes for a stage performance with the Judson Living Theatre in 1961. The "performer" he chose and constructed was a hollow column which appeared alone on the stage. Standing vertical for three and a half minutes, the column was then made to topple, where it rested, horizontal, for the remaining amount of time.

The column was a basis for much of Morris's subsequent thinking about sculpture. But one is struck by the parallels between it and the work of Oldenburg—no matter how differently shaped. In being an actor, it is anthropomorphized—made into a kind of model of the self—at the same time that, being an object, it is made completely inexpressive or deadpan.[30] And, like the soft toilet, it strikes out at the viewer's conventional assumptions about how his experience is formed. The column does this with stunning simplicity. For its only "action" within the course of the performance is to change its position. It falls. In so doing it changes from an upright object to one that is prone. Our normal assumptions about this "action" is that it changes nothing, or that it changes nothing essential about the object. The object persists through time and space as *the same*. Indeed, Morris's later work, which exploits this kind of variation of position undergone by the same shape (fig. 198), has been described in terms of the very theories of knowledge that the column wishes to defy. The works have been described as being like "a child's manipulation of forms, as though they were huge building blocks. The urge to alter, to see many possibilities inherent in a single shape,

175. LEFT *Yvonne Rainer (1934–   ): Parts of Some Sextets, March 24, 1965, Judson Church, New York. (Photo, Peter Moore)*

176. BELOW *Morris:* Waterman Switch, 1965. *Robert Morris, left; Lucinda Childs, right. (Photo, Peter Moore)*

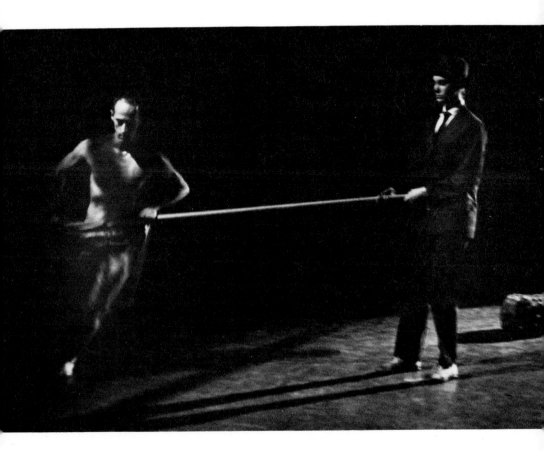

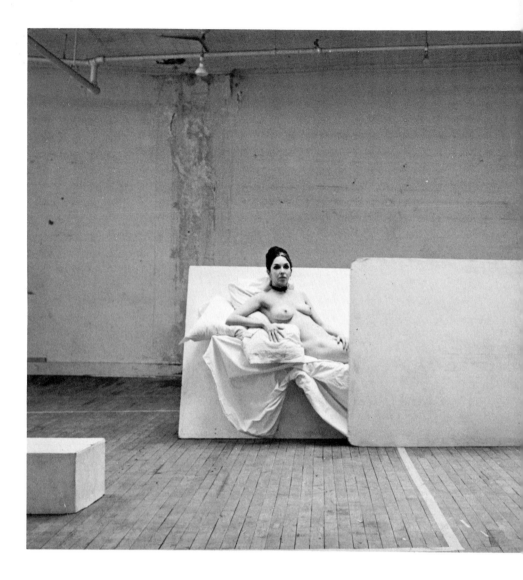

is typical of a child's syncretistic vision, whereby learning of one specific form can be transferred to any variation of that form."[31] But the reason the above description seems inadequate is that it does not fit one's actual experience of the column.

Upright, the column seems light and thin, its erectness unburdened by the downward pressure of weight. It seems fluid, linear, and without mass. But in a prone position, the column changes *in kind*. It appears massive, constricted and heavy; it seems to be *about* weight. The

177. *Morris: Site, 1963. Performed by Carolee Schneeman and Robert Morris. (Photo, Hans Namuth)*

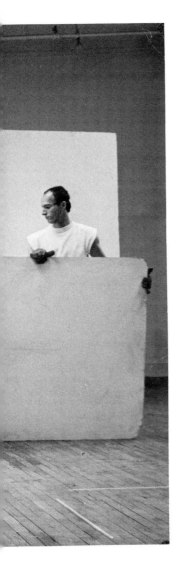

import of the column is, then, not that it is the same throughout "any variation of that form," but that it is different. And this difference strikes at the heart of the idea that the meaning of a shape is to be found in its abstractness, or separability, in its detachment from an actual situation, in the possibility that we can transfer it intact from one place and orientation to another. Merleau-Ponty, in *The Phenomenology of Perception*, attacks just this notion of abstractable aspects of the senses, when he talks about the way color, for example, *signifies*:

> This red patch which I see on the carpet is red only in virtue of a shadow which lies across it, its quality is apparent only in relation to the play of light upon it, and hence as an element in a spatial configuration. Moreover the colour can be said to be there only if it occupies an area of a certain size, too small an area not being describable in these terms. Finally this red would literally not be the same if it were not the "woolly red" of a carpet.[32]

It is only on a color chart that the red of the rug and the red of the wall could be thought to be the same red. And then, on the color chart—or rather, *for* the color chart—the very concept of redness signifies something else.

To see the column as the same, despite its change in positions, is to imagine that one's knowledge of space leaps over the specifics of one's perspective, that space itself is laid out before one as an ideal grid. We explain space in terms of this grid, rationalizing the way its parallel arms seem to converge in depth, by thinking that we are badly placed to see the whole of the grid. We attempt to clarify this apparent contradiction by imagining ourselves suspended above the grid in order to correct the "distortions" of our perspective, and to recapture the absoluteness of its total parallelism. But the meaning of depth is nowhere to be found in this suspension. "When I look at a road which sweeps before me towards the horizon," Merleau-Ponty cautions, "I must not say either that the sides of the road are given to me as convergent or that they are given to me as parallel: They are *parallel in depth*. The perspective appearance is not posited, but neither is the parallelism. *I am engrossed in the road itself*, and I cling to it through its virtual distortion, and depth is this intention itself which posits neither the perspective projection of the road, nor the 'real' road."[33]

The notion of the axiomatic coordinates, which allows one to think of oneself as capable of reconstituting the object, from all around itself, regardless of one's own position, or its, is a notion that wants to forget that meaning arises only from *this* position, and *this* perspective; and that one has no knowledge of these things beforehand. The column insists that only phantoms appear to "the syncretic vision"; but *its* meaning is specific and is a function of lived time.

Two things are important. One is that this sculptural attack on a classical explanation of how things are known has precedents in the work of Rodin and Brancusi—which means not that it is dependent upon them but merely that it is continuous with a deep and serious vein in the tradition of modern sculpture. The second is that it was the very dependency of theater on a variable situation that was able to put pressure on and disrupt the conventions of classicism lodged so deeply within their twentieth-century variants, in futurism, constructivism, and their technological extensions. By the mid-1960s it was clear that theatricality and performance could produce an operational divide between the sculptural object and the preconceptions about knowledge that the viewer might have about both it and himself.

Bruce Nauman's Wilder Gallery Installation (1970), for example, puts pressure on the viewer's notion of *himself* as "axiomatically coordinated"—as stable and unchanging in and for himself. The installation is a pair of long narrow corridors through which the viewer moves (fig. 178). High on the wall at one end of one corridor is a video camera while at the floor at the far end is a monitor relaying the immediate image the camera intercepts. This is of course the image of the viewer as he advances down the corridor toward the video screen. But the image of himself toward which the viewer walks is an image of his back; and as he comes over closer to his own reflection, the picture of "himself" recedes. The nearer he comes, the smaller it gets, since he is resolutely moving away from the camera that is the image's source. This sense of a moving center within the viewer's own

178. *Bruce Nauman (1941–): Corridor, 1968–70. Live taped video corridor, 204" x 480" x 36" (variable). Collection, Dr. Giuseppe Ponza. (Photo, Rudolph Burckhardt)*

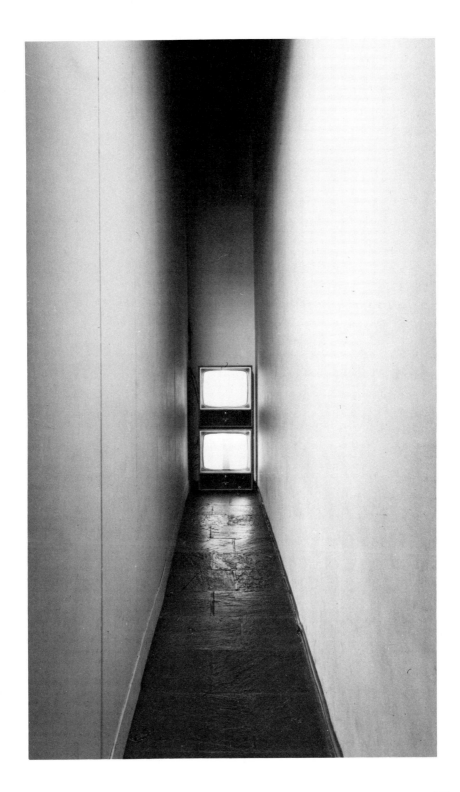

body is yet another attack on the conventions of sculpture as they had been maintained throughout the century. Its fulfillment in the work of a whole range of sculptors is a subject the next chapter will take up. But the fact that is essential here is that the kind of theatricality one finds in the work of Oldenburg, Morris, and Nauman is central to the reformulation of the sculptural enterprise: what the object is, how we know it, and what it means to "know it."

So we are brought full circle back to the polemic against theater with which this chapter opened. Fried had asserted that theatricality must work to the detriment of sculpture—muddying the sense of what sculpture uniquely was, depriving it thereby of meaning that was *sculptural*, and depriving it at the same time of seriousness. But the sculpture I have just been talking about is predicated on the feeling that what sculpture *was* is insufficient because founded on an idealist myth. And in trying to find out what sculpture *is*, or what it can be, it has used theater and its relation to the context of the viewer as a tool to destroy, to investigate, and to reconstruct.

The *Double Negative:*
a new syntax for sculpture

In 1969 a young sculptor named Richard Serra made *Hand Catching Lead* (fig. 179), a three-minute film which is repetitive, austere, and nearly without incident. Extending in from screen-right to almost fill the frame are a hand and forearm that perform the totality of the action, which is Serra's attempt to catch a sequence of falling strips of metal as they drop through the space of the image. The pulsating rhythm from open hand to clenched fist, as Serra tries to stop the falling objects, is the sole punctuation of the temporal/spatial sequence of the film. Sometimes his hand misses its target and the lead slips by it. Sometimes he makes his catch, arresting the strip for a moment before opening his hand once more to allow the lead to continue its fall. The film is composed entirely of those catches and misses—that, and the sense of the visually disembodied hand's intense concentration on the deed.

One of the striking aspects of this film is its quality of relentless persistence—of doing something over and over again without regarding "success" as any particular kind of climax—of simply adding one very specific action to the next, the way a nautilus adds on the chambers of its shell. In regarding repetition as a way of composing, as a demonstration of almost absurd tenacity, Serra's film is continuous with a sculptural tradition that had developed during the seven or eight years prior to his film. And not only his film, but also some of the sculpture he did in that year as well: such pieces as the 1969 *Casting* (fig. 180) made by flinging molten lead into the angle between floor and wall, pulling away the hardened shape into the center of the room, repeating the gesture, and thereby building a succession of lead strips, as sequential and near alike as waves following one another toward shore.

In 1964 Donald Judd spoke of that quality of repetition, both in his own sculpture (fig. 181) and in the paintings of Frank Stella (see fig. 196). "The order," he wrote, "is not rationalistic and underlying, but is simply order, like that of continuity, one thing after another."[1] Somewhat later in a joint interview, he and Stella elaborated on their interest in this composition by means of "one thing after another." It was, they said, a strategy to escape relational composition which they identified with European art. "The basis of their whole idea is balance," Stella said of European formalism. "You do something in one corner and you balance it with something in the other corner."[2] In explaining why he objected to relational composition, Judd followed with, "It is that they're linked up with a philosophy—rationalism, rationalist philosophy. . . . All that art is based on systems built beforehand, *a priori* systems; they express a certain type of thinking and logic that is pretty much discredited now as a way of finding out what the world's like."

So "one thing after another" was a way to escape from setting up relations. It was at work in the paintings Stella

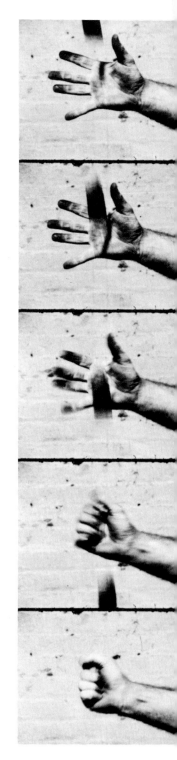

made after 1960, with their concentric or parallel rows of identical stripes, filling out the canvas surface with what appeared to be mechanical repetitiveness. One found it in the early 1960s in the sculpture of Donald Judd, through wall-bound rows of boxes in which the sameness of the units and the regularity of the intervals between them seemed to drive the possibility of "significance" out of the act of placing or arranging forms. Dan Flavin's use of commercially produced fluorescent tubes (fig. 182) continued the approach of Stella and Judd. Like the prosaically painted four-inch-wide band or the mundane prefabricated box, the tube seems not to have been shaped or given special significance by the artist. The resistance to meaning that is a feature of the single tube carries over into the compositions Flavin built from groups of them. The tubes are mounted on the wall in simple sequences: one tube isolated, then a space, then a pair of tubes, and then, after another interval of wall, a triple unit. What is characteristic of the approach taken by the minimalist sculptors is that they exploited a kind of found object for its possibilities as an element in a repetitive structure. This is true not only of the works just described but also of Carl Andre's rows of Styrofoam planks (fig. 183) or fire-bricks, and of Robert Smithson's stacks of plate-glass panes (fig. 184). In the late 1960s one finds it as well in certain of the works of Serra and in Mel Bochner's use of written numbers extended in a chain across the space of a wall (fig. 185). "One thing after another" was undeniably present as a compositional strategy, but that it might be in Judd's words, "a way of finding out what the world's like," is far more open to doubt.

That is because we tend to think that the act of finding out what something is like means that we give it a shape, propose for it a model or an image that will organize what seems on the surface merely an incoherent array of phenomena. This was obviously the conviction held by the constructivists as they proceeded to build abstract models through which to depict the organization of matter. "One thing after another" seems, on the other hand, like days simply following each other without anything having given them a form or a direction, without their being

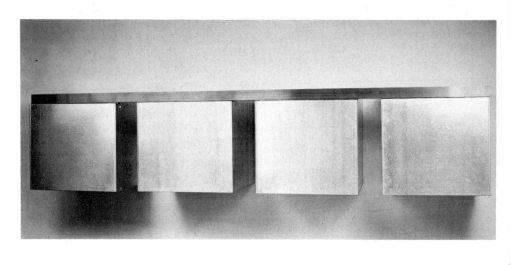

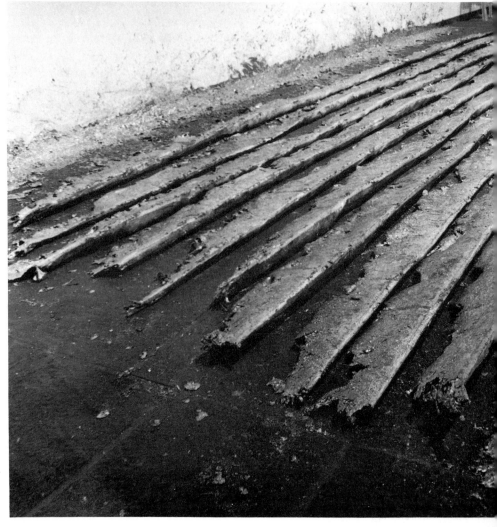

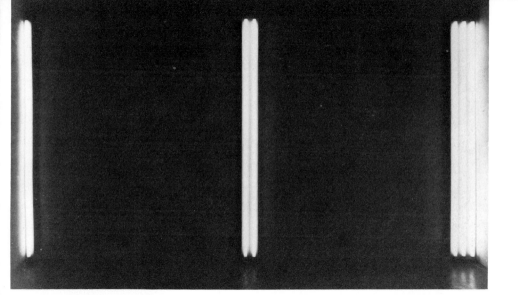

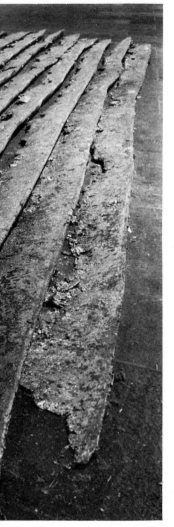

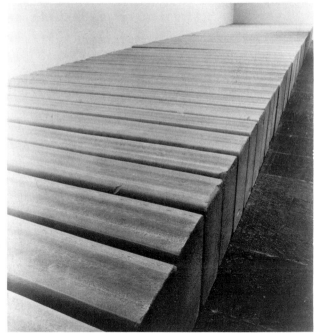

180. LEFT *Serra:* Casting, 1969. Lead, 4" x 210" x 300" (now destroyed). (Photo, Peter Moore for Leo Castelli Gallery, New York)

181. OPPOSITE PAGE TOP *Donald Judd (1928–   ):* Untitled *(four boxes),* 1965. Galvanized iron and painted aluminum, 33" x 141" x 30" Collection, Philip Johnson, Connecticut. (Photo, Leo Castelli Gallery)

182. THIS PAGE TOP *Dan Flavin (1933–   ):* The Nominal Three (To William of Ockham), *1963–64.* Cool white fluorescent light, 96" x 264" x 4". John Weber Gallery, New York. (Photo, John Weber Gallery)

183. THIS PAGE BOTTOM *Carl Andre (1935–   ):* Reef, 1969. Sixty-five Styrofoam planks, 20" x 9" x 10". John Weber Gallery, New York. (Photo, John Weber Gallery)

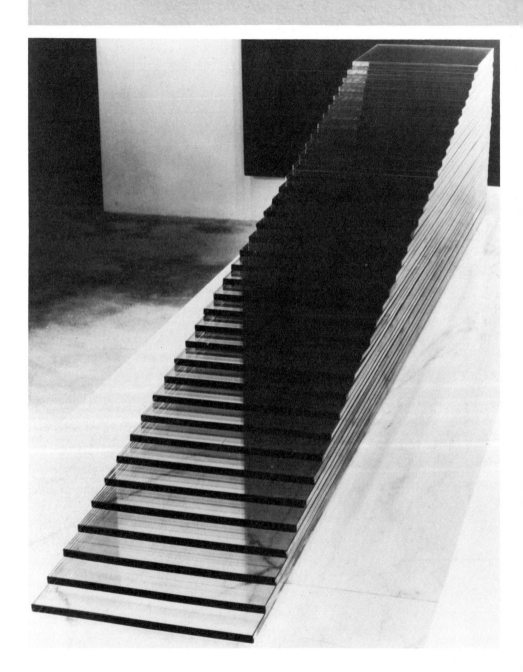

inhabited, or lived, or meant. With that thought, we might be led to ask whether Judd is proposing, by his row of identical boxes, an analogy with inert matter—with things untouched by thought or unmediated by personality? In asking the question in that way, we begin to find a connection between what Judd is doing with his rows or stacks of boxes and what Duchamp did almost fifty years earlier in his readymades.

Given its tendency to employ elements drawn from commercial sources, minimal art thus shares with pop art a common source: a newly awakened interest in the Duchampian readymade, which the work of Jasper Johns in the late 1950s had made available to artists of the early 1960s (fig. 193). But there is an important difference between the attitude of the minimal and the pop artists toward the cultural readymade. The pop artists worked with images that were already highly inflected (fig. 186), such as photographs of movie stars or frames from comic books, while the minimalists used elements

184. LEFT *Smithson:* Glass Stratum, *1967. Glass, 12" x 108". John Weber Gallery, New York. (Photo, John Weber Gallery)*

185. ABOVE *Mel Bochner (1940–   ): Three Ideas and Seven Procedures (now destroyed/dismantled), 1971. Felt pen on 1" masking tape on wall at the Museum of Modern Art, New York, Sept. 27–Nov. 1, 1971. (Photo, Eric Pollitzer)*

186. RIGHT *Andy Warhol (1928–   ): Brillo Boxes, 1964. Acrylic silk-screened on wood, each box 17" x 17" x 14". Collection, Peter M. Brant, New York.*

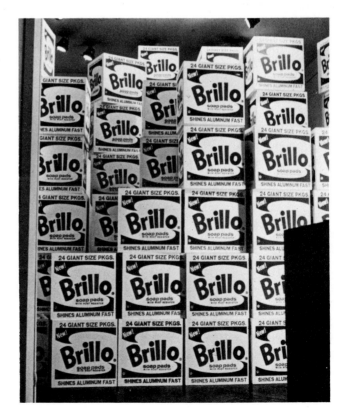

into which content of a specific kind had not been built. Because of this they were able to deal with the readymade as an abstract unit and to focus attention on the more general questions of the way it could be deployed. What they were doing was exploiting the idea of the readymade in a far less anecdotal way than the pop artists, considering its structural rather than its thematic implications.

The first of these implications concerns the basic units of a sculpture and the discovery that certain elements— fire-bricks for example—will resist the appearance of manipulation. The idea that they were not fabricated by the artist but were made instead for some other use within society at large—constructing buildings—gives to those elements a natural opacity. It will be difficult, that is, to read them illusionistically or to see them as alluding to an inner life of form (the way eroded or chiselled rock in a sculptural context might allude to inner biological forces). Instead the fire-bricks remain obdurately external, as objects of use rather than vehicles of expression. In this sense the readymade elements can convey, on a purely abstract level, the idea of simple externality.

In combining several of these elements together to form a grouping that might be called a sculptural composition, the minimal artists exploited yet another implication of the readymade element. Mass production insures that each object will have an identical size and shape, allowing no hierarchical relationships among them. Therefore, the compositional orders that seem to be called for by these units are those of repetition or serial progression: orders that are without either logically determined points of focus or internally dictated outer limits. We have already seen how the minimalists were attracted to sheer repetition as a way of avoiding the inferences of relational composition. To string elements together without emphasis or logical termination is clearly to defeat the idea of a center or a focus toward which forms point or build. One arrives at a mode of composition from which the idea of *inner* necessity has been removed: the idea that the explanation for a particular configuration of forms or textures on the surface of an object is to be looked for at its center. In structural or abstract terms, compositional devices of the minimalists deny the logical importance of

187. *Andre: Lever, 1966. Fire-bricks, 4" x 360" x 4". Installation, "Primary Structures," Jewish Museum, New York. (Photo, John Weber Gallery)*

250

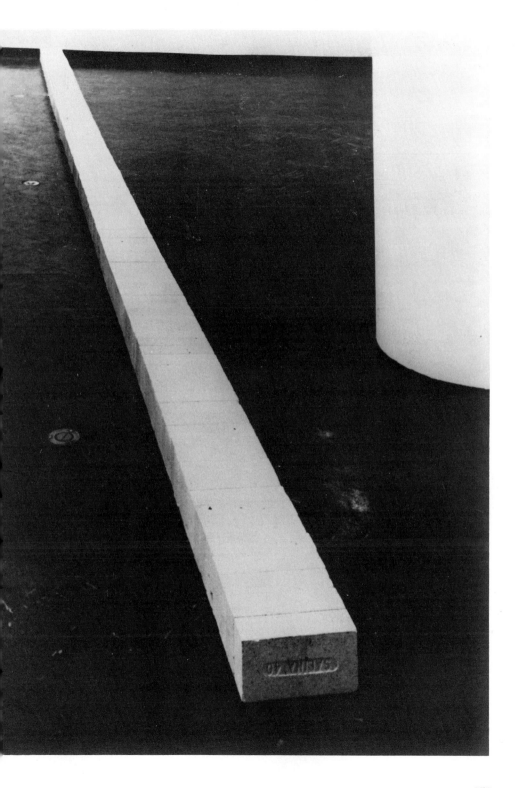

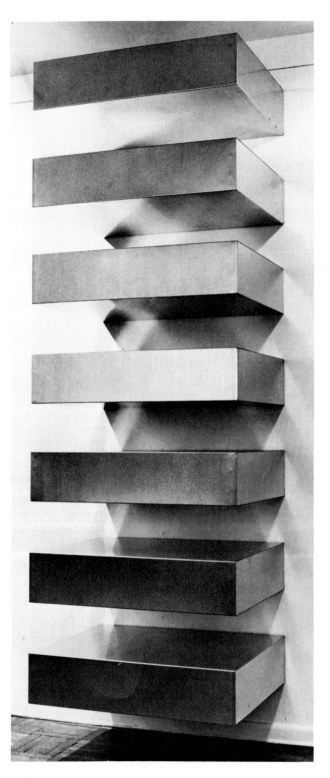

188. LEFT *Judd:* Untitled, *1965. Galvanized iron, 9" x 40" x 31" (each block; 9" between each block). Collection, Gordon Locksley. (Photo, Rudolph Burckhardt)*

189. RIGHT *Moore:* Internal and External Forms, *1953–54. Elm wood, 103" x 36". Albright-Knox Art Gallery, Buffalo, N.Y. Consolidated Purchase Fund. (Photo, Greenberg-May Prod. Inc.)*

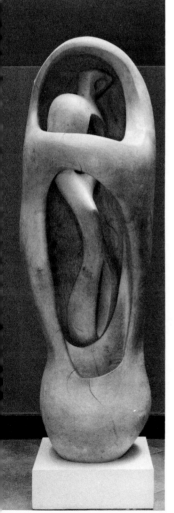

the interior space of forms—an interior space which much of previous twentieth-century sculpture had celebrated.

The symbolic importance of a central, interior space from which the energy of living matter derives, from which its organization develops as do the concentric rings that annually build outward from the tree trunk's core, had played a crucial role for modern sculpture. Because, as twentieth-century sculpture discarded realistic representation as a source of major ambition and turned to far more generalized and abstracted plays of form, the possibility arose—as it had not for naturalistic sculpture —that the sculpted object might be seen as nothing but inert material. If Henry Moore or Jean Arp made conspicuous use of eroded stone or rough-hewn wooden block (fig. 189), it was not to serve this material, untransformed, to the viewer of their work. Instead, they wished to create the illusion that at the center of this inert matter there was a source of energy which shaped it and gave it life. They wanted to establish an analogy between the slow formation of the rock's strata or the wood's fibers, and the growth of organic life from the tiny seed that is its inception. In using sculpture to create this metaphor, they were establishing the abstract meaning of their work; they were saying that the process of creating form is, for the sculptor, a visual meditation on the logic of organic growth itself.

In the case of artists such as Gabo and Pevsner, who employed a much more geometric vocabulary and used the synthetic materials of the industrial age, the immediate content of the work is different, but the ultimate meaning is similar. Gabo's (fig. 190) and Pevsner's sculpture is no more *about* plastic and plywood and sheet tin than Moore's is *about* limestone or oak. For the Russians, the logic of construction, with its symmetrical building outward from revealed centers, was a way of presenting visually the creative power of thought, a meditation on the growth and development of Idea. *Behind* the surface of their abstract forms an interior was always indicated, and it was from this interior that the life of the sculpture emanated. This was the kind of order, or constructive principle, that Judd had spoken of as being "rationalistic and underlying" and tied to an idealist philosophy.

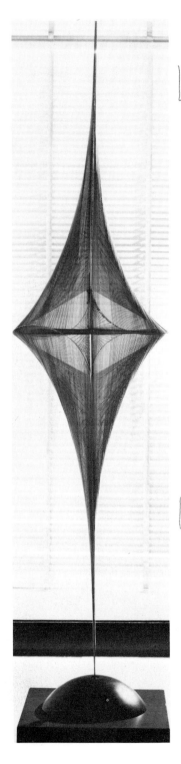

Contrary to the procedures of Gabo or Moore, the minimalist sculptors, in both their choice of materials and their method of assembling them, were intent to deny the interiority of the sculpted form—or at least to repudiate the interior of forms as a source of their significance. Their notion of what it really meant to find out "what the world's like" precluded our making any aesthetic hypotheses by which to plumb to the center of matter and metaphorically bring it to life.

Not surprisingly this stance affected the critical response of these artists to the work of their contemporaries. Writing about the sculpture of Mark di Suvero (fig. 191), for example, Donald Judd objected that "[he] uses beams as if they were brushstrokes, imitating movement, as Franz Kline did. The material never has its own movement. A beam thrusts; a piece of iron follows a gesture; together they form a naturalistic and anthropomorphic image."[3]

In the early 1960s, when Judd issued that negative judgment, most of the public for modern sculpture found the terms of his criticism highly perverse. If, they argued, meaning is not to derive from the illusion of human movement, or of human intelligence attaching itself to material through the power of the sculptor to create metaphor, then how is the work of art to transcend its status as mere stuff, as inert and meaningless matter? Isn't Judd, in his critical stance, denying to sculpture its only source of significance? Isn't he advocating that sculpture has no meaning at all? Indeed, this assumption that minimalism stood for an attack on the very possibility of art's meaningfulness formed the basis of the initial response to minimalism—both by its supporters and its detractors. The very term minimalism itself points to this idea of a reduction of art to a point of emptiness, as do the other terms such as "neo-dadaism" and "nihilism" that were used to characterize the works of these artists.[4]

Yet Judd was being neither perverse nor nihilistic in his assessment of di Suvero. He was simply looking at the work of a contemporary with an entirely new set of values in mind. In order to understand the nature of Judd's objection, and thus to become a little clearer

190. LEFT *Gabo:* Vertical
Construction and Kinetic with
Motor No. 2, *(Photo, Musées
Nationaux)*

191. BELOW *di Suvero:* Ladder
Piece, *1961–62. Wood and
steel, 75". Collection of Philip
Johnson, Connecticut. (Photo,
Rudolph Burckhardt)*

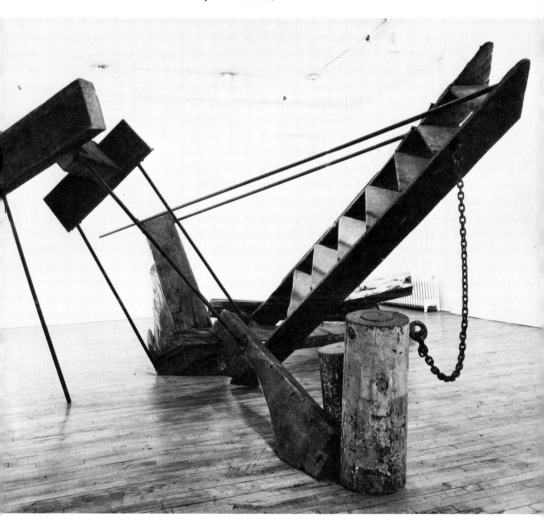

about what minimalism was working toward as the positive value of a newly conceived sculpture, it might be well to look again at what he says about di Suvero. The important key in Judd's assessment is the reference he makes to Franz Kline and the parallel he draws between Kline's slashes of black paint on a white ground and di Suvero's juxtapositions of steel and wooden beams. Judd's accusation, if spelled out, is that it is no longer possible to work with the rhetoric of Kline's art—a rhetoric identified with the American artists of the 1950s, the abstract-expressionists—for, as Judd continues, "[a] fair amount of their meaning isn't credible."[5]

The meaning that Judd is talking about as not being "credible" is a meaning that was attached to abstract-expressionism by some of its earliest supporters. Harold Rosenberg, for example, described this meaning as the transcription of an artist's inner emotions by means of a pictorial or sculptural "act." "A painting that is an act," Rosenberg wrote, "is inseparable from the biography of the artist. The painting itself is a 'moment' in the adulterated mixture of his life." Or, again, "Art . . . comes back into painting by way of psychology. As Wallace Stevens says of poetry, 'it is a process of the personality of the poet.' "[6]

In speaking this way Rosenberg is equating the painting itself with the physical body of the artist who made it. Just as the artist is made up of a physiognomic exterior and an inner psychological space, the painting consists of a material surface and an interior which opens illusionistically behind that surface. This analogy between the psychological interior of the artist and the illusionistic interior of the picture makes it possible to see the pictorial object as a metaphor for human emotions that well up from the depths of those two parallel inner spaces (fig. 192). In the case of abstract-expressionism Rosenberg sees every mark on the canvas or angled placement of steel in the context of an intense inner experience. For him, the outer surface of the work demanded that one look at it as a map on which could be read the privately held cross-currents of personality—a kind of testimony to the artist's inner, inviolable self. Because the sculpture or the picture was understood as a surrogate for the

192. *Willem De Kooning (1904–): Door to the River, 1960. Oil on canvas, 80" x 70". Collection of The Whitney Museum of American Art, New York. Gift of the Friends of The Whitney Museum of American Art. (Photo, Oliver Baker Associates)*

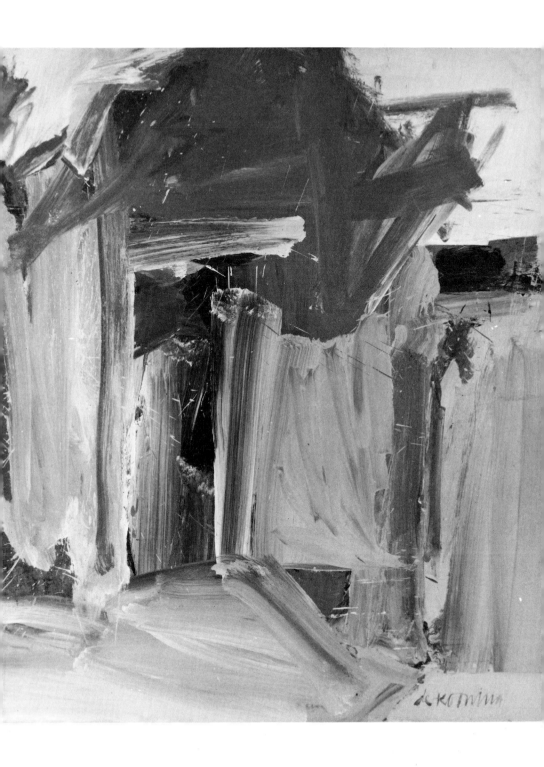

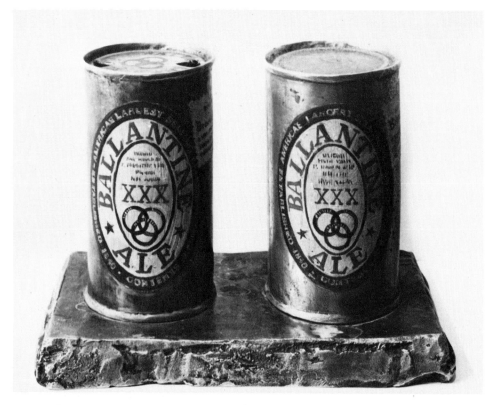

artist, who uses the language of form to report on his
experience, the meanings that were read into abstract-
expressionism depended on the analogy between the inaccessibility of illusionistic space and an intense experience
of the privacy of the individual self.

By claiming that these meanings are no longer credible,
Judd is rejecting a notion of the individual self that sup-
poses personality, emotion, and meaning as elements existing within each of us separately. As a corollary to his
rejection of this model of the self, Judd wants to repudiate
an art that bases its meanings on illusionism as a metaphor for that privileged (because private) psychological
moment.

In thinking about that attack on the credibility of an
illusionistic (or interior) model of meaning in art, it is
useful to consider the immediate sources of minimalism,
particularly the work of Jasper Johns, which developed
in the mid-1950s and constituted a radical critique of
abstract-expressionism. Sculpturally, this critique was

258

performed through such works as the 1960 Ale Cans (fig. 193) in which Johns cast two cans of Ballantine Ale in bronze and then painted their surfaces to replicate the appearance of the tin originals. In painting Johns used a similar method. In the 1955 *Target with Four Faces* (fig. 194), for example, Johns's drawing simply replicates the internal divisions of a commercially produced object; his exploitation of the design of a ready-made, flat target deprives the painting of the specific kind of suggestive illusionistic space that had infected postwar American art.

Johns's *Target* or *Ale Cans*, in negating the internality of the abstract-expressionist picture, simultaneously rejects the innerness of its space and the privacy of the self for which that space was a model. His was a rejection of an ideal space that exists prior to experience, waiting to be filled, and of a psychological model in which a self exists replete with its meanings prior to contact with its world. Johns's reading of the readymade reinforced his opposition to the whole idea of art as pure expression; his understanding of it led not toward but away from the expression of the self. Indeed, Johns saw the readymade as pointing to the fact that there need be *no* connection between a final art object and the psychological matrix from which it issued, since in the case of the readymade this possibility is precluded from the start. The *Fountain* (fig. 195), for example, was not made by Duchamp, only selected by him. Therefore, there is no way in which the urinal can "express" the artist. It is like a sentence that is put into the world unsanctioned by the voice of a speaker standing behind it. Because maker and artist are evidently separate, there is no way for the urinal to serve as the externalization of the state or states of mind of the artist as he made it. And by not functioning within the grammar of the aesthetic personality, the *Fountain* can be seen as putting distance between itself and the notion of personality *per se*.

Johns and the minimal artists insisted on making work that would refute the uniqueness, privacy, and inaccessibility of experience. In this refutation they were echoing, within the visual arts, questions that had been raised by philosophers concerned with the way verbal language

193. *Jasper Johns (1930–   ): Untitled (Ale Cans), 1960. Painted bronze, 5½" x 8" x 4¾". Collection, Dr. Peter Ludwig, New York. (Photo Rudolph Burckhardt)*

259

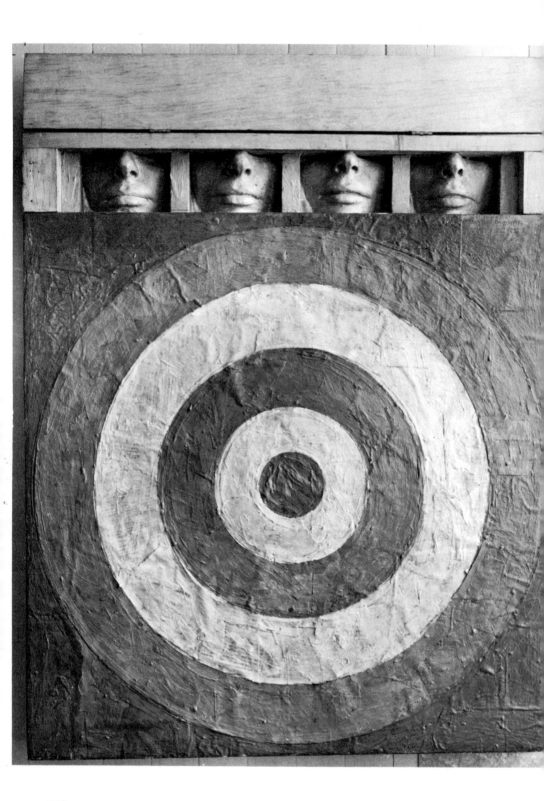

communicates internal, personal experience. The late work of Ludwig Wittgenstein, for example, questions the notion that there can be something we might call a private language—a language in which meaning is determined by the uniqueness of an individual's internal experience in such a way that, if others cannot *have* that experience, they cannot really know what a person means by the words he uses to describe it.

Focusing on the language of psychological response—the words used to describe sense-impressions, mental images, and private sensations—he asked if it were true that there could be no possible outside verification of the meaning of words we used to point to our private experience—whether meaning itself had to be hostage to that separate video of impressions registered across the screen of each individual's mental monitor. For if this were true, language would be mired in a kind of solipsism in which the "real" meaning of words would be conferred on them by each of us separately. In that sense, my "green" and my "headache" would point to what *I* see and feel, just as your "green" and your "headache" would name only

194. LEFT *Johns:* Target with Four Faces, 1955. Encaustic on newspaper over canvas, 26" x 26"—surmounted by four plaster faces. Museum of Modern Art, New York. Gift of Mr. and Mrs. Robert Scull.

195. RIGHT *Duchamp:* Fountain (second view, see fig. 58).

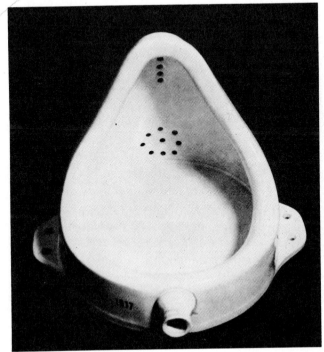

what you alone sense. Since neither of us has any way of verifying the separate data to which these words point, neither of us can verify the meanings of these words, and thus the words that operate in a public space—passing between individuals—have meaning conferred upon them from what is, in fact, a private space within each speaker.

This question of language and meaning helps us by analogy to see the positive side of minimalism's endeavor, for in refusing to give the work of art an illusionistic center or interior, minimal artists are simply re-evaluating the logic of a particular *source* of meaning rather than denying meaning to the aesthetic object altogether. They are asking that meaning be seen as arising from—to continue the analogy with language—a public, rather than a private space.

To see how this is done in a visual medium, it might be helpful to examine a pictorial example before turning to the sculpture produced by the minimalists and the artists who succeeded them in the early 1970s. The work of Frank Stella performed an important service to sculpture in showing how Johns' use of the readymade cultural object could be employed for more abstract, more wholly generalized purposes.

Die Fahne Hoch! (fig. 196) a black painting by Stella from 1959 is related to Johns's exploitation of the readymade as an externally given structure, particularly the series Johns based on the American flag. However, instead of using a known flag-pattern, Stella arrives at his own configuration by deriving a pattern of stripes from the external, physical fact of the canvas's own shape. Beginning with the midpoints of the vertical and horizontal sides, he forces the stripes into a repetitive, unbroken declaration of the expanse of the painting's four quadrants in a double set of mirror reversals. In the later aluminum paintings, where the canvases are shaped, with notches cut out of the traditional pictorial rectangle, the stripes perform a more self-evident reverberation inward from the shape of the frame, and thereby seem even more nakedly dependent upon this literal feature of the picture's support. The effect of this kind of surface, flashed continually with the sign of its edge, purges itself of illusionistic space, achieving a flatness that is an adamant

196. *Frank Stella (1936–   ): Die Fahne Hoch! 1959. Enamel on canvas, 121½" x 73". Collection, Mr. and Mrs. Eugene M. Schwartz, New York. (Photo, Rudolph Burckhardt)*

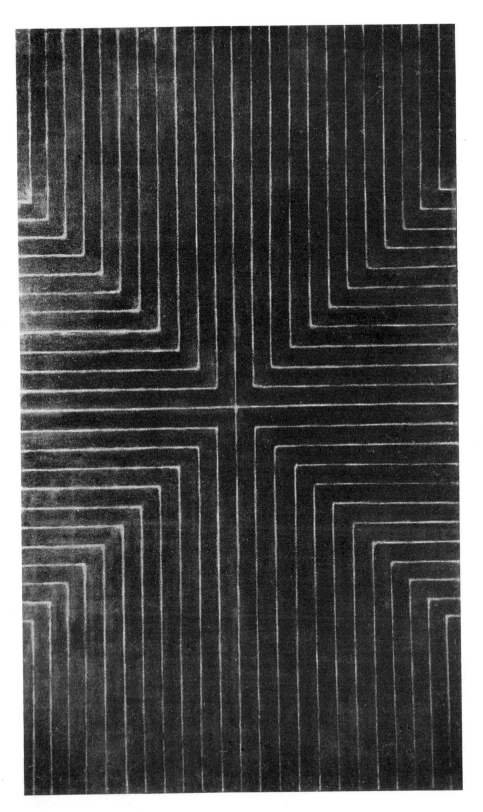

presentation of the painting's space as something external only.

But the signs that haunt Stella's early striped paintings are more than simply signifiers of their literal shapes or the flatness of their surfaces. *Die Fahne Hoch!* (like many other of Stella's canvases) arrives at a particular configuration, which is the configuration of a cross. We could call this accidental, of course, just as we could conceive it as accidental that the Cross itself relates to that most primitive sign of an object in space: the vertical of the figure projected against the horizon-line of an implicit background. But the three-way relationship that fuses along the striped surface of these pictures is a kind of argument for the logical connection between the cruciform of all pictoriality, of all intention to locate a thing

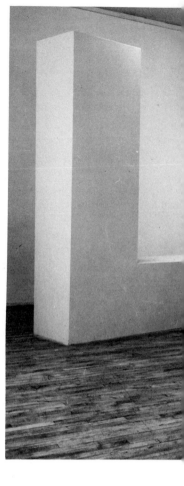

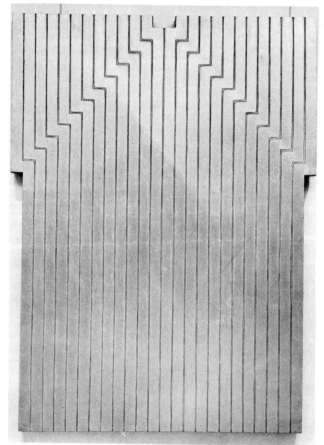

197. LEFT *Stella:* Luis Miguel Dominguin, *1960. Aluminum paint on canvas, 96" x 72". Collection, Mr. and Mrs. Burton L. Tremaine, Connecticut. (Photo, Rudolph Burckhardt)*

198. ABOVE *Morris:* Untitled (L-beams). *1965. Painted plywood, 96" x 96" x 24" (each). Collection, Philip Johnson, Connecticut. (Photo, Rudolph Burckhardt)*

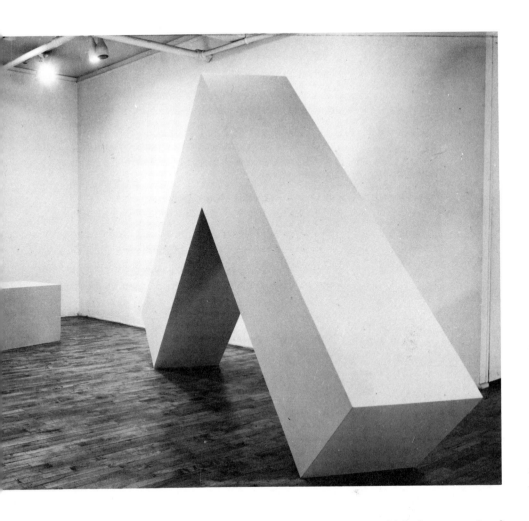

within its world, and the way in which the conventional sign—in this case the Cross—arises naturally from a referent in the world. In canvas after canvas one finds oneself in the presence of a particular emblem, drawn from the common repertory of signs—stars, crosses (fig. 197), ring-interlocks, etc.—part of a language that belongs, so to speak, to the world rather than to the private, originating capacity of Stella to invent shapes. What Stella convinces us of is an account of the initial genesis of those signs. Because in these paintings we see how they are given birth through a series of natural and logical operations.

The logic of the compositional structure is therefore shown to be inseparable from the logic of the sign. Both

[handwritten margin note: cross is part of natural world. to universal world rather than private]

265

seem to sponsor one another and in so doing ask one to grasp the natural history of pictorial language as such. The real achievement of these paintings is that they have fully immersed themselves in meaning, but still succeed in making meaning itself a function of surface—of the external, public space that is in no way a signifier of the contents of a psychologically private space. The meaning of Stella's expurgation of illusionism is unintelligible apart from this intention to lodge all meanings within the conventions of a public space.

The significance of the art that emerged in this country in the early 1960s is that it staked everything on the accuracy of a model of meaning severed from the legitimizing claims of a private self. This is the sense in which these artists understood their ambition to be tied to a new set of propositions about "what the world's like." Therefore, if we read the work of Stella, Judd, Morris, Andre, Flavin, or LeWitt merely as part of a text of formal reordering, we miss the meaning that is most central to that work.

Minimalist sculptors began with a procedure for declaring the externality of meaning. As we saw, these artists reacted against a sculptural illusionism which converts one material into the signifier for another: stone, for example, into flesh—an illusionism that withdraws the sculptural object from literal space and places it in a metaphorical one. These artists refused to use edges and planes to shape an object so that its external image would suggest an underlying principle of cohesion or order or tension. As with metaphor, the implication of this order is that it lies beyond the simple externals of the object— its shape or substance—endowing that object with a kind of intentional or private center.

This extraordinary dependence upon the facts of an object's exterior, in order to determine *what it is*, occurs in the untitled sculpture that Robert Morris made in 1965 using three large plywood Ls. In this work (fig. 198), Morris presents three identical forms in different positions relative to the ground. One L is up-ended, the second lies on its side, the third is poised on its two ends. This placement visually alters each of the forms, thickening the lower element of the first unit or bowing the sides of the third. Thus no matter how clearly we might *understand* that the three Ls are identical (in structure and dimension), it is impossible to see them as the same. Therefore, Morris seems to be saying, the "fact" of the objects' similarity belongs to a logic that exists *prior* to experience; because at the moment of experience, or *in* experience, the Ls defeat this logic and are "different." Their "sameness" belongs only to an ideal structure— an inner being that we cannot see. Their difference belongs to their exterior—to the point at which they surface into the public world of our experience. This "difference" is their sculptural meaning; and this meaning is dependent upon the connection of these shapes to the space of experience.

Insofar as sculpture is constantly forming an analogy with the human body, Morris's work addresses itself to the meaning projected by our own bodies, questioning the relationship of that meaning to the idea of psychological privacy. He is suggesting that the meanings we make—and express through our bodies and our gestures—are fully dependent on the other beings to whom we make them and on whose vision of them we depend for them to make sense. He is suggesting that the picture of the self as a contained whole (transparent only to itself and the truths which it is capable of constituting) crumbles before the act of connecting with other selves and other minds. Morris's L-beams serve as a certain kind of cognate for this naked dependence of intention and meaning upon the body as it surfaces into the world in every external particular of its movements and gestures— of the self understood, that is, only in experience.

In focusing on the work's moment of appearing within a public space, Morris defeats the way that surface in traditional sculpture is understood to be a reflection of a pre-existent, internal armature or structure. In his sectional Fiberglas sculptures of 1967, he creates a type of structure (figs. 199a, b, and c) that has no fixed internal order, for each sculpture can be (and was) continually rearranged.[7] Therefore, the notion of a rigid, internal armature that could mirror the viewer's own self—fully formed prior to experience—founders on the capacity of the separable parts to shift, to formulate a notion of the self which exists only in *that* moment of externality within *that* experience.

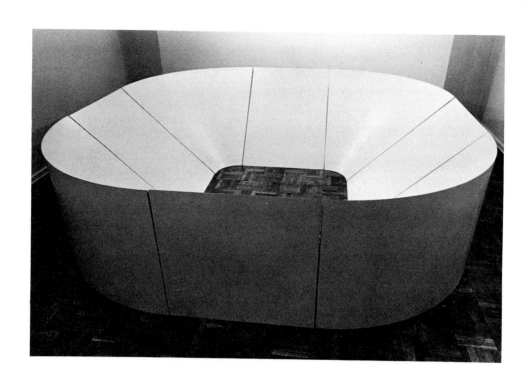

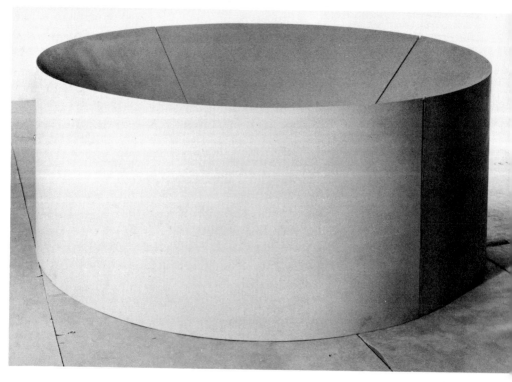

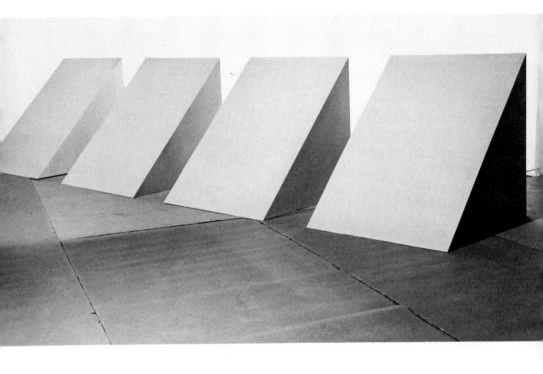

Richard Serra's *One-Ton Prop (House of Cards)* of
1969 (fig. 200) continues the protest of Morris's work
against sculpture as a metaphor for a body divided into
inside and outside, with the meaning of that body dependent upon the idea of the private, inner self. The simplicity of the sculpture's shape initially suggests the
presence of an underlying, ideal armature, for it assumes
the configuration of a cube, a form that seems to belong
to a timeless logic, rather than a moment of experience.
But Serra's aim is to defeat the very idea of this idealism
or this timelessness, and to make the sculpture visibly
dependent on each passing moment for its very existence.
To this end, Serra constructs the *House of Cards* by bal-
ancing four five-hundred-pound plates of lead against
one another, creating points of contact only at their upper corners and using no permanent means of locking
them into position. In this way, Serra creates an image
of the sculpture as something that is constantly having to
renew its structural integrity by keeping its balance. In
place of the cube as an "idea"—determined a priori—he
substitutes the cube as an existent—creating itself in time,

269

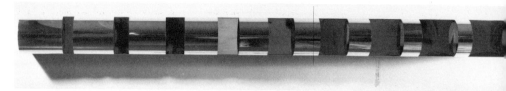

totally dependent upon the facts of its surface in tension.

With this work Serra seems to be declaring that we ourselves are like the *Prop*. We are not a set of private meanings that we can choose or not choose to make public to others. We are the sum of our visible gestures. We are as available to others as to ourselves. Our gestures are themselves formed by the public world, by its conventions, its language, the repertory of its emotions, from which we learn our own. It is no accident that the work of Morris and Serra was being made at the time when novelists in France were declaring, "I do not write. I am written."

The ambition of minimalism was, then, to relocate the origins of a sculpture's meaning to the outside, no longer modeling its structure on the privacy of psychological space but on the public, conventional nature of what might be called cultural space. To this end the minimalists employed a host of compositional strategies. One of these was to use conventional systems of ordering to determine composition. As with Stella's use of conventional signs, these systems resist being interpreted as something that wells up from within the personality of the sculptor and, by extension, from within the body of the sculptural form. Instead, the ordering system is recognized as coming from outside the work.

Judd's wall sculpture in which arithmetic progressions are used is a good example of this (fig. 201). The progression itself determines the size of the elements, which project serially, from smallest to largest, along the expanse of the sculpture. The same progression determines (but in reverse order) the size of the negative spaces between the elements. The visual interpenetration of the two progressions—one of volumes and the other of voids —itself becomes a metaphor for the dependence of the sculpture on the conditions of external space, for it is impossible to determine whether it is the positive volume of

200. RIGHT *Serra:* One-Ton Prop (House of Cards), *1969. Lead, 48" x 60" x 60". Whitney Museum of American Art, New York. (Photo, Peter Moore)*

201. ABOVE *Judd:* Untitled, *1970. Copper, 5" x 69" x 8¾". Leo Castelli Gallery, New York. (Photo, Eric Pollitzer)*

the work that brings the intervals into being, or whether it is the rhythm of the intervals that establishes the contours of the work. In this way Judd is depicting the reciprocity between the integral body of the sculpture and the cultural space that surrounds it. The systems of permutation that Sol LeWitt (figs. 202a and 202b) explored in his sculpture of the 1960s are another instance of this strategy to externalize the meaning of the work.

For Carl Andre, divesting sculpture of the implications of an internal space was not only a matter of additive composition but involved exploiting the real weight of materials as well. Confronted by one of Andre's "rugs," in which plates of differing metals are laid edge to edge to form flat, extended squares that rest directly on the floor (fig. 203), the viewer comes to feel that internal space is literally being squeezed out of the sculptural object. The strategy of this work is to make weight a function of material even while the materials themselves

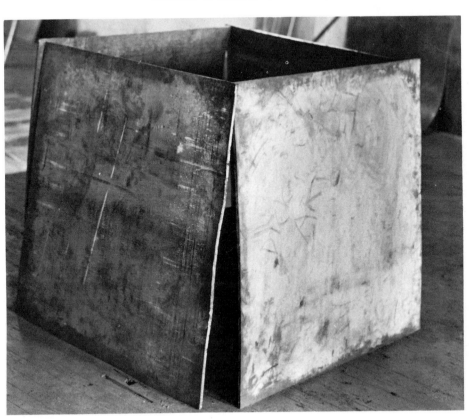

seem paradoxically to be stripped of mass. The flatness of the rugs leave these sculptures with no sense of depth or thickness, and therefore with no appearance of inside or center.[8] Rather, they seem to be coextensive with the very floor on which the viewer stands. Yet the difference that reads from plate to plate is a difference in the color and the reflectivity of the separate metals, so that what one sees in the works is the registration of material as a kind of absolute. The quality of specific weight, of differing pressures with which each metal plate pushes against the floor, presses illusionistic space out of the sculpture.

Generative for much that was important to younger artists, Andre's work touched off speculation about sculptural composition that would be neither relational nor "one thing after another," in a potentially endless chain. Instead, the properties inherent to a specific material could be used to compose the work, as though what was being tapped was nature as a readymade, instead of some aspect of culture. This work, which came to be known as process art, of which Eva Hesse was a major proponent (fig. 204), was interested in the principle of transformation as the observable logic of the work.[9] The kinds of transformation that were employed were mainly those that cultures use to incorporate the raw materials of nature, such as melting, in order to refine, or stacking in order to build. Working with processes of melting and rolling, or melting and molding, Hesse gives her objects an anthropological imagery, as though attention to that initial change from raw to processed brought her into a sculptural space that was itself extremely archaic.

Similarly, Serra's work with molten lead is involved with the forms created as the material solidified, although, as we saw earlier, the arrangement of the hardened waves of lead in *Casting* had less to do with the inherent properties of the metal than with the minimalist compositional device of repetition. But the stacked steel pieces Serra made later in the same year combine Andre's use of weight to force illusionism out of the work, with a use of the evident properties of material to determine from inside the sculpture where its composition ends. For Serra's 1969 *Stacked Steel Slabs* (Fig. 205) terminates

202a and 202b. *Sol LeWitt (1928–): Open Modular Cube (two views), 1966. Painted aluminum, 60" x 60" x 60". Collection, Art Gallery of Ontario, Canada. (Photo a. John D. Schiff; b. Ron Vickers Ltd.)*

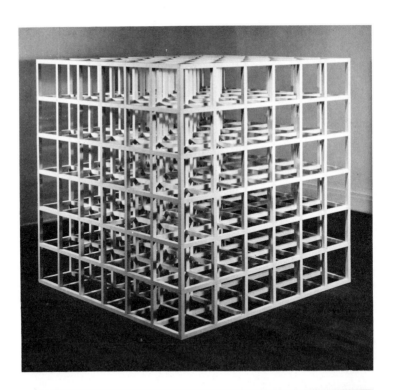

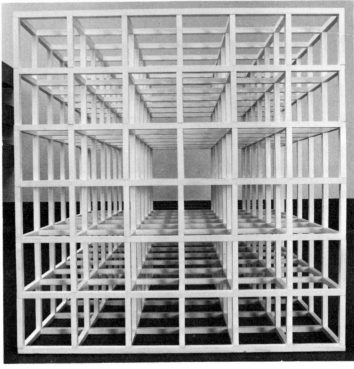

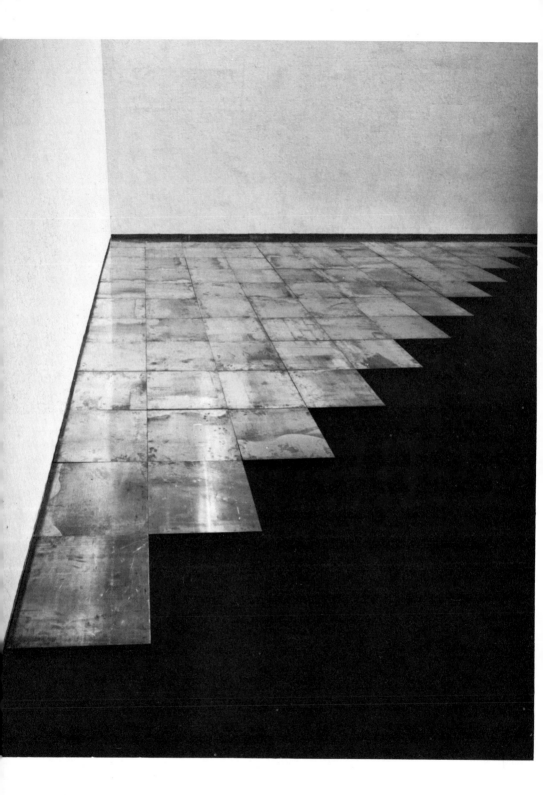

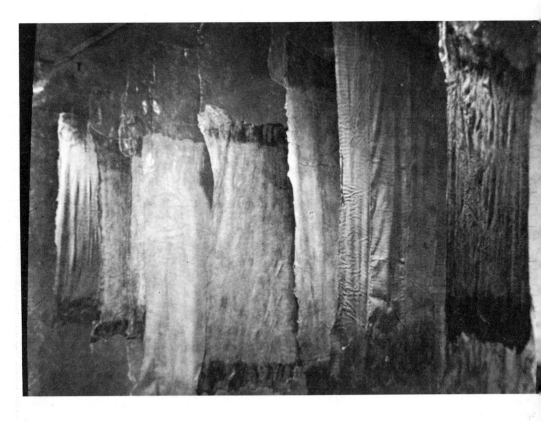

when the addition of one more to their number would unbalance and destroy the structure. In that each slab's response to gravity is the only stabilizing (and potentially destabilizing) aspect of the sculpture, Serra's work is limited to another of Andre's notions of how to make sculptural composition a function of materials: "My first problem," Andre says, "has been to find a set of particles, a set of units, and then to combine them according to laws which are particular to each particle, rather than a law which is applied to the whole set, like glue or riveting or welding."[10]

Despite their similarity of principle—the principle of nonartificial adherence of the separate units of the work—Serra's *Stacked Steel Slabs* and Andre's floor-bound pieces are grammatically distinct. Serra's work seems to inhabit the realm of the transitive verb, with its image of activity and effect, while Andre's sculpture occupies an intransitive state: materials perceived as expressions of their own being. Because of this, one encounters without

surprise a long list that Serra made for himself in 1967–68
—a working notation, the beginning of which reads:

TO ROLL
TO CREASE
TO FOLD
TO STORE
TO BEND
TO SHORTEN
TO TWIST
TO TWINE
TO DAPPLE
TO DAPPLE
TO CRUMPLE
TO SHAVE
TO TEAR
TO CHIP
TO SPLIT
TO CUT
TO SEVER
TO DROP . . .[11]

205. *Serra:* Stacked Steel Slabs, *1969. Steel, 240" x 96" x 120". Leo Castelli Gallery, New York.*

Contemplating that chain of transitive verbs, each one specifying a particular action to be performed on an unspecified material, one senses the conceptual distance that separates this from what one would normally expect to find in a sculptor's notebook. In place of an inventory of forms, Serra has substituted a list of behavioral attitudes. Yet one realizes that those verbs are themselves the generators of art forms: they are like machines which, set into motion, are capable of constructing a work. They remind one of Duchamp's admiration for Raymond Roussel's art-making machines in *Impressions of Africa,* and of Duchamp's own insistence on a speculative attitude toward the procedures of making. In this sense one can see the last direction—"to drop"—paired with a later member of Serra's list—"to grasp"—as the double-image that produced the film *Hand Catching Lead* (fig. 179).

By meditating on the action of a (visually) disembodied hand, the film explores a very particular definition of the human body throughout the three minutes of its projection. As one watches, one shares the real time of the sculptor's concentration on his task and one has a sense that during this time, the artist's body *is* that task: his very being is represented by this outward show of

276

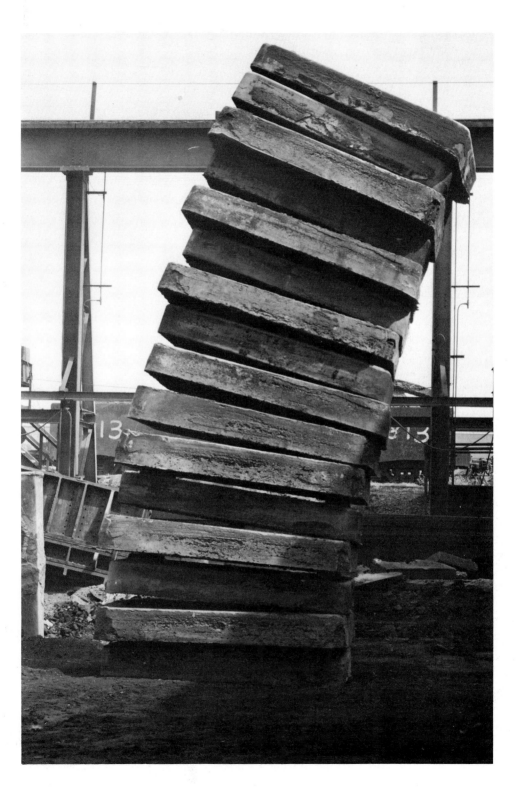

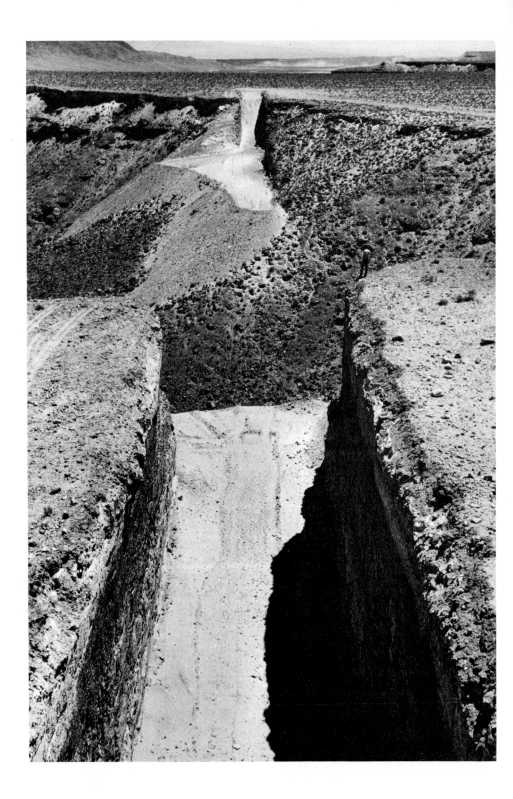

behavior contracted down to a single extremity. The time of this film is the "operation time" of the "new dance" described in Chapter 6, and its image of the body is similarly contoured by "task-performance." Like Serra's *One-Ton Prop* (or Morris's three Ls) the film presents an image of the self as something arrived at, something defined in and through experience. In severing the hand from the body, Serra's film participates as well in a lesson taught previously by Rodin and by Brancusi: the fragmentation of the body is one way of freeing the meaning of a particular gesture from a sense that it is preconditioned by the underlying structure of the body understood as a coherent whole. Though its style is very different, *Hand Catching Lead* is close in meaning to works such as the *Balzac* (fig. 25) in which Rodin visually frees the head from the pedestal of its body or the *Torso of a Young Man* (figs. 75 and 76) in which Brancusi renders the adolescent figure as a moment of pure eroticism by use of a fragment.

If I have been presenting the minimalist-based work of the last ten years as a radical development in the history of sculpture, that is because of the break it declares from the dominant styles that immediately precede it, and because of the profound abstractness of its conception.[12] But there is another level at which this work can be seen as renewing and continuing the thinking of those two crucial figures in the early history of modern sculpture: Rodin and Brancusi. The art of both men represented a relocation of the point of origin of the body's meaning—from its inner core to its surface—a radical act of decentering that would include the space to which the body appeared and the time of its appearing. What I have been arguing is that the sculpture of our own time continues this project of decentering through a vocabulary of form that is radically abstract. The abstractness of minimalism makes it less easy to recognize the human body in those works and therefore less easy to project ourselves into the space of that sculpture with all of our settled prejudices left intact. Yet our bodies and our experience of our bodies continue to be the subject of this sculpture—even when a work is made of several hundred tons of earth.

206a. *Michael Heizer (1944–): Double Negative, 1969. Mohave Desert, Nev. (Photo, Gianfranco Gorgoni)*

The *Double Negative* (figs. 206a and 206b), an earth-work sculpture by Michael Heizer, was made in 1969 in the Nevada desert. It consists of two slots, each forty feet deep and a hundred feet long, dug into the tops of two mesas, sited opposite one another and separated by a deep ravine. Because of its enormous size, and its location, the only means of experiencing this work is to be in it—to inhabit it the way we think of ourselves as inhabiting the space of our bodies. Yet the image we have of our own relation to our bodies is that we are *centered* inside them; we have knowledge of ourselves that places us, so to speak, at our own absolute core; we are wholly trans-parent to our own consciousness in a manner that seems to permit us to say, "I know what *I* think and feel but *he* does not." In this sense the *Double Negative* does not resemble the picture that we have of the way we inhabit ourselves. For, although it is symmetrical and has a center (the mid-point of the ravine separating the two slots), the center is one we cannot occupy. We can only stand in one slotted space and look across to the other. Indeed, it is only by looking at the other that we can form a picture of the space in which we stand.

By forcing on us this eccentric position relative to the center of the work, the *Double Negative* suggests an alter-native to the picture we have of how we know ourselves. It causes us to meditate on a knowledge of ourselves that is formed by looking outward toward the responses of others as they look back at us. It is a metaphor for the self as it is known through its appearance to the other.

The effect of the *Double Negative* is to declare the eccentricity of the position we occupy relative to our physical and psychological centers. But it goes even fur-ther than that. Because we must look across the ravine to see the mirror image of the space we occupy, the expanse of the ravine itself must be incorporated into the enclosure formed by the sculpture. Heizer's image therefore depicts the intervention of the outer world into the body's internal being, taking up residence there and forming its motiva-tions and its meanings.

Both the notion of eccentricity and the idea of the invasion of a world into the closed space of form re-appears in another earthwork, conceived contemporane-

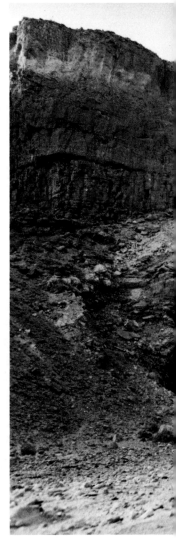

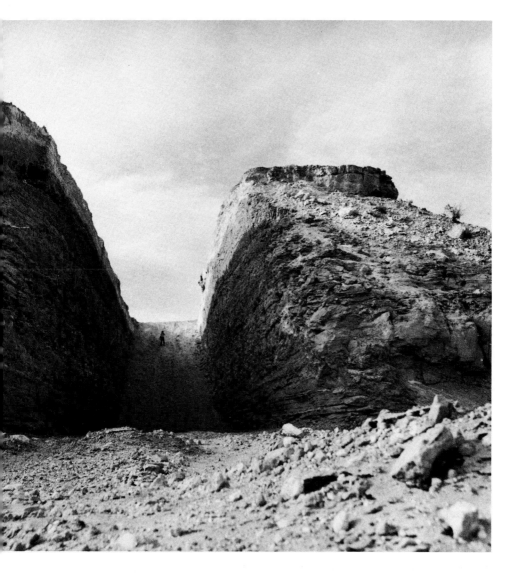

206b. *Heizer:* Double
Negative *(second view).*

ously with the *Double Negative* but executed the following year in the Great Salt Lake in Utah. Robert Smithson's *Spiral Jetty* (1970) is a heaped runway of basalt
rock and dirt, fifteen feet wide, which corkscrews fifteen
hundred feet out into the red water of the lake off Rozelle
Point (figs. 2 and 207). Like the *Double Negative*, the
Spiral Jetty is physically meant to be entered. One can
only see the work by moving along it in narrowing arcs
toward its terminus.

As a spiral this configuration does have a center which

we as spectators can actually occupy. Yet the experience of the work is one of continually being decentered within the great expanse of lake and sky. Smithson himself, in writing about his first contact with the site of this work, evokes the vertiginal response to perceiving himself as de-centered: "As I looked at the site, it reverberated out to the horizons only to suggest an immobile cyclone while flickering light made the entire landscape appear to quake. A dormant earthquake spread into an immense roundness. From that gyrating space emerged the possibility of the Spiral Jetty. No idea, no concepts, no systems, no structures, no abstractions could hold themselves together in the actuality of that phenomenological evidence."[13] *anything apprehended by senses*

The "phenomenological evidence" out of which Smithson's idea for the *Jetty* came, derived not only from the visual appearance of the lake, but also from what we might call its mythological setting, which Smithson refers to in his terms "immobile cylone" and "gyrating space." The occurrence of a huge interior salt lake had for centuries seemed to be a freak of nature, and the early inhabitants of the region sought its explanation in myth. One such myth was that the lake had originally been connected to the Pacific Ocean through a huge underground waterway, the presence of which caused treacherous whirlpools to form at the lake's center. In using the form of the spiral to imitate the settlers' mythic whirlpool, Smithson incorporates the existence of the myth into the space of the work. In doing so he expands on the nature of that external space located at our bodies' centers which had been part of the *Double Negative*'s image. Smithson creates an image of our psychological response to time and of the way we are determined to control it by the creation of historical fantasies. But the *Spiral Jetty* attempts to supplant historical formulas with the experience of a moment-to-moment passage through space and time.

Contemporary sculpture is indeed obsessed with this idea of passage. We find it in Nauman's *Corridor* (fig. 178), in Morris's *Labyrinth* (fig. 209), in Serra's *Shift* (figs. 211a and 211b), in Smithson's *Jetty*. And with these images of passage, the transformation of sculpture —from a static, idealized medium to a temporal and

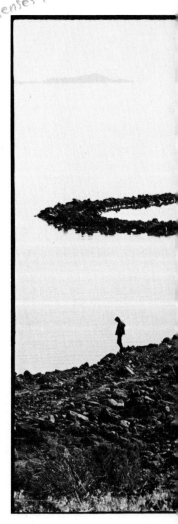

material one—that had begun with Rodin is fully achieved. In every case the image of passage serves to place both viewer and artist before the work, and the world, in an attitude of primary humility in order to encounter the deep reciprocity between himself and it.

There is nothing new in this attempt. Proust speaks of it in the incident in which the adult Marcel tastes the *madeleine* and, through the involuntary memory triggered by this object, re-experiences his childhood in Combray. Proust tells us that he had often attempted in vain to will these memories. But, he says of the voluntary

207. *Smithson:* Spiral Jetty *(second view, see fig. 2). (Photo, Gianfranco Gorgoni)*

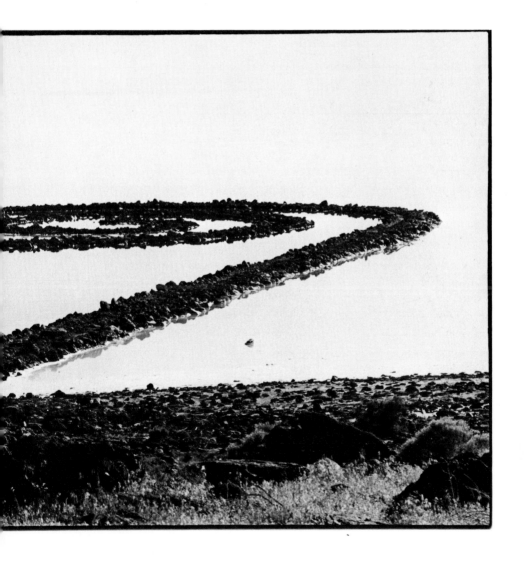

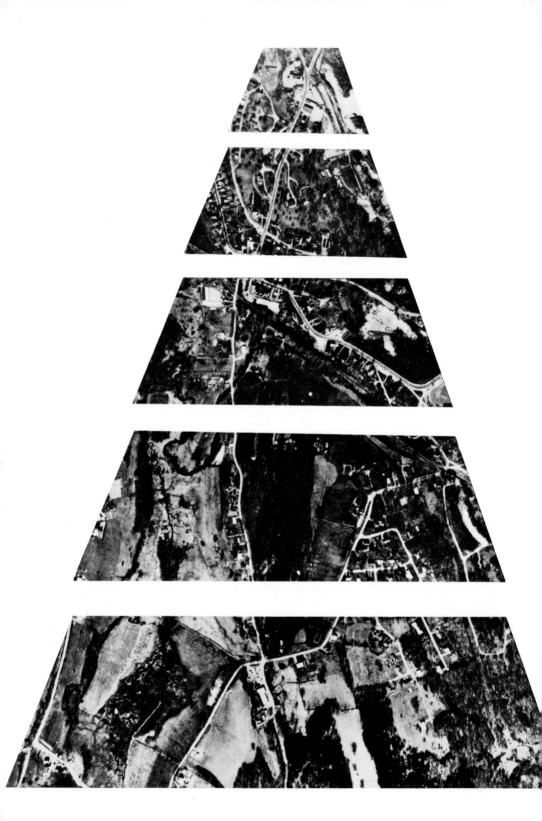

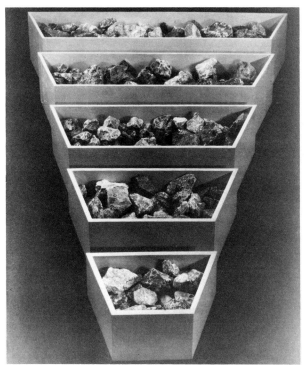

208a and **208b.** *Smithson:* A Non-Site (Franklin, New Jersey), *1968. a. Aerial map; b. Beige-painted wood bins filled with rocks, 16½" x 110" x 11". Estate of the artist. (Photos, John Weber Gallery)*

209. BELOW *Morris:* Labyrinth, *1974. Painted masonite, plywood, and two-by-fours, 96" x 360" (diameter). Institute of Contemporary Art, University of Pennsylvania, Philadelphia. (Photo, Will Brown)*

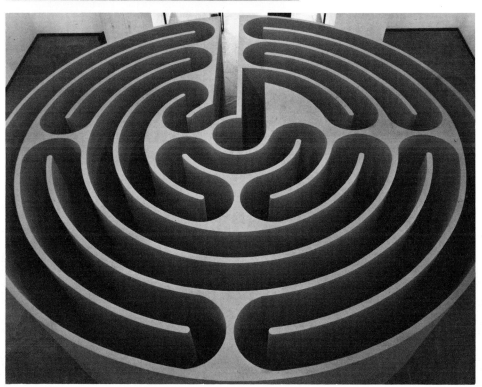

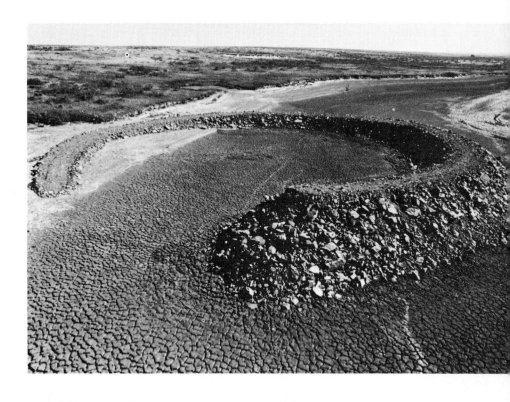

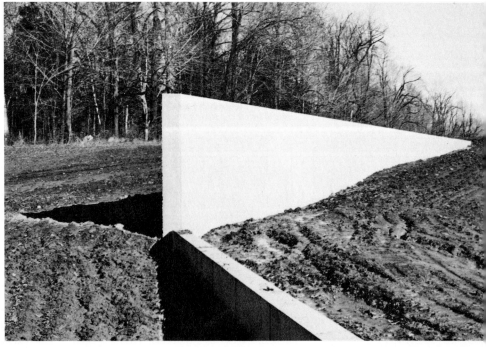

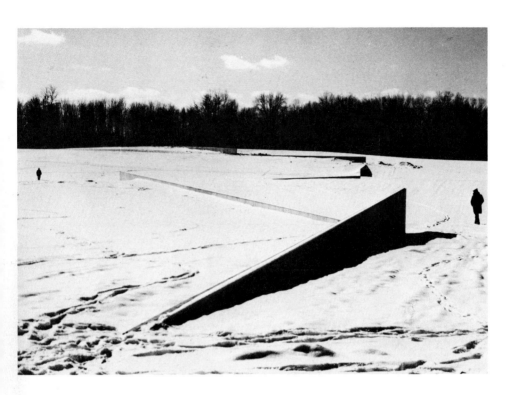

210. ABOVE LEFT *Smithson: Amarillo Ramp, 1973. Red sandstone shale, 1800" (diameter at top). Estate of the artist. (Photo, Gianfranco Gorgoni)*

211a and **211b.** *Serra: Shift (two views), 1970–72. Cement, six rectilinear sections, each 60" x 8". Collection of the artist, King City, Ontario. (Photo b., Gianfranco Gorgoni)*

memory, "it is characteristic that the information which it gives about the past retains no trace of it."[14] We might think of classical ideas of formal organization as a species of voluntary memory, in which there is "no trace" of experience as it is lived. And we might analogize the modes of cognition formulated by modern sculpture to the encounter with the *madeleine.* That sculpture asks us to experience the present in the way that Proust finds the past: "somewhere beyond the reach of the intellect, and unmistakably present in some material object (or in the sensation which such an object arouses in us), though we have no idea which one it is. As for that object, it depends entirely on chance whether we come upon it before we die, or whether we never encounter it."[15]

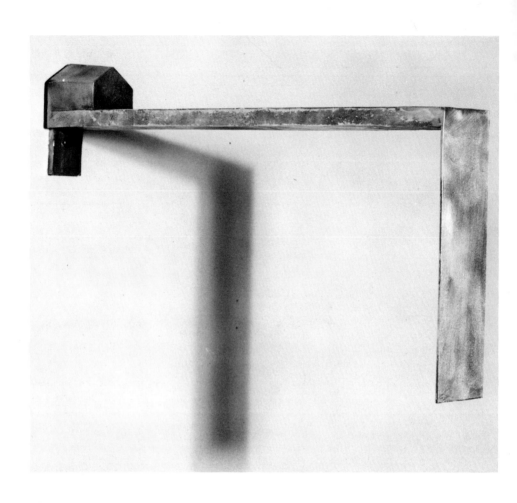

212. *Joel Shapiro (1941–):*
Untitled, *1974. Bronze, 13½" x*
27¾" x 2½". Museum of
Modern Art, New York.
(Photo, Geoffrey Clements)

notes

Introduction

1. Gotthold Lessing, *Laocoön*, tr. Ellen Frothingham (New York: Noonday, 1957).

2. Carola Giedion-Welcker, *Modern Plastic Art* (New York: Wittenborn, 1955; London: Faber, 1956).

3. Ibid., p. 9.

4. Lessing, op. cit., p. 91.

Chapter 1   Narrative Time: the question of the *Gates of Hell*

1. In *The Dialogues Concerning Natural Religion*, David Hume has one of the speakers rehearse this argument:

   Look around the world: contemplate the whole and every part of it: you will find it to be nothing but one great machine, subdivided into an infinite number of lesser machines . . . All of these various machines, and even their most minute parts, are adjusted to each other with an accuracy, which ravishes into admiration all men who have ever contemplated them. The curious adapting of means to ends, throughout all nature, resembles exactly, though it much exceeds, the productions of human contrivance; of human design, thought, wisdom, and intelligence. Since therefore the effects resemble each other, we are led to infer, by all the rules of analogy, that the cases also resemble; and that the Author of Nature is somewhat similar to the mind of men; though possessed of much larger faculties, proportioned to the grandeur of the work, which he has executed . . . The most agreeable reflection, which it is possible for human imagination to suggest, is that of genuine theism, which represents us as the workmanship of a Being perfectly good, wise, and powerful; who created us for happiness, and who, having implanted in us immeasurable desires for good, will prolong our existence to all eternity. David Hume, *The Philosophical Works*, Vol. II, ed. Thomas Hill Green (Darmstadt: Scientia Verlag Aalen, 1964), p. 392.

2. Eisenstein writes specifically about his use of sculpture in *October* as a way of denoting and then examining particular concepts of religion or history. In analyzing the sequence of statues employed in the section of the film called "In the Name of God and Country," Eisenstein says, "A chain of images attempted to achieve a purely intellectual resolution, resulting from a conflict between a preconception and *a gradual discrediting of it in purposeful steps.*" See Sergei Eisenstein, *Film Form*, tr. Jay Leyda (New York: Meridian, 1957), p. 62.

3. Lessing, op. cit., p. 92.

4. Adolf von Hildebrand, *The Problem of Form* (New York: Stechart, 1907), p. 95.

5. The Ministry of Fine Arts had planned to construct a museum of decorative arts in Paris that was to have been financed by a state lottery. The Undersecretary of the Ministry, Edmond Turquet, had become personally involved with Rodin's work in the years just prior to 1880, when the plans for the museum were consolidated. Turquet had headed an investigative committee that had been convened at the young sculptor's request to clear his 1877 *Age of Bronze* from accusations that it had been cast from life. Turquet's committee vindicated Rodin and then bought the sculpture, which was installed in the Luxembourg Gardens in 1880. That year Rodin received his first official honor from the Salon: a third-prize medal for his *St. John*. Soon afterward Rodin and Turquet met. When Rodin learned of the possibility of the commission for the sculptural portal, he asked Turquet to intercede on his behalf. The commission, granted to Rodin in 1880, brought him an initial fee of 8000 francs and, more important, a free

studio which the government provided for the task. This large space in the State marble deposit was the first large, heated work space Rodin had ever had.

6. Leo Steinberg's essay on Rodin details this use of doubling and tripling of figures in the section headed "Multiplication." I am particularly indebted to that and to a further section entitled "Sculpture Itself," for the argument that is developed here. Professor Steinberg's essay is reprinted in *Other Criteria* (New York: Oxford, 1972), pp. 322–403.

7. What can be seen in the *Mother and Child Sleeping* (1883) is also apparent in *Flesh of Others* from the same year and in *The Golden Age* (1886). In both these works cast shadow is a datum of the sculptural whole. Although to my knowledge there is no photograph of *Mother and Child Sleeping* taken by the sculptor himself, there exist several original photographs of the two other sculptures from Rosso's own hand. (See Mino Borghi, *Medardo Rosso* [Milan: Edizioni del Milione, 1950], Plates 11, 14, and 15.) These photographs emphasize to an even greater extent that the function of the internal cast shadow was to gesture toward the unseeable sides of objects. In her monograph, Margaret S. Barr notes that "Rosso insisted that his sculpture be reproduced only from photographs taken by himself because he felt that his impressions should be seen in one light and at one angle. . . ." (*Medardo Rosso* [New York: Museum of Modern Art, 1963], p. 46.)

8. The title of this work is taken from the first line of "La Beauté," a poem in Baudelaire's *Les Fleurs du mal* (1857): "Je suis belle, ô mortels! Comme un rêve de pierre."

9. See Edmund Husserl, "The transcendental problems of intersubjectivity and the intersubjective world," *Formal and Transcendental Logic*, tr. Dorion Cairns

(The Hague: Martinus Nijhoff, 1969), pp. 237–43; also Edmund Husserl, *Ideas*, tr. W. R. Boyce Gibson (New York: Macmillan, 1962), p. 94.

10. Steinberg, op. cit., 385 ff.

11. Rainer Maria Rilke, *Rodin*, tr. Jessie Lemont & Hans Transil (London: Grey Wall Press, 1946), p. 58.

12. Rosso's *The Kiss on the Tomb* (1886) joins with much of nineteenth-century funerary sculpture in its quality of theatricalized narrative and its dependence on the scenographic possibilities of relief. The work vividly incorporates an imagined space which, though it is unseeable, is the focus of all the elements of the sculpture. The central metaphor of the work links what is physically beyond the reach of both viewer and participant with an absolute Beyond, the space of death.

13. In his *Gauguin's Paradise Lost* (New York: Viking, 1971), Wayne Andersen has reconstructed the intricate but fragmented narratives of many of these sculptures.

Chapter 2 Analytic Space: futurism and constructivism

1. F. T. Marinetti, "The Founding and Manifesto of Futurism, 1909," reprinted in Umbro Apollonio, ed., *Futurist Manifestos* (London: Thames & Hudson, 1973; New York: Viking, 1973, p. 19).

2. Marianne W. Martin, *Futurist Art and Theory, 1909–1915* (Oxford: Clarendon Press, 1968), p. 169.

3. "Futurist Painting: Technical Manifesto 1910," *Futurist Manifestos*, op. cit., p. 28.

4. In 1912 Boccioni composed the "Technical Manifesto of Futurist Sculpture," where he salutes "the genius of Medardo Rosso . . . the only great modern sculptor who has tried to open up a whole new field of sculpture, by his representation in plastic art of the influences of the environment and the

atmospheric links which bind it to his subject," in ibid., p. 61.

5. In the "Technical Manifesto of Futurist Sculpture," Boccioni exhorted, "Destroy the literary and traditional 'dignity' of marble and bronze statues. Refuse to accept the exclusive nature of a single material in the construction of a sculptural whole. Insist that even twenty different types of materials can be used in a single work of art in order to achieve plastic movement. To mention a few examples: glass, wood, cardboard, iron, cement, hair, leather, cloth, mirrors, electric lights, etc.," ibid., p. 65.

6. Martin, op. cit., p. 105.

7. "The Program of the Productivist Group" was published in 1920. It is reprinted in *The Tradition of Constructivism*, ed. Stephen Bann (London: Thames and Hudson, 1974; New York: Viking, 1974, pp. 18–20).

8. Reprinted in *The Tradition of Constructivism*, pp. 5–11.

9. Pevsner's own sculptural production did not begin until after the 1925 removal to Paris. See Alexei Pevsner, *Naum Gabo and Antoine Pevsner: A Biographical Sketch of My Brothers* (Amsterdam: Augustin and Schoonman, 1964), p. 51.

10. The most complete account of Tatlin's work on this monument and of its reception in the USSR is in Troels Andersen, *Vladimir Tatlin* (Stockholm: Moderna Museet, 1968).

11. Jeremy Gilbert-Rolfe has analyzed the relationship between the monument and Marxist-Leninist thought in the following:

Many of the charges leveled by Soviet officialdom against the Russian avant-garde—many of whom had (like Trotsky) been associated with the Mensheviks or the left Social Revolutionaries before and during the events of October 1917—do not seem to apply to Tatlin's proposed work. Not only does one recognize it as Marxist but as, quite precisely, Marxist-Leninist. It sought to concretize Lenin's view of the party and its relationship to the world, and in this it was concerned with providing a model (in the land of the icon) for the administration of revolutionary life. The frame came from Marx, the core from Lenin, or perhaps one should say from the commitment to bureaucratic centralization that the latter had inherited from the French revolutionary thinker Blanqui.

Accordingly the general frame of the work is a spiral, but within that one encounters a hierarchy of physical movements and social functions which qualify and specify its significance in a revealing way. The spiral itself is readily grasped as a framework which incorporates within itself the notion of dialectic progression, and has been popular with artists on the left throughout the century partly for this reason. At each point on a spiral one is uniquely situated with regard to the rest, while remaining connected to a progression which proceeds towards its ultimate goal through being pushed and pulled to either side. As Brecht was to say a decade later, in describing the spiral as the "Epic" drama's chosen device, as a narrative resource the spiral constantly offers moments for reconsideration where the "linear progression"—others would say the positivism—of bourgeois drama had none. The spiral, too, imitates nature. Plants grow in spirals, and the spiral is therefore a model which allows for the identification of materialist thinking with the organic world, an identification which—as we know from his letters to Darwin—Marx cared about as much as anyone.

If (as I'm suggesting) the spiral is to be taken as history seen as a corollary of natural evolution—as a parallel current obeying laws that are ultimately analogous—then the contents of the spiral—the cube, the cone and the cylinder—continue this theme by equating the relationship between the party and the people with that of the movements of the heavenly bodies. The cube was to revolve once a day, the cone once a month, and the cylinder once a year. The ritual significance of this can hardly be ignored. In a stroke worthy of the man himself, Lenin is made to be continuous with Marx through a maneuver which identifies the party structure (or the structure of the party's relationship to its base) with the natural order at a level which precedes that to which the latter was drawn, i.e., at the level of astronomy rather than biology.

The executive was to sit suspended in the cone at the middle, poised between the slower moving deliberations of the party conferences which were to be housed in the cylinder below—input from the rank and file—and the information broadcasting station that Tatlin intended to house in the cube above—output to same. The analogy of a spider in its web is unavoidable, but locating the executive here also completes the dialectic proposed by the work as a whole. Earlier spirals also pointed to the stars, e.g., ziggurats, so that in being placed at the core of the edifice the party leadership was put in the same relationship to the structure of history (to the spiral) as a whole as it is to the administration of the day-to-day. At about the same time that Tatlin made his model, the literary critic Eichenbaum wrote, "The difference between life before and life after the revolution is that after the revolution everything is *felt*." (Unpublished manuscript.)

12. Theo van Doesburg, "Sixteen Points of a Plastic Architecture," quoted in Theodore M. Brown, *The Work of G. Rietveld Architect* (Utrecht: A. W. Bruna & Zoon, 1958), pp. 66–69.

13. Carola Giedion-Welcker, op. cit., p. 100.

Chapter 3 Forms of Readymade: Duchamp and Brancusi

1. Pierre Cabanne, *Dialogues with Marcel Duchamp* (London: Thames and Hudson, 1971; New York: Viking, 1971, p. 33).

2. Raymond Roussel, *Impressions of Africa*, tr. Lindy Foord and Rayner Heppenstall (Berkeley: University of California Press, 1967), p. 93.

3. Cabanne, op. cit., p. 24.

4. Ibid., p. 34.

5. For a discussion of Roussel's methods of writing see Rayner Heppenstall, *Raymond Roussel* (Berkeley: University of California Press, 1967). The account of this particular transformation is on page 40.

6. Ibid., p. 28.

7. Cabanne, op. cit. In discussing Duchamp's use of homophones and puns, Arturo Schwarz quotes the artist's references to Roussel and to Jean-Pierre Brisset, whose work Duchamp described as "a philological analysis of language —an analysis worked out by means of an incredible network of puns." See Schwarz, *Marcel Duchamp* (New York: Harry N. Abrams, 1969), p. 80.

8. In 1926 Duchamp used these discs, along with ones carrying graphic designs, in the film *Anemic-Cinéma* which he made in collaboration with Man Ray and Marc Allegret.

9. The sentence roughly translates as: The aspiring one lives in Javel and me I (was living) in the spiral. An amalgam of syllables, the line is symmetrical around "*et moi.*" Because the first syllable corresponds to the last, and so on inward toward the center, the sentence itself takes a spiral form.

10. In the quoted sentence there is, for example, the pun on "*l'habite*" which sounds like *la bitte*, French slang for penis. This causes the sentence to read ". . . and me, I had my penis in the spiral." In an essay on the puns in *Anemic-Cinéma*, Katrina Martin further analyzes the erotic subtext of this line: "Javel is the place where *eau de Javel*, a bleach, comes from. It can be that water itself. In slang, *blanc d'oeuf* (egg white) refers to sperm, while *eau de Javel* refers to cum. 'The aspiring one lives in Javel,' or in a woman, 'And me I had my domicile (my penis) in the spiral' seems more onanistic." (Katrina Martin, "Marcel Duchamp's Anémic-cinéma," *Studio International*, clxxxix [January 1975], pp. 53–60.)

11. The most important of these are: Robert Lebel, *Marcel Duchamp*, (Paris: Trianon Press, 1959); Arturo Schwarz, op. cit.; and Lawrence D. Steefel, Jr., "The Position of 'La Mariée mise à nu par ses célibataires, même' (1915–1923) in the Stylistic and Iconographic

Development of the Art of Marcel Duchamp" (unpublished Ph.D. dissertation, Princeton University, 1960).

12. Sidney Geist, *Brancusi* (New York: Grossman, 1967), p. 178.

13. Geist writes, "*Torment* (in plaster) was exhibited in the spring of 1907 at the Société Nationale. The refinement of the modeling may well reflect an interest in Medardo Rosso. The Italian sculptor had been one of the founders of the Salon d'Automne; in the Salon's second appearance, the exhibition of the fall of 1906 where Brancusi showed three works, Rosso had exhibited a boy's head in wax, the magical *Ecce Puer*" (ibid., pp. 22–23).

14. *The First Step*, a wooden sculpture of 1913, expressed the head of a young child through the strong central feature of an opened mouth. By 1914 this feature was imparted to *The First Cry*, a sculpture which, like the *Prometheus*, expressed the figure entirely through the fragmented head presented as the total object. In 1915 Brancusi schematized this vehicle of expression—the mouth—to a plane sliced across one end of the ovoid, thus closing off in *The Newborn* the possibility of a break in the nearly uniform surface tension of the sculptural object.

15. Geist, op. cit., p. 48.

16. Geist, ibid., p. 141.

17. Brancusi was instructed in photography by Man Ray. Photographs of his sculpture, taken by himself, were published in *Cahiers d'Art*, IV (1929), pp. 384–96.

18. See Chapter 4, p. 143.

19. Geist, op. cit., p. 59.

Chapter 4 A Game Plan: the terms of surrealism

1. Read by Tristan Tzara at Picabia's exhibition in Paris, December 1920 (this statement originally in *Littérature*, July 1920).

2. Jean Arp, *On My Way: Poetry and Essays 1912–1914* (New York: Wittenborn, 1948), p. 91.

3. Tristan Tzara, "Lecture on Dada," in Robert Motherwell, ed., *The Dada Painters and Poets* (New York: Wittenborn, 1951), pp. 246–51.

4. The *3 Standard Stoppages* (1913–14) are perhaps Duchamp's most single-minded investigation of this mode. Duchamp's working note for this object, collected in *The Green Box*, reads:

   3 Standard Stops=
         canned chance
   1914.
   the Idea of the Fabrication
       horizontal
         If a thread one meter long falls
         straight
         from a height of one meter to a
         horizontal plane
         twisting as it pleases and creates
         a new image of the unit of length.

   (*The Bride Stripped Bare by Her Bachelors, Even*, Richard Hamilton, ed., George Heard Hamilton, tr. [New York: Wittenborn, n.d.]). In his long interview with Duchamp, Pierre Cabanne refers to the fact that his major work, *The Large Glass*, was "completed" by the accident of its breakage in transit in 1925, and comments that this is an example of "the intervention of chance that you count on so often." Duchamp simply replied, "I respect it; I have ended up loving it." (Cabanne, op. cit., p. 76).

5. André Breton, *Nadja*, tr. Richard Howard (New York: Grove Press, 1960), p. 32.

6. In the first *Surrealist Manifesto*, Breton had written, "Surrealism is based on the belief in the higher reality of certain types of association previously neglected, in the omnipotence of dreams, and the free unmotivated play of the mind. It tends to undermine all

other psychic mechanisms and to take their place in the resolution of the principal problems of life" (*Manifestos of Surrealism*, Richard L. Seaver, ed., [Ann Arbor; University of Michigan Press, 1969], p. 26).

7. Breton, *L'Amour fou* (Paris: Gallimard, 1937), pp. 32–38.

8. "Entretien avec Alberto Giacometti," Georges Chardonnier, ed., 1959, cited in William Rubin, *Dada and Surrealist Art* (London: Thames and Hudson, 1969; New York: Abrams, 1971, p. 251).

9. Maurice Nadeau, *Histoire du surréalisme* (Paris: 1958), p. 176.

10. Peter Selz, *Alberto Giacometti* (New York: Museum of Modern Art, 1965), p. 20.

11. Breton, *Nadja*, p. 39.

12. In this connection Giacometti's own account of the inception and development of *The Palace at 4 A.M.* (1932–33) (fig. 83) is particularly interesting. He describes it as an image in which was encapsulated a particular relationship he had had the year before. This image formed itself for him as though in a dream—revealing itself seemingly without his own conscious design or intervention. He recalls: "This object took shape little by little in the late summer of 1932; it revealed itself to me slowly, the various parts taking their exact form and their precise place within the whole. By autumn it had attained such reality that its actual execution in space took no more than one day. It is related without any doubt to a period in my life that had come to an end a year before, when for six whole months hour after hour was passed in the company of a woman who, concentrating all life in herself, magically transformed my every moment. We used to construct a fantastic palace at night—days and nights had the same color, as if everything happened just before daybreak; throughout the whole time I never saw the sun—a very fragile palace of matchsticks..." (Selz, op. cit., p. 44). In the rest of this statement Giacometti continues to try to analyze the various contents of the *Palace*.

13. Rubin, op. cit., p. 251.

14. Annette Michelson, "Breton's Surrealism," *Artforum*, V (September 1966), p. 77.

15. From Lautréamont's long prose poem the *Chants de Maldoror*, of which Breton said: "nothing, not even Rimbaud, had up to that time [1919] affected me as much. Even today, I am absolutely incapable of coldly, analytically, examining that astonishing message which, to me, seems in every way to surpass man's potential." (*Entretiens* [Paris: Gallimard, 1952], p. 42).

16. The sculpture that most prefigured the openness and linearity of Gonzalez' and Picasso's welded sculpture of the 1930s was the series of "transparencies" that Lipchitz concentrated on in the mid-1920s. In some of these works, which are of cast bronze, Lipchitz achieves that sense of spontaneity in handling and of linearity that seems only possible through direct welding. During the late teens and twenties much of Constructivist sculpture pointed in this direction, but with rare exceptions the works were not executed in metal.

17. Andrew C. Ritchie, *Julio Gonzalez* (New York: Museum of Modern Art, 1956), p. 42.

18. The "Exposition Surréaliste d'Objets" was held at the Charles Ratton Gallery in Paris during the last week in May 1936. The exhibition was announced as containing: "*objets mathématiques, objets naturels, objets sauvages, objets trouvés, objets irrationnels, objets ready-made, objets interprétés, objets incorporés,* and *objets mobiles.*" That the Ratton Gallery should have been the context for this exhibition is interesting since M. Ratton was mainly a dealer in primitive art. On the occasion

of this demonstration of the *"objet surréaliste à fonctionnement symbolique,"* Breton published his important essay "Crisis of the Object," *Cahiers d'Art*, VI (1936), 21–26. See also Salvador Dali, "Objets Surréalistes" and Alberto Giacometti, "Objets Mobiles et muets," both in *Le Surréalisme au Service de la Révolution*, no. 3 (1930), pp. 16–19.

19. See Annabelle Henkin Melzer, "The Dada Actor and Performance Theory," *Artforum*, XII (December 1973), pp. 51–57.

20. Herbert Read, *Art of Jean Arp* (London: Thames and Hudson, 1968; New York: Abrams, 1968, pp. 38–39).

21. James T. Soby, *Arp* (New York: Museum of Modern Art, 1958), pp. 14–15.

22. For a discussion of the relationship between vitalism and early-twentieth-century sculpture, see Jack Burnham, *Beyond Modern Sculpture* (New York: George Braziller, n.d.).

23. J. L. Martin, Ben Nicholson, and Naum Gabo, eds., *Circle* (London: Faber, 1937), p. 113.

24. Herbert Read, *Henry Moore, Sculptor* (London: Zwemmer, 1934), p. 29.

25. ———, *The Art of Sculpture* (New York: Pantheon, 1956), p. 74.

Chapter 5   *Tanktotem*: welded images

1. For a more detailed discussion of Smith's work see Rosalind Krauss, *Terminal Iron Works: The Sculpture of David Smith* (Cambridge: MIT Press, 1971).

2. In the early 1950s, Smith embodied this theme in works such as *Sacrifice* (1950) and *Cathedral* (1951).

3. Clement Greenberg wrote that "Smith returned periodically to the scheme— not so much the forms or contours—of the human figure as though to a base of operations." However, Greenberg viewed much of the late work as escap-

ing direct figurative reference. Of the 1961 *Zig IV*, Greenberg said, "In it he escapes entirely from the allusions to the natural world (which includes man) that abound elsewhere in his art." (See Greenberg, "David Smith," *Art in America*, LIV (January–February 1966), p. 32 and p. 28, respectively. Yet *Zig IV* is as referential as anything else in Smith's oeuvre. It extends yet another theme that grew within his art over a period of three decades: the theme of the phallic cannon.

4. Elaine de Kooning, "David Smith Makes a Sculpture," *Art News*, L (September 1951), p. 40.

5. *Art Journal*, XXXV (Winter 1975), p. 127.

6. Michael Fried, *Anthony Caro* (London: The Arts Council, Hayward Gallery, 1969), p. 5.

7. Phyllis Tuchman, "An Interview with Anthony Caro," *Artforum*, X (June 1972), p. 56.

8. Richard Wollheim, "Minimal Art," *Arts Magazine* (January 1956). Reprinted in Gregory Battcock, ed., *Minimal Art* (London: Studio Vista, 1969; New York: Dutton, 1968, p. 387).

9. This argument was given its first and fullest presentation by Michael Fried in 1967. See Michael Fried, "Art and Objecthood," *Artforum*, V (Summer 1967), pp. 12–23; reprinted in *Minimal Art*, op. cit.

10. Ibid., p. 22.

Chapter 6   Mechanical Ballets: light, motion, theater

1. This was for a series of seven-minute performances organized by the composer LaMonte Young at the Living Theater in 1961.

2. Michael Fried, "Art and Objecthood," op. cit., p. 31.

3. Clement Greenberg, the major contemporary spokesman for this position as it applies to the visual arts, stated it

most clearly when he wrote, "The essence of Modernism lies, as I see it, in the use of the characteristic methods of a discipline to criticize the discipline itself—not in order to subvert it, but to entrench it more firmly in its area of competence. . . . Each art had to determine, through the operation peculiar to itself, the effect peculiar and exclusive to itself. . . . It quickly emerged that the unique and proper area of competence of each art coincided with all that was unique to the nature of its medium. The task of self-criticism became to eliminate from the effects of each art any and every effect that might conceivably be borrowed from or by the medium of any other art," "Modernist Painting," *Arts Yearbook 4* (1963); reprinted in Gregory Battcock, ed., *The New Art* (New York: Dutton, 1966), pp. 101–102.

4. Fried, "Art and Objecthood," p. 31.

5. Jack Burnham, op. cit., p. 185.

6. Ibid.

7. Ibid., p. 314.

8. This is the argument of Noam Chomsky's *American Power and the New Mandarins* (New York: Pantheon, 1967), particularly the chapter entitled "Objectivity and Liberal Scholarship."

9. Antonin Artaud, *The Theatre and Its Double* (New York: Grove Press, 1958), p. 92. Artaud adds, "With an element of cruelty at the root of every spectacle, the theatre is now possible. In our present state of degeneration it is through the skin that metaphysics must be made to re-enter our minds."

10. Burnham, op. cit., p. 341.

11. The "New Tendency" is a term used to refer to a pan-European sensibility that self-consciously identified itself with the values of science and technology. It gathered force in the late 1950s and early 1960s and was represented by various national groups. In Germany Group Zero was led by Otto Piene,

Heinz Mack, and Günther Uecker. In France the Groupe de Recherche d'Art Visuel (or GRAV) included Julio Le Parc and François Morellet, among others, with strong connections to Vasarely and Schöffer. In Italy similar collectives were formed in the early 1960s: Group N in Padua and Group T in Milan. The Dutch arm of this movement called itself NUL. The independent artists who have contributed to new tendency exhibitions include Pol Bury, Yaacov Agam, Bruno Munari, Piero Dorazio, Luis Tomasello, Dieter Rot, and Yayoi Kusama. (See Burnham, op. cit., pp. 238–62). The New Tendency attracted adherents in Eastern Europe—Yugoslavia and Poland. The first New Tendency exhibition at Zagreb, in 1961, was organized by a young Marxist critic, Matko Mestrovic. (See Donald Drew Egbert, *Social Radicalism and the Arts* [New York: Alfred A. Knopf, 1970], pp. 371ff.)

12. Statement in "What Abstract Art Means to Me," *The Bulletin of the Museum of Modern Art*, XVIII (Spring 1958), p. 8.

13. *Calder, an Autobiography with Pictures* (London: Allen Lane, 1967; New York: Pantheon, 1966, pp. 126–27).

14. Burnham, op. cit., p. 270.

15. Peter Selz, *Directions in Kinetic Sculpture* (Berkeley, Calif.: University Art Gallery, March–May 1966), p. 27.

16. Burnham, op. cit., pp. 272–73.

17. See Chapter 4, pp. 109–117.

18. See Chapter 1, pp. 26–28.

19. While there were many contributors to happenings, perhaps the five most central figures were Jim Dine, Red Grooms, Allan Kaprow, Claes Oldenburg, and Robert Whitman. See Michael Kirby, *Happenings* (New York: Dutton, 1965).

20. Susan Sontag, *Against Interpretation* (London: Eyre, 1967; New York: Farrar, Straus & Giroux, 1967, p. 273).

21. Ibid., p. 265.

22. Ibid., p. 266.

23. For instance, in Kaprow's *Untitled Happening*, March 1962, a naked woman lies motionless throughout the performance on a ladder suspended above the action.

24. Sontag, op. cit., p. 268.

25. Annette Michelson, "Yvonne Rainer," *Artforum*, XII (January 1974), p. 58.

26. In July 1962 the first public performances were held of a group of dancers who had studied at Merce Cunningham's studio primarily under the tutelage of Robert Dunn. These include Yvonne Rainer, Simone Forti, Trisha Brown, Deborah Hay, and Steve Paxton. Some of the contributions were made by performers not trained as dancers such as Robert Morris, Robert Rauschenberg, and Alex Hay. See Don McDonagh, "Notes on Recent Dance," *Artforum*, XI (December 1972), pp. 48–52.

27. In describing her work, *The Mind is a Muscle, Trio A*, Yvonne Rainer writes: "What is seen is a control that seems geared to the *actual* time it takes the *actual* weight of the body to go through the prescribed motion, rather than an adherence to an imposed ordering of time. In other words, the demands made on the body's (actual) energy resources *appear* to be commensurate with the task—be it getting up from the floor, raising an arm, tilting the pelvis, etc.— much as one would get out of a chair, reach for a high shelf, or walk downstairs when one is not in a hurry. The movements are not mimetic, so they do not remind one of such actions, but I like to think that in their manner of execution they have the factual quality of such actions." Yvonne Rainer, "A Quasi Survey of Some 'Minimalist' Tendencies in the Quantitatively Minimal Dance Activity Midst the Plethora, or an Analysis of Trio A," Battcock, ed., *Minimal Art*, p. 270.

28. In the same essay Rainer writes, "The artifice of performance has been reevaluated in that action, or what one does, is more interesting and important than the exhibition of character and attitude, and that action can best be focused on through the submerging of the personality; so ideally one is not even oneself, one is a neutral 'doer.'" Ibid., p. 267.

29. The sculptors who have conventionally been grouped under this name are Carl Andre, Richard Artschwager, Larry Bell, Ronald Bladen, Walter De Maria, Robert Grossner, Donald Judd, Sol Lewitt, James McCracken, Robert Morris, Tony Smith, and Robert Smithson. Although they do not consider their work to be sculpture, Dan Flavin and Robert Irwin are also included.

30. For the performance of *Site* (1963) Morris wore a mask of his own face molded for him by Jasper Johns (fig. 177). Because in this work Morris had to lift and carry heavy sheets of plywood, he used the mask so that the viewer could not see the expressions of strain, exertion or fatigue that might register on his face.

31. Marcia Tucker, *Robert Morris* (New York: Whitney Museum, 1970), p. 25.

32. Maurice Merleau-Ponty, *Phenomenology of Perception* (London: Routledge & Kegan Paul, 1962), p. 5.

33. Ibid., p. xii.

Chapter 7   The *Double Negative*: a new syntax for sculpture

1. Donald Judd, "Specific Objects," *Arts Yearbook 8* (1965), p. 82.

2. Bruce Glaser, "Questions to Stella and Judd," in Battcock, op. cit., p. 149.

3. Judd, "Specific Objects," p. 78.

4. "Nihilism" was the term Barbara Rose used in one of the first attempts to characterize the general intentions of the minimal artists. See, "A B C Art,"

in Battcock, op. cit., reprinted from *Art in America* (October 1965).

5. Judd, "Specific Objects," p. 78.

6. Harold Rosenberg, "The American Action Painters," *The Tradition of the New*, (New York: Horizon Press) p. 27. Reprinted from *Art News*, LI (December 1952).

7. When they were exhibited in 1967, Morris himself rearranged the sculptures each day to form new configurations.

8. The sense here that Andre's works exist completely at their surface, that depth or interior has been expelled, is analogous to the flatness that Stella achieves in his striped canvases.

9. Robert Morris's essay, "Some Notes on the Phenomenology of Making," discusses the importance of finding the form of a work through the procedures of its making. He writes:

   What is particular to Donatello and shared by many 20th-century artists is that some part of the systematic making process has been automated. The employment of gravity and a kind of "controlled chance" has been shared by many since Donatello in the materials/process interaction. However it is employed, the automation serves to remove taste and the personal touch by coopting forces, images, processes, to replace a step formerly taken in a directing or deciding way by the artist. Such moves are innovative and are located in prior means but are revealed in the *a posteriori* images as information. Whether this is draping wax-soaked cloth to replace modeling [as in Donatello's *Judith and Holofernes*], identifying prior "found" flat images with the totality of a painting, employing chance in an endless number of ways to structure relationships, constructing rather than arranging, allowing gravity to shape or complete some phase of the work—all such diverse methods involve what can only be called automation and imply the process of making back from the finished work. (*Artforum*, VIII [April 1970], p. 65.

10. Carl Andre, "Interview," *Artforum*, VIII (June 1970), p. 55.

11. The entire list is reprinted in Gregoire Müller, *The New Avant-Garde* (London: Pall Mall, 1972; New York: Praeger, 1973, unpaged).

12. I have been treating the sculptural movement that begins roughly in 1964 and continues to the present as the manifestation of a single sensibility, which for simplicity's sake I am calling minimalism. The critical writing of Robert Pincus-Witten, which forms one of the earliest coherent and important responses to the younger members of this movement, was careful to differentiate work done after 1969 from work made prior to that date. To this end he used the term "Post-Minimalism" to distinguish the more pictorial handling of material in, say, Serra's cast lead pieces or Hesse's latex hangings from the severity of early Morris or Judd. "Post-Minimalism" also referred to the more overtly theoretical cast of the post-1969 work of LeWitt and to younger artists like Mel Bochner or Dorothea Rockburne. See, "Eva Hesse: Post-Minimalism into Sublime," *Artforum*, X (November 1971); "Bruce Nauman: Another Kind of Reasoning," *Artforum*, X (February 1972); "Mel Bochner: The Constant as Variable," *Artforum*, XI (December 1972); "Sol LeWitt: Word ⟷ Object," *Artforum*, XI (February 1973).

13. Robert Smithson, "The Spiral Jetty," unpublished manuscript.

14. Walter Benjamin says this in describing Proust's writing as a major source for Bergson's attempt to "lay hold of the 'true' experience as opposed to the kind that manifests itself in the standardized, denatured life of the civilized masses." In *Illuminations* (New York: Harcourt, 1969), p. 158.

15. Marcel Proust, *Swann's Way*, tr. C. K. Scott-Moncrieff (London: Chatto, 1929; New York: Random House, 1928, p. 61).

bibliography

Andre, Carl
  Carl Andre, Sculpture 1958–1974. Berne: The
    Kunsthalle, 1975.
  Waldman, Diane. *Carl Andre.* New York: The
    Solomon R. Guggenheim Museum, 1970.
Arp, Jean
  Giedion-Welcker, Carola. *Jean Arp.* New
    York: Abrams, 1957.
  Jean, Marcel, ed. *Arp on Arp.* New York:
    Viking, 1972.
  Read, Sir Herbert. *The Art of Jean Arp.* New
    York: Abrams, 1968.
  Soby, James Thrall, ed. *Arp.* New York: The
    Museum of Modern Art, 1958.
Bill, Max
  Max Bill, Oeuvres 1928–1969. Paris: Centre
    National d'Art Contemporain (CNAC), 1969.
  Staber, Margit. "Max Bill." *Art International,*
    X (May 1966), 25–31.
Boccioni, Umberto
  Golding, John. *Boccioni's Unique Forms of
    Continuity in Space.* Newcastle upon Tyne:
    University of Newcastle upon Tyne, 1972.
  Martin, Marianne W. *Futurist Art and
    Theory, 1909–1915.* Oxford: Oxford Univer-
    sity Press, 1968.
Bochner, Mel
  Richardson, Brenda. *Mel Bochner.* Baltimore:
    Baltimore Museum of Art, 1976.
Bourgeois, Louise
  Lippard, Lucy R. "Louise Bourgeois." *Art-
    forum,* XIII (March 1975), 26–33.
  Robbins, Daniel. "Sculpture by Louise
    Bourgeois." *Art International,* VIII (October
    1964), 29–31.
Brancusi, Constantin
  Geist, Sidney. *Brancusi.* New York: Grossman,
    1968.
  Giedion-Welcker, Carola. *Constantin Brancusi.*
    New York: Braziller, 1959.
  Lewis, David. *Brancusi.* New York: Witten-
    born, 1957.
  Paleolog, V. G. C. *Brancusi.* Bucharest, 1947.
  Pound, Ezra. "Brancusi." *The Little Review*
    (Autumn 1921), 3–7.
Bury, Pol
  Ashton, Dore. *Pol Bury.* Paris: Maeght
    Editeur, 1970.
  Pol Bury. Berkeley: University of California
    at Berkeley Art Museum, 1970.
Calder, Alexander
  Arnason, H. H. *Calder.* New York: Van
    Nostrand, 1966; and London: Studio Vista,
    1966.
  Calder, Alexander. "Statement." *Tiger's Eye,*
    no. 4 (June 1948), 74.
  ———. "What Abstract Art Means to Me."
    Museum of Modern Art Bulletin, XVIII
    (Spring 1951), 8–9.
  Lipman, Jean. *Calder's Universe.* New York:
    Viking, 1976; and London: Thames & Hud-
    son, 1977.

Sartre, Jean-Paul. "Existentialist on Mobilist;
    Calder's Newest Works Judged by France's
    Newest Philosopher." *Art News.* XLVI
    (December 1947), 22–23, 55–56.
  Sweeney, James Johnson. *Alexander Calder.*
    New York: The Museum of Modern Art,
    1951.
Chamberlain, John
  Waldman, Diane. *John Chamberlain.* New
    York: The Solomon R. Guggenheim Museum,
    1971.
Cornell, Joseph
  Ashton, Dore. *A Joseph Cornell Album.* New
    York: Viking, 1974.
  Levy, Julien. *Surrealism.* New York: The
    Black Sun Press, 1936 (includes "Monsieur
    Phot," a scenario by Joseph Cornell, pp.
    77–88).
  Michelson, Annette. "Rose Hobart and
    Monsieur Phot: Early Films from Utopia
    Parkway." *Artforum,* XI (June 1973), 47–57.
  Waldman, Diane. *Joseph Cornell.* New York:
    The Solomon R. Guggenheim Museum, 1967.
Di Suvero, Mark
  Monte, James. *Di Suvero.* New York: The
    Whitney Museum of American Art, 1975.
Duchamp, Marcel
  Duchamp, Marcel, ed. Sanouillet, Michel, and
    Peterson, Elmer. *Salt Seller.* New York:
    Oxford University Press, 1973.
  d'Harnoncourt, Anne, and McShine, Kynaston,
    ed. *Marcel Duchamp.* New York: The
    Museum of Modern Art, 1973.
  Lebel, Robert. *Marcel Duchamp.* New York:
    Grove Press, 1959.
  Schwarz, Arturo. *The Complete Works of
    Marcel Duchamp.* New York: Abrams, 1969;
    London: Thames & Hudson, 1969.
Eakins, Thomas
  Goodrich, Lloyd. *Thomas Eakins, His Life
    and Work.* New York: The Whitney Museum
    of American Art, 1933.
  Hendricks, Gordon. *The Life and Works of
    Thomas Eakins.* New York: Grossman, 1974.
  Porter, Fairfield. *Thomas Eakins.* New York:
    Braziller, 1959.
Ernst, Max
  Diehl, Gaston. *Max Ernst.* New York: Crown
    Publishers, 1973.
  Ernst, Max. *Beyond Painting and Other
    Writings.* New York: Wittenborn, Schultz,
    Inc., 1948.
  "Max Ernst." *View Magazine,* II (April
    1942), special issue on Max Ernst.
  Russell, John. *Max Ernst, Life and Work.*
    New York: Abrams, 1967; London: Thames
    & Hudson, 1967.
Ferber, Herbert
  Anderson, Wayne. *The Sculpture of Herbert
    Ferber.* Minneapolis: The Walker Art
    Center, 1962.
  Goosen, E. C.; Goldwater, Robert; and

Sandler, Irving. *Three American Sculptors: Ferber, Hare, Lassaw.* New York: Grove Press, 1959.

Flavin, Dan
Dan Flavin, Fluorescent Light, Etc. Ottawa: National Gallery of Canada, 1969.

Gabo, Naum
Gabo, Naum, *Of Divers Arts,* New York: Bollingen, 1962; London: Faber & Faber, 1962.
Olson, Ruth, and Chanin, Abraham. *Naum Gabo—Antoine Pevsner.* New York: The Museum of Modern Art, 1948.
Pevsner, Alexei. *A Biographical Sketch of My Brothers Naum Gabo and Antoine Pevsner.* Amsterdam: Augustin & Schooman, 1964.
Read, Sir Herbert. *Gabo.* Cambridge: Harvard University Press, 1957; London: Lund, Humphries, 1957.

Gauguin, Paul
Andersen, Wayne. *Gauguin's Paradise Lost.* New York: Viking, 1971.
Gauguin: Paintings, Drawings, Prints, Sculpture. Chicago: The Art Institute of Chicago, 1959.
Goldwater, Robert. *Gauguin.* New York: Abrams, 1957.
Gray, Christopher. *Sculpture and Ceramics of Paul Gauguin.* Baltimore: Johns Hopkins Press, 1963.

Giacometti, Alberto
Genet, Jean. *Alberto Giacometti.* Zurich: Scheidegger, 1962.
Giacometti, Alberto. *Schriften, Briefe, Zeichnungen.* Zurich: Arche, 1958.
Hohl, Reinhold. *Alberto Giacometti.* London: Thames & Hudson, 1972.
Sartre, Jean-Paul. "Giacometti in Search of Space." *Art News,* LIV (September 1955), 26–29, 63–65.
Selz, Peter. *Alberto Giacometti.* New York: The Museum of Modern Art, 1965.

Gonzalez, Julio
Julio Gonzalez. London: The Tate Gallery, 1970.
Perez Alfonseca, Ricardo. *Julio Gonzalez.* Madrid, 1934.
Ritchie, Andrew Carnduff. *Sculpture of Julio Gonzalez.* New York: The Museum of Modern Art, 1956.

Hare, David
Goosen, E. C.; Goldwater, Robert; and Sandler, Irving. *Three American Sculptors: Ferber, Hare, Lassaw.* New York: Grove Press, 1959.
Modern Artists in America. New York: Wittenborn Schultz, Inc., 1951.
Sartre, Jean-Paul. "N-Dimensional Sculpture." In *Women, A Collaboration of Artists and Writers.* New York: Kootz Editions, 1948.

Hepworth, Barbara
Browse, Lillian, ed. *Barbara Hepworth, Sculptures.* London: Faber & Faber, 1946.
Hepworth, Barbara, *Barbara Hepworth: A Pictorial Autobiography.* New York: Praeger, 1970; and Somerset-Adams & Dart, 1970.
Hodin, J. P. *Barbara Hepworth.* New York: David McKay, 1962; London: Lund, Humphries, 1962.

Read, Sir Herbert. *Barbara Hepworth, Carvings and Drawings.* London: Lund, Humphries, 1952.

Hesse, Eva
Pincus-Witten, Robert and Shearer, Linda. *Eva Hesse.* New York: The Solomon R. Guggenheim Museum, 1972.

Johns, Jasper
Kozloff, Max. *Jasper Johns.* New York: Abrams, 1967.
Solmon, Alan R. *Jasper Johns.* New York: The Jewish Museum, 1964.
Steinberg, Leo. *Jasper Johns.* New York: Wittenborn, 1963. Reprinted in Leo Steinberg, *Other Criteria,* New York: Oxford University Press, 1972.

Judd, Donald
Agee, William C. *Donald Judd.* New York: The Whitney Museum of American Art, 1968.
Judd, Donald. *Complete Writings 1959–1975.* New York: New York University Press, 1975.
Smith, Brydon, ed. *Donald Judd.* Ottawa: National Gallery of Canada, 1975 (includes a *catalogue raisonné* and essay by Roberta Smith).

Kaprow, Allan
Kaprow, Allan. *Assemblages, Environments & Happenings.* New York: Abrams, 1966.

Kienholz, Edward
Tuchman, Maurice. *Edward Kienholz.* Los Angeles: The Los Angeles County Museum of Art, 1966.

King, Philip
Philip King. Otterlo: Rijksmuseum Kröller-Müller, 1974.

Lassaw, Ibram
Goosen, E. C.; Goldwater, Robert; and Sandler, Irving. *Three American Sculptors: Ferber, Hare, Lassaw.* New York: Grove Press, 1959.

LeWitt, Sol
Sol LeWitt. The Hague: Gemeentemuseum, 1970.

Lipchitz, Jacques
Arnason, H. H. *Jacques Lipchitz: Sketches in Bronze.* New York: Praeger, 1969.
Goldwater, Robert. *Lipchitz,* New York: Universe Books, 1959; London: A. Zwemmer, 1959.
Lipchitz, Jacques; with Arnason, H. H., *My Life in Sculpture.* New York: Viking, 1972.
Patai, Irene. *Encounters: The Life of Jacques Lipchitz.* New York: Funk & Wagnalls, 1961.

Lipton, Seymour
Elsen, Albert. *Seymour Lipton.* New York: Abrams, 1972.

Maillol, Aristide
Cladel, Judith. *Aristide Maillol: Sa vie, son œuvre, ses idées.* Paris: Grasset, 1937.
Denis, Maurice. *A. Maillol.* Paris: Crès, 1925.
Rewald, John. *Maillol,* New York: Hyperion, 1939; London: Imperia, 1939.
Waldemar, George. *Aristide Maillol.* London: Cory, Adams & McKay, 1965.

Man Ray
Man Ray. *Self-Portrait.* Boston: Little, Brown, 1963; London: André Deutsch, 1963.

Man Ray. Los Angeles: The Los Angeles County Museum of Art, 1966 (includes texts by Jules Langsner and Man Ray).

Matisse, Henri
Barr, Alfred H., Jr. *Matisse: His Art and His Public.* New York: The Museum of Modern Art, 1951.
Elsen, Albert. *The Sculpture of Henri Matisse.* New York: Abrams, 1972.
Jacobus, John. *Henri Matisse.* New York: Abrams, 1973.
Legg, Alicia. *The Sculpture of Matisse.* New York: The Museum of Modern Art, 1972.

Modigliani, Amedeo
Lipchitz, Jacques. *Amedeo Modigliani.* New York: Abrams, 1954.
Modigliani, New York: The Museum of Modern Art, 1951.
Salmon, André. *Modigliani.* New York: G. P. Putnam, 1961.

Moholy-Nagy, László
Kostelanetz, Richard, ed. *Moholy-Nagy.* New York: Praeger, 1970.
Moholy-Nagy, László. *The New Vision.* New York: Wittenborn & Co., 1946.
Moholy-Nagy, László; Schlemmer, Oscar; and Nolnar, Farkas. *The Theatre of the Bauhaus.* Middletown, Conn.: Wesleyan University Press, 1961.
Moholy-Nagy, Sibyl. *Moholy-Nagy.* Cambridge, Mass.: MIT Press, 1969.

Moore, Henry
Argan, Giulio Carlo. *Henry Moore.* New York: Abrams, 1973.
Moore, Henry, ed. Philip James. *Henry Moore on Sculpture.* New York: Viking, 1966; London: McDonald, 1966.
Neumann, Erich. *The Archetypal World of Henry Moore.* New York: Pantheon, 1959; London: Routledge & Kegan, 1959.
Read, Sir Herbert. *Henry Moore.* New York: Praeger, 1965; London: Thames & Hudson, 1965.
Russell, John. *Henry Moore.* New York: G. P. Putnam, 1968.

Morris, Robert
Battcock, Gregory, ed. *Minimal Art.* New York: Dutton, 1968 (includes Robert Morris, "Notes on Sculpture").
Compton, Michael, and Sylvester, David. *Robert Morris.* London: The Tate Gallery, 1971.
Michelson, Annette. *Robert Morris.* Washington. D.C.: The Corcoran Gallery of Art, 1969.
Tucker, Marcia. *Robert Morris.* New York: The Whitney Museum of American Art, 1970.

Nauman, Bruce
Livingston, Jane, and Tucker, Marcia. *Bruce Nauman, Work from 1965 to 1972.* Los Angeles: The Los Angeles County Museum of Art, 1972.

Nevelson, Louise
Friedman, Martin. *Nevelson.* Minneapolis: The Walker Art Center, 1973.
Glincher, Arnold. *Louise Nevelson.* New York: Praeger, 1972.

Noguchi, Isamu
Gordon, John. *Isamu Noguchi.* New York: The Whitney Museum of American Art, 1968.
Noguchi, Isamo. *A Sculptor's World.* New York: Harper & Row, 1968; London: Thames & Hudson, 1968.

Oldenburg, Claes
Johnson, Ellen. *Claes Oldenburg.* Baltimore: Penguin Books, 1971.
Oldenburg, Claes. *Raw Notes,* Halifax: Nova Scotia College of Art and Design, 1973.
Rose, Barbara. *Claes Oldenburg.* New York: The Museum of Modern Art, 1970.

Pepper, Beverly
Fry, Edward. *Beverly Pepper.* San Francisco: San Francisco Museum of Art, 1976.

Pevsner, Antoine
Olson, Ruth, and Chanin, Abraham. *Naum Gabo—Antoine Pevsner.* New York: The Museum of Modern Art, 1948.
Pevsner, Alexei. *A Biographical Sketch of My Brothers Naum Gabo and Antoine Pevsner.* Amsterdam: Augustin & Schooman, 1964.

Picabia, Francis
Camfield, William. *Francis Picabia.* New York: The Solomon R. Guggenheim Museum, 1970.
Little Review, VIII (Spring 1922). Special issue on Picabia.
Schwarz, Arturo. *New York Dada: Duchamp, Man Ray, Picabia.* Munich: Prestel-Verlag, 1973.

Picasso, Pablo
Johnson, Ron. *The Early Sculpture of Picasso.* New York: Garland Press, 1976.
Penrose, Roland. *The Sculpture of Picasso.* New York: The Museum of Modern Art, 1967.
Spies, Werner. *Sculpture by Picasso.* New York: Abrams, 1971.

Rickey, George
Rickey, George. *Constructivism.* London: Studio Vista, 1967; New York: Braziller, 1967.
Rosenthal, Nan. *George Rickey.* New York: Abrams, 1977.

Rodin, Auguste
Bourdelle, Emile Antoine. *La Sculpture et Rodin.* Paris: Emile-Paul, 1937.
Cladel, Judith. *Rodin: The Man and His Art.* New York: Century, 1917.
Elsen, Albert. *Rodin's Gates of Hell.* Minneapolis: University of Minnesota Press, 1960.
———. *Rodin.* New York: The Museum of Modern Art, 1963.
———. *Auguste Rodin, Readings on His Life and Work.* Englewood Cliffs, N.J.: Prentice-Hall, 1965.
Rilke, Rainer Maria. *Auguste Rodin.* London: Grey Walls Press, 1917.
Rodin, Auguste. *On Art and Artists.* New York: Philosophical Library, 1957; London: Peter Owen, 1958.
Steinberg, Leo. "Rodin." In *Other Criteria,* New York: Oxford University Press, 1972.

Rosso, Medardo
Barr, Margaret S. *Medardo Rosso.* New York: The Museum of Modern Art, 1963.

Borghi, Nino. *Medardo Rosso*. Milan: Ed. de Milione, 1950.
Soffici, Ardengo. *Medardo Rosso*. Florence: Vallecchi, 1929.
Roszak, Theodore
Arnason, H. H. *Theodore Roszak*. Minneapolis: The Walker Art Center, 1956.
Schöffer, Nicolas
Habasque, Guy. *Nicolas Schöffer*. Neuchâtel: Editions du Griffon, 1963.
Schöffer, Nicolas. *La Ville Cybernétique*. Paris: Tchou, 1969.
Schwitters, Kurt
Schmalenback, Werner. *Kurt Schwitters*. New York: Abrams, 1967.
Steinitz, Kate. *Kurt Schwitters: A Portrait from Life*. Berkeley: University of California Press, 1968.
Scott, Tim
Tim Scott. London: Whitechapel Gallery, 1967.
Segal, George
Marck, Jan van der. *George Segal*. New York: Abrams, 1975.
Seitz, William. *Segal*. New York: Abrams, 1972.
Serra, Richard
Richard Serra. Pasadena: Pasadena Art Museum, 1970.
Smith, David
Cone, Jan Harrison. *David Smith*. Cambridge, Mass.: The Fogg Art Museum, 1966.
Fry, Edward. *David Smith*. New York: The Solomon R. Guggenheim Museum, 1969.
Gray, Cleve, ed. *David Smith by David Smith*. New York: Holt, Rinehart, 1968.
Krauss, Rosalind. *Terminal Iron Works, The Sculpture of David Smith*. Cambridge, Mass.: MIT Press, 1971.
———. *David Smith, A Catalogue Raisonné of the Sculpture*. New York: Garland Press, 1977.
Smithson, Robert
Robert Smithson: Drawings. New York: The New York Cultural Center, 1974.
Smithson, Robert. "The Monuments of Passaic." *Artforum*, VI (December 1967), pp. 48–51.
———. "A Sedimentation of the Mind: Earth Projects." *Artforum*, VII (September 1968), pp. 44–50.
Stankiewicz, Richard
Sawin, Marticia. "Richard Stankiewicz." *Arts Yearbook 3*, 1959, pp. 156–159.
Tatlin, Vladimir
Andersen, Troels. *Vladimir Tatlin*. Stockholm: Moderna Museet, 1968.
Tinguely, Jean
Jean Tinguely. Amsterdam: Stedelijk Museum, 1973.
Tomkins, Calvin. *The Bride and the Bachelors*. New York: Viking, 1965; London: Weidenfield & Nicolson, 1966.
Two Kinetic Sculptors, Nicolas Schöffer and Jean Tinguely. New York: The Jewish Museum, 1965.
Tucker, William
Tucker, William. *The Language of Sculpture*. London: Thames & Hudson, 1974; New York: Oxford University Press, 1974 (as *Early Modern Sculpture*).
———. *Space. Illusion. Sculpture*. London: Mains, 1974.
William Tucker, Sculpture 1970–73. London: The Arts Council, 1973.

index

Abstract expressionism, 148, 150, 256, 258, 259
Abstraction and Empathy (Worringer), 41
Abstraction-Création, 140
Adam (Rodin), 26, *27*
Aesthetic transformation, 77–80, 83, 117
Afternoon of a Faun, The (Gauguin), 34
Ale Cans (Johns), *258*, 259
Amarillo Ramp (Smithson), *286*
Ambiguity, 195–96
Andre, Carl, 198, 245, *247*, *251*, 266, 271, 272, *274*, 275
Anemic-Cinéma (Duchamp), 81
Annesley, David, 195, *196*, 197
Antiquarian plaques (von Hildebrand), *16*, 22
Apollinaire, Guillaume, 69, 71, 108
Aragon, Louis, 108
Arch of Triumph (Rude), *10–12*, 14
Archery Lesson (von Hildebrand), *21*
Arnold, Matthew, 203
Arp, Jean, 100, 105, *136*, 137–40, *138*, *139*, *141*, 142, 253
"Art and Objecthood" (Fried), 203
Artaud, Antonin, 212, 232
Art as ideology, 9, 211
Artforum, vi
Art nouveau, 33–34
Audience, 78, 79–80, 83, 105–106, 123, 150, 201, 203, 212–13, 221, 229, 240
Automaton, 8–9, 14, 62–63, 208, *209*, 210, 211–12

Ballets Suédois, 207
Balzac (Rodin), 30, *31*, 96, 279
Bases, sculptural, 99
Bauhaus, 57, 63–64, 65, 67
Be in Love, You Will Be Happy (Gauguin), 34, *35*
Bedroom Ensemble (Oldenburg), *227*
Beginning of the World (Brancusi), 86, 87, 88, 92, 96
Bell and Navels (Arp), *136*, 138
Bellmer, Hans 124, 153
Bergson, Henri, 141
Beyond Modern Sculpture (Burnham), 209, 212
Bicycle, The (Calder), *222*
Bill, Max, 65, *66*, 67
Bird (Brancusi), *97*
Bird in Space (Brancusi), *84*, 85, 96, 99, 100
Blackburn: Song of an Irish Blacksmith (Smith), *154*, *155*, 156, 157–58, 159, 161, 165
Boccioni, Umberto, 41–43, *43*, *44*, 45–47, 51, 53, 55, 56–57, 58, 106, 113, 114, 124, 139, 144, 157
Bochner, Mel, vi, 245, *248–49*
Bolus, Michael, 195, 197
Bottle Rack (Duchamp), *73*
Bourgeois, Louise, 148, *151*
Brancusi, Constantin, 1, 4, 67, *84–93*, 85, *87*, *89*, *90*, *91*, *92*, *96–97*, *98*, 99, *100*, *101*, *102*, 103, 106, 240, 279

Braque, Georges, 53, 72
Breton, André, 108, 109–10, 111, 117, 123, 132, 135, 140, 146, 229–30
Bride, The (Duchamp), 72
Brummer Gallery, New York, 99
Buffet-Picabia, Gabrielle, 69
Burnham, Jack, 209–11, 212, 221
Bury, Pol, 220–21, *225*

Café Voltaire, Zurich, 137
Calder, Alexander, 213, *215*, *216–17*, *218*, *219*, 220, 222
Calligraph in Cage with Cluster No. 2 (Ferber), 173, *176*
Canova, Antonio, *18*, 19, 20, 21, *24*, 25
Caro, Anthony, 181–83, *184*, *185*, 186–90, *187*, *188*, *189*, *190–91*, 192, *193*, *194*, 195, 196, 199, 200
Carpeaux, Jean-Baptiste, *19*, 20
Carriage (Caro), 192, *193*
Case study method, 6
Casting (Serra), 244, *246–47*, 272
Caught Hand (Giacometti), 124, *127*
Cercle et Carré, 140
Chamberlain, John, 181, *183*
Chance, 108, 109–11, 117, 137
Chants du crépuscule, Les (Hugo), 75
Characteristics, sculptural, 3, 191, 197–98, 199–200, 201, 203
Charioteer of Delphi, 134
Che Farò Senza Eurydice (di Suvero), *178–79*
Cinema (Segal), *226*
Circuit for a Square (Giacometti), *117*, 118
Clerk, The (Jaquet-Droz), *209*
Cloak, The (Lipton), 173, *177*
Color, sculptural, 165, 192, 196
Column (Gabo), *60*, 61–62, 131, 144, 207
Columns (Morris), *202*
Comment j'ai écrit certains de mes livres (Roussel), 76
Communication through art, 76, 77–78, 79, 203, 259, 261–62
Composition of sculpture, 20, 67, 80, 83, 86–87, 88, 90, 91, 92, 93, 96, 99, 113, 118, 124, 128, 140, 143, 148, 157–58, 169, 171, 191, 244, 250, 275
Condensation Cube (Haacke), *225*
Constructed Head (Gabo), *58*, 59
Construction in an Egg (Pevsner), *63*
Construction in Metal Wire (Picasso), *133*, 134
Constructive technique, 75–76, 83, 250, 275
Constructivism, 4, 55–56, 57–58, 67, 77–78, 103, 110, 124, 132, 134, 141–42, 143, 146, 156, 157, 158, 159, 161, 173, 178, 216, 240, 245, 253
Contingent (Hesse), *275*
Cornell, Joseph, 124, *127*, 128, *129*, 131
Corner Relief (Tatlin), *54–55*, 55
Corridor (Nauman), *241*, 282
Creative act, 79, 88, 111, 113

Creative Evolution (Bergson), 141
Creative procedures, 71, 72, 76, 79, 119
Crest, The (Gottlieb), *153*
Cubi VI (Smith), 165, *166*
Cubi XIX (Smith), 161, 165, *167*
Cubism, 46–47, 51, 53, 71, 72, 77–78, 103, 195
Cunningham, Merce, 204, 233
CYSP I (Schöffer), 213

Dada, 105–106, 137, 139
Dali, Salvador, 120, *121*, 124, 153, 173
Dance, The (Carpeaux), *19*, 20
Dance Movement, A (Rodin), *36*
Dancer (Rodin), *36*
"Dawn's Wedding Feast" (Nevelson), *149*
De Kooning, Willem, *257*
Departing Volunteer. See *La Marseillaise*
Development of a Bottle in Space (Boccioni), 42–47, *43*, 53, 55, 58, 61, 113, 144, 146, 157
Disagreeable Object (Giacometti), 118, *119*, 120
Discontinuity, 158, 165, 171, 173, 182, 186, 197
Di Suvero, Mark, *178–79*, 181, 254, *255*, 256
Divine Comedy (Dante), 15, *16*, 17
Door to the River (De Kooning), *257*
Double Negative (Heizer), *278*, *280–81*, 282
Drawing (Boccioni), 41–42, *44*
Drawing (Van Doesburg), *64*
Dreams, 117, 233
Duchamp, Marcel, 1, 67, 69, 70, 71–75, *73*, *74*, 76, 77, 78, 79, 80–81, *82*, 83–84, 85, 100, 103, 106, *107*, 108, 109, 120, 131, 138, 197, 211, 219–20, 249, 259, *261*, 276

Eakins, Thomas, *21*, 22
Early One Morning (Caro), 187–91, *188*, *189*, 190–192
Ecce Puer! (Rosso), *32*, 33, 88, 91
18 Superimposed Balls (Bury), *225*
Eisenstein, Sergei, 7, *8*, 9, 62–63, 211–12
Eliot, T. S., 203
Endless Loop I (Bill), *66*
Ernst, Max, *114*, 115, 117, 131
Eternal Idol, The (Rodin), *9*
Expression, sculptural, 5, 27–28, 99, 141–42, 170–71, 191, 254, 256

Fahne Hoch!, Die (Stella), 262, *263*, 264–65
Fauvism, 71
Femme 100 Têtes, La (Ernst), *114*, 115, 117, 131
Ferber, Herbert, 171–73, *174*, *176*
Figure (Lipchitz), *156*, 157, 158, 173
Fish, The (Brancusi), *85*
Flavin, Dan, 198, 245, *247*, 266
Flesh of Others (Rosso). See *Sick Boy*
Flying Figure (Rodin), *30*
Formation, sculptural, 29–30, 37, 99, 124, 181, 253, 276
Fountain (Duchamp), 72, 76, 77, 78, 79–80, 81, 100, 197, *259*, *261*

Freud, Sigmund, 80, 109, 154, 155
Fried, Michael, 186, 203–204, 242
"From the Height of a Little Shoe Forming One Body with Her" (Ray), *110*
Fugit Amor (Rodin), *16*, 17
Fur-Lined Teacup (Oppenheim), *122*, 123
Furniture, carved (Guimard), *32*, 33
Futurism, 40, 41, 45–46, 47, 51, 53, 67, 103, 157, 240
Futurist Manifesto (Marinetti), 39–41, 46, 53

Gabo, Naum, 1, 4, *56*, 57–63, *58*, *59*, *60*, *62*, 65, 67, 106, 114, 124, 131, 132, 139, 143, 144, 157, 159, 161, 207, 216, *221*, 253, *254*
Gallée, Emile, 33
Gates of Hell (Rodin), *13*, 14, *15*, *16*, 17, *18*, 22, 26, 28, 34–35, 51
Gates of Paradise (Ghiberti), 15, 16
Gaudí, Antonio, 33
Gauguin, Paul, *34*, 35
Ghiberti, 15
Geist, Sidney, 84, 100
"Ghost" Toilet (Oldenburg), *228*
Giacometti, Alberto, *111*, *112*, 113, 114, *115*, *116*, *117*, 118, *119*, 120, 124, *127*, 128, 138–39, 146, 153, *164*, 165, 172, 173
Giant Fag Ends (Oldenburg), *227*
Giedion-Welcker, Carola, 3
Gift (Ray), *122*, 124
Glass of Absinthe, The (Picasso), *135*
Glass Stratum (Smithson), *248*
Glider Containing a Water Mill in Neighboring Metals (Duchamp), *82*, 83
Golden Age, The (Rosso), *31*, 32
Gonzalez, Julio, *130*, 131–32, 134
Gottlieb, Adolph, 148, *153*
Graham, Martha, 218
Grass Field (Hay), *205*
Gropius, Walter, 65
Growth (Arp), *141*
Guimard, Hector, *32*, 33
Guitar (Picasso), 48, *50*, 51

Haacke, Hans, *225*
Hand Catching Lead (Serra), 243, *244*, 276, 279
Hanging Lamp (Gropius), *65*
Hanging Mobile (Calder), *216–17*, *218*, 219
Happenings, 204, *231*, 232–33
Hare, David, 148, *150*, 171–72, 173
Hay, Alex, *205*
Head (Brancusi), 87, *89*
Head (Gonzalez), *130*, 131–32, 134
Head (Modigliani), 93, *95*
Head of a Sleeping Child (Brancusi), *91*
Head of a Woman (Gabo), *59*
Head of a Woman (Picasso), *135*, 137
Heads as Still Life (Smith), 161, *162*
Head with Annoying Objects (Arp), 138, *139*

Heizer, Michael, *278*, *280–81*
Hepworth, Barbara, 141, *142*
Hercules and Antaeus (Pollaiuolo), *24*
Hercules and Lichas (Canova), *24*, 25
Hesse, Eva, 272, *275*
Hildebrand. *See* Von Hildebrand, Adolf
Historic narrative, 10–13
History painting, 10
Homage to Bernini (Rickey), *223*
Homage to New York (Tinguely), *224*
Homage to the Romantic Ballet (Cornell), *127*
Horoscope (Jean), 124, *125*
Horta, Victor, 33
Hugo, Victor, 75
Husserl, Edmund, 28

Impressions of Africa (Roussel), 69–70, 71, 72, 73, 74, 75, 276
Imprisoned Figure (Lipton), *150*
In Advance of a Broken Arm (Duchamp), 72, *73*
Independents show, New York, 76–77
Internal and External Forms (Moore), *145*, 253
Interpretation of Dreams, The (Freud), 109

Jacob, Max, 71
Jaquet-Droz, Pierre, *209*
Jean, Marcel, 124, *125*
Jeannette I-V (Matisse), *37*
Je suis belle (Rodin), *22*, 24, 25
Johns, Jasper, 249, *258*, 259, *260*, 262
Judd, Donald, 181, 198, 245, *246*, 249, *252*, 253, 254, 256, 258, 266, *270*, 271
Judson Living Theatre, 233, 236
Jurassic Bird (Smith), 169

Kant, Immanuel, 71
Kaprow, Allan, 232, *234*
Kerensky, Aleksandr, 8–9, 211
Kienholz, Edward, 221, *226*
Kinetic Construction (Gabo), 216, *221*
Kinetic sculpture, 204, 207, 216, 218, 220–21
King, Philip, 181, *184*, 195, *197*
King and Queen Surrounded by Swift Nudes, The (Duchamp), 72, *73*
Kiss, The (Rodin), 9
Kline, Franz, 254, 256

Ls (Morris), *264–65*, 266–67, 279
Labyrinth (Morris), 282, *285*
Lachaise, Gaston, 93, *94*
Ladder Piece (di Suvero), *255*
Lady-of-Waiting (Hare), 173
L'Amour fou (Breton), 111, 115
Laocoön (Lessing), 1, 2, 3, 4
Laocoön and His Sons, *2*
Larionov, Mikhail, 56
Lassaw, Ibram, *159*, 173
Lautréamont, 123
Léger, Fernand, 72
Lessing, Gotthold, 1–3, 4, 10

Lever (Andre), *251*
LeWitt, Sol, 266, 271, *273*
Light-art, 204, 207
Light Ballet from "Fireflowers" (Piene), *214*
Light Prop (Moholy-Nagy), *206*, 207–209, 211, 212, 213, 219, 230
Linguistics, structural, 4–5, 261
Linoleum (Rauschenberg), 234
Lipchitz, Jacques, 59, *156*, 157, 158, 173
Lippold, Richard, 173
Lipton, Seymour, 148, *150*, 159, 171–72, 173, 177
Lissitzky, Eliezer, 57, *63*, 64, 67
Littérature, 108
Lonely Avenue (Annesley), *196*
Loop, The (Lye), 220, *223*
Luis Miguel Dominguin (Stella), *264*
Lye, Len, 220, *223*

Magician's Game (Hare), *150*
Magritte, René, 124, *126*, 173
Maillol, Aristide, 90, *91*
Malevich, Kasimir, 53
Mallarmé, Stéphane, 71
Mamelles de Tirésias, Les (Apollinaire), 108
Man Taking Off His Shirt (Caro), 186, *187*
Man, Woman and Child (Giacometti), *116*, 118
Man's Torso (Rodin), *29*
Marinetti, Filippo, 39–40, 41
Marseillaise, La (Rude), 10, *11*, 12, 14, 15, 37, 41, 42
Materials of sculpture, 3, 100, 113, 132, 143–44, 170, 181, 207, 253, 271–72, 275
Matisse, Henri, 35, *36*, 37
Mechanistic view, 140, 212
Medals for Dishonor (Smith), 169, *171*
Medici Slot Machine (Cornell), 128, *129*
Merleau-Ponty, 239–40
Michelson, Annette, 233
Microtemps 16 (Schöffer), *210–11*
Milky Way (Lassaw), vi, 173
Minimal art, 181, 198–99, 236, 245, 249–50, 254, 256, 258, 259, 262, 266, 270, 272, 279
Mlle. Pogany (Brancusi), *98*
Mobiles, 213, *215*, *216*, *217*, *218*, *219*, 220, *222*, *223*
Modern Plastic Arts (Giedion-Welcker), 3
Modigliani, Amedeo, 93, *95*
Moholy-Nagy, László, 57, 64, 65, *66*, 67, *206*, 207, 213, 230
Monument to Heros (Noguchi), *151*
Monument to the Third International (Tatlin), *60*, 61–62, 211
Moore, Henry, 100, 141, *142*, 143, *144*, *145*, 146, 156, 182, *253*, 254
Morris, Robert, vi, 198, 201, *202*, 203, 236, *237*, *238–39*, 242, *264–65*, 266–67, *268*, *269*, 270, 279, 282, *285*
Mother and Child Sleeping (Rosso), *22*, 23, 32, 88
Motion pictures, 7–9, 243

Movement, 201, 216, 220, 233, 236–39, 243–44
Multiple viewpoints, 18
Museum of Modern Art, New York, 220
Musical Instruments (Picasso), *52*
Mutt, R., 76

Nadeau, Maurice, 113
Nadja (Breton), 109–10, 115
Narrative in art, 41, 78, 81
Nauman, Bruce, 240, *241*, 242, 282
Necktie and Navel (Arp), *138*, 139–40
Neoclassicism, 9–10, 18, 46, 106
Nevelson, Louise, 148, *149*
Newborn, The (Brancusi), 85, 93, *96–97*
Newman, Barnett, 148, 150
Nickel Construction (Moholy-Nagy), *66*
No More Play (Giacometti), *116*, 118
Noguchi, Isamu, 148, *151*, *205*
Nominal Three, The (Flavin), *247*
Nonrepresentation, 165
Non-Site, A (Smithson), *284*, *285*

Object to Be Destroyed (Ray), *120*
October (Eisenstein), 7, *8*, 9, 14, 63, 211
Oldenburg, Claes, 227, *228*, 229, 230, *231*, 232, *234*, 236–37, 242
One-Ton Prop (Serra), 269–70, *271*, 279
Open Modular Cube (LeWitt), *273*
Oppenheim, Meret, *122*, 123
Optical Machine (Duchamp), *74*
Other Criteria (Steinberg), vi

Palace at 4 A.M., The (Giacometti), *115*
Paolo and Francesca (Rodin), 15, *16*
Paris Opera façade, 19
Parts of Some Sextets (Rainer), *236*
Pelagos (Hepworth), *142*
Pelican (Rauschenberg), *235*
Pepper, Beverly, 178, *182*
Pesarea Maiastra (Brancusi), 96
Pevsner, Antoine, 57, *63*, 65, 143, 253
Phaedra set (Noguchi), *205*
Phenomenology, 4–5
Phenomenology of Perception, The (Merleau-Ponty), 239–40
Picabia, Francis, 69, 207, *208*, 212, 230
Picasso, Pablo, 47–48, *49*, *50*, 51, *52*, 53, 72, *133*, 134, *135*, 137, 192, 211
Piene, Otto, *214*
Pollaiuolo, Antonio, *24*, 25
Pollock, Jackson, 148, 150, *152*, 165
Pop art, 249, 250
Pot in the Shape of the Head and Shoulders of a Young Girl (Gauguin), *34*
Princess X (Brancusi), 100, *102*, 103
Problem of Form, The (Von Hildebrand), 41
Prodigal Son, The (Rodin), *17*
Profiles (Gabo), *58*, *59*
Prometheus (Brancusi), *91*, *92*, 93, 96
Proun-the-Town (Lissitzky), *63*
Proust, Marcel, 283, 287

Psychoanalysis, 80
Psychopathology of Everyday Life, The (Freud), 80

Quantic of Sakkara (Scott), 195–96, *198–99*

Rainer, Yvonne, *236*
Rape, The (Smith), 169, *170*
Rationalism, 9–10, 71, 106, 124, 132, 140, 244, 253
Rauschenberg, Robert, 204, *234*, *235*
Ray, Man, *110*, *120*, *122*, 123, 124
Read, Sir Herbert, 144–46
Ready-made art, 72–73, 79–80, 81, 83, 84, 88, 106, 109, *120*, 211, 245, 249–50, 259, 262, 272
Realistic Manifesto, The (Gabo), 57
Real motion of sculpture, 204, 213, 216, 218, 220, 221, 233, 236–37, *238–39*
Reclining Figure (Moore), 143, *144*, 146
Reclining Woman (Giacometti), 111
Red Splash (Caro), 192, *193*
Reef (Andre), *247*
Relâche (Picabia), 207, *208*, 212–13, 230
"*Relation of Horizontal and Vertical Planes, The*" (van Doesburg and van Eesteren), *64*
Relief sculpture, 12, 14, 15, 20–21, 191–92
Repetition, 17, 19, 20, 35, 244–45, 249, 250, 272
Rickey, George, 220, *223*
Rilke, Rainer Maria, 31, 96
Rodin, Auguste, vi, 9, *13*, 14–15, *16*, *17*, *18*, 20–21, 22, 23, 24, 25–26, 27, 28, *29*, *30*, *31*, 34, 35, *36*, 96, 99, 230, 240, 279, 283
Rosenberg, Harold, 256
Rosso, Medardo, 22, 23, *31*, *32*, 46, 88, *89*, 90, 91
Rothko, Mark, 148
Rotoreliefs (Duchamp), 81
Roussel, Raymond, 69, 70, 71, 72, 73, 74, 75–76, 78, 276
Rrose Sélavy (Duchamp), *74*, 78–79, 81
Rude, François, 10, *11*, 12, 14, 22, 37, 41, 42, 114

Salon des Indépendants, Paris, 100
Satie, Eric, 219
Schöffer, Nicolas, *210–11*, 213
Scott, Tim, 195, 196, 197, *198–99*
Sculpture
    audience and, 4, 12, 20, 45, 51, 61–62, 67, 78–80, 83, 196, 203, 212, 221, 229, 230, 240, 242, 254
    communication and, 26–28, 79, 87–88, 158
    material properties and, 56, 57, 132, 269–70, 271–72
    motion and, 41–42, 43, 45, 47, 53, 113, 123, 128, 229
    narrative and, 10–12, 14, 15, 17, 23, 41, 81, 103, 106, 123, 283
    technology and, 46, 62–63, 100, 209–210, 213
    theater and, 201, 203–204, 207, 212–13, 218, 221, 229, 230, 236–39, 240, 242

time and, 4, 5, 10, 12, 15, 17, 23, 61–62, 106, 108, 113–14, 146, 198, 203–204, 233
  See also Composition of sculpture; Materials of sculpture; Real motion of sculpture; Spatial aspects of sculpture; Structure of sculpture; Viewing sculpture
Segal, George, 221, *226*
Self, notion of the, 28, 30, 256, 258, 259, 266, 267, 270, 279, 280
Sentinel (von Schlegell), *180*
Serf (Matisse), 36
Serpentine, The (Matisse), *36*
Serra, Richard, vi, 243, *244*, 245, *246–47*, 269–70, *271*, *272*, 275–76, *277*, 279, 282, *286*, *287*
Service for the Dead, A (Kaprow), *234*
Shadows, sculptural, 22–23
Shapiro, Joel, *288*
Shchukin, Sergei, 53
Shift (Serra), 282, *286–87*
Sick Boy (Rosso), 88, *89*
Signs, 148, 150–52, 264–66, 270
Simultaneity, 3, 4, 5, 12, 19, 45, 117
Site (Morris), *238–39*
Sketches (Smith), 169–70, *172*
Slant (King), *197*
Sleeping Figure (Bourgeois), *151*
Sleeping Muse (Brancusi), *89*
Smith, David, 147, *149*, 152, 153, *154*, *155*, 156–58, *160*, *161*, *162*, *163*, 165, *166*, *167*, *168*, 169, *170*, *171*, *172*, 173, *175*, 178, 181–82, 183, 186
Smith, Tony, 198
Smithson, Robert, vi, 4–5, 245, *248*, 281, *282–283*, *284*, *285*, *286*
Socrate (Satie), 219
Soffici, 47
Some Shadows: Portrait of Tristan Tzara (Arp), *136*, 137
Sontag, Susan, 232
Soupault, Philippe, 108
Space in art, 7–8, 17, 41, 55, 64–65, 114–15, 117, 204, 239–40, 259, 262, 266, 270, 279, 280
Spatial aspects of sculpture, 3–4, 12, 17, 23, 45, 51, 53, 55, 56, 58, 60, 61, 64–65, 81, 106, 114, 118, 128, 146, 191, 204, 250, 253, 266, 270–71, 272, 279, 280, 282
Specter of War (Smith), 169
Spinning (Eakins), *21*
Spiral Jetty (Smithson), 4–5, 281, *282–83*
Spring Happening, A (Kaprow), 232
Stacked Steel Slabs (Serra), 272–75, 277
Standing Nude with Arms Raised (Matisse), 36
Standing Personage (Lipchitz), *59*
Star Cradle (Lassaw), *159*, 161
Steinberg, Leo, vi
Stella, Frank, 244, 245, 262, *263*, *264*, 265–66, 270
Stereometric diagram (Gabo), *56*, 57–58, 161
Stereometry, 57–58, 63, 131–32, 159, 161
Stevens, Wallace, 256
Still, Clyfford, 148

Stokes, Adrian, 191–92
Stones of Rimini, The (Stokes), 191–92
Store, The (Oldenburg), *231*, 232
Structural values, 106, 110–11, 158
Structure of sculpture, 4, 20–21, 43, 55–56, 58, 60, 61, 63, 67, 88, 93, 96, 124, 128, 131, 134, 139–40, 141–43, 147, 157, 161, 187–88, 192, 195, 207–208, 216, 230, 250, 254, 266–67, 269
Study for "Thought" (Maillol), 90, *91*
Sun (Lippold), 173
Surface, sculptural, 33, 34, 48, 61, 86–87, 91, 93, 96, 99, 103, 106, 124, 137, 141, 178, 181, 267, 279
Surface quality, 34, 47–48, 86, 99–100, 106, 165
Surrational Zeus II (Ferber), 172, *174*
Surrealism, 103, 108, 110, 111, 114, 117, 120, 123, 124, 131, 132, 134, 139, 142, 152–53, 165, 172, 173, 229–30
Surrealism, Manifesto of (Breton), 108, 123
Surrealist objects, 120, 124, 138, 139
Surrogate performer, 201, *202*, 203, 204, *205*, *206*, 207–208
Suspended Ball (Giacometti), *112*, 113, 118, 120, 138, 146, 165
Symbolists, 71

Table (Giacometti), *164*, 165
Table and Bottle and Block of Houses (Boccioni), *44*
Table Piece (Caro), *194*
Table Torso (Smith), 161, *163*
Takis, 213
Tanktotem I (Smith), 147–48, *149*, 171
Target with Four Faces (Johns), 259, *260*
Tatlin, Vladimir, 51, 53, *54–55*, 56, 57, 58, *60*, 61–63, 211
Technology, influence of, 100, 209–212
Temporal values, 4, 5, 10, 12, 15, 17, 61–62, 106, 108, 113–14, 123, 140, 142, 198, 203, 283
"Theatre of Cruelty, A" (Artaud), 212
Thinker, The (Rodin), 15
Thirteen Spines (Calder), *215*
Thorwaldsen, Bertel, *19*
Thought (Maillol), 90, *91*
Three Graces, The (Canova), *18*, 19, 21
Three Graces, The (Thorwaldsen), *19*
Three Ideas and Seven Procedures (Bochner), *248–49*
Three Shades, The (Rodin), 17, *18*, 20–21, 35, 36
3 Standard Stoppages (Duchamp), *107*
Through (King), *184*, 195
Tiffany, Louis, 33, 34
Time, real, 10, 15, 17, 41, 106, 108, 113–14, 123, 128, 203, 233, 236, 240, 276, 279
Tinguely, Jean, 213, 220, *224*
Torment (Brancusi), 88, *89*, 91, 92, 93, 96
Torso (Lachaise), 93, *94*
Torso of a Young Man (Brancusi), 85, *100*, *101*, 103, 279

Totem and Taboo (Freud), 154–55
Totem: Lesson II, The (Pollock), *152*
Totemism, 154, 155, 158, 161–62, 171
Translucent Variation of Spheric Theme (Gabo), *62*
Trefoil (Caro), *190–91*
Tucker, William, 195, 197
Twelfth Copper Corner (Andre), *274*
Twenty-four Hours (Caro), 183, *184, 185*
Tzara, Tristan, 105, 106, 108–109, 137, 138, 230

Ugolino and His Sons (Rodin), 15, *16*
Uncatalogued Page in the Archive (Smith), *172*

Van der Velde, Henry, 33
Van Doesburg, Theo, *64*, 65
Van Eesteren, Cornelis, *64*
Van Gogh, Vincent, 70, 81
Vaucanson, 209
V–B XXIII (Smith), *160, 161,* 165
Veiled Woman (Rosso), 32
Velvet White (Chamberlain), 181, *183*
Venezia Blu (Pepper), 178, *182*
Venus de Milo with Drawers (Dali), 120, *121,* 123, 124
Vertical Construction and Kinetic with Motor No. 2 (Gabo), *254*
Victory of Samothrace, 40
Viewer, relation of the, 110, 118, 120, 123, 128, 138, 144, 150, 155–56, 158–59, 191, 195, 196, 203, 212–13, 221, 229, 230, 240–42, 267, 283, 287
Viewing sculpture, 4, 12, 18, 42, 43–45, 47, 67, 76, 78, 83, 105–106, 148, 152, 195, 280
Violin (Picasso), 48, *49*, 192
Vitalism, 140–41
Voltri XVII (Smith), *175*
Volume, sculptural, 4, 86, 90, 134, 141, 143, 147, 172, 178, 181, 216, 270–71
Von Hildebrand, Adolf, 14, 20, *21*, 22, 41, 46, 114, 144
Von Schlegell, David, 178, *180*

Wadsworth Atheneum, Hartford, 219
Walking Man, The (Rodin), *29*, 36
War Landscape (Smith), 169
Warhol, Andy, *249*
Waterman Switch (Morris), *237*
Wilder Gallery Installation (Nauman), 240, *241*
Wittgenstein, Ludwig, 261
Wollheim, Richard, 198
Woman, The (Magritte), 124, *126*
Woman with Her Throat Cut (Giacometti), 118, *119*, 124, 153, 172
Worringer, 41

Year 1915 Exhibition, Moscow, 56

Zig IV (Smith), 165, *168*, 169
Zig VII (Smith), 169
Zig VIII (Smith), 169